Playford's Soham Magazine, And Friendly Monitor

William Playford

PLAYFORD'S

SOHAM MAGAZINE,

AND

FRIENDLY MONITOR.

1847.

Soham, Cambridgeshire:

PUBLISHED BY WILLIAM PLAYFORD;

LONDON: MESSRS. WHITTAKER & CO., AVE-MARIA LANE;

AND MAY BE HAD OF ALL BOOKSELLERS.

INDEX.

LIST OF ENGRAVINGS.

FRONTISPIECE (Steel Engraving).—North View of Soham Church.

PLAYFORD'S

SOHAM MAGAZINE,

AND

Friendly Monitor.

JANUARY, 1847.

VERY sincere friend of morality and social order, has much reason for anxiety in these eventful times. The Press—that powerful engine for good or evil, while, on the one hand, it pours the streams of sound principle and religious belief through the land, poisons, on the other, the pure fountain of truth with the deadly weeds of infidelity and vice. It is no libel, except so far as *truth* may be a libel, to say, that a large proportion of the publications that find their way into the libraries of the rich, and the cottages of the poor—either with the view of gain, by pandering to the lowest propensities of fallen humanity, or by a neglect and indifference almost equally culpable—are silently, but surely loosening the bands of society, or heaping fuel upon the flame of man's insatiable desires. But while so grave a charge may be too easily supported even against many periodicals which have far different ends in view, are there not others which present one uniform picture of immorality and crime? What writings are those which are read, with such avidity, at the houses of resort

No. 1. Vol. I.   B

of the labourer and the artisan?   Go from the gilded spirit shop of the Metropolis to its squalid associate in the fen, and is the tone of the blackened journal, that lies upon the table, most calculated to humanize, or to degrade its readers?   Are they likely to become more intelligent, more upright, more pure from its perusal, or, from the depth of their depravity, to sink to a deeper still?   How strangely distorted must be the views of those who maintain that the sight of vice will prove its effectual antidote!   That because the Stage may sometimes faintly echo with some moral sentiment, the scenes of profligacy, which have been so broadly played before a vicious audience, will tend to check them in their career of sin!   But when we find the crimes, into which our fallen nature is too often betrayed, recounted with every particularity of circumstance that can agravate their enormity, and yet the perpetrator made, so frequently, the object of interest and commiseration, it must surely be time for all who have any regard, either for the temporal or eternal condition of their fellow creatures, to cast, if but a handful, to the barrier that may repel so great a flood of evil.

It is with such a design that this little publication is set on foot, and now pleads with the Public for their countenance and support.   It proposes to supply an hour's instruction, connected more immediately with the associations of the neighbourhood but still of a sufficiently general character to render it more extensively useful.

It is not, unhappily, to ephemeral publications alone, that the mischief to which we have alluded, is confined.   It is interwoven alike with works of history and fiction of so established a reputation, as to find a ready access to all classes of society, and every grade of life.

If it might, with justice, have been said of a celebrated Poet, that he had " poisoned the fount of human felicity," the remark is, at least, equally applicable to many a fashionable novelist of the day; while others, whose professed aim is to administer an antidote in disguise, do but bring truth and soberness into caricature, and forget " that every idle word that men shall speak they shall give an account thereof in the day of judgment."

This Magazine is intended to form a channel through which may be conveyed the sentiments and views of all those who desire to meliorate the condition of the people.

It has been said that if every man should write a simple statement of the knowledge he may have acquired in his own station of life, it would form a volume, at once amusing and instructive. This is precisely the opinion we entertain, and, to a certain extent, desire to verify. The knowledge derived from experience is peculiarly valuable, and if all who have gone before us had left a record of the problems they had solved, many an investigation, which now perplexes the learned and the wise, might have been saved. But, there are certain great lessons of morality and truth of such infinite importance to mankind, that, to withold them, were to inflict an irreparable— an eternal injury. How sublime, for example, and of what unspeakable obligation is that precept, laid down by the author of our holy Religion, "thou shalt love thy neighbour as thyself." And yet, if we go into any of the different walks of life, how rarely do we find it exercising habitual influence. *Selfishness* is the curse that blights the fairest flowers of human bliss, that bars the heart of man against his fellow, and, unless removed by the hand of Almighty Love, will close the door of Heaven against us all.

Let it be then our aim to diffuse a kindly and a Christian spirit. Let us endeavour to meet upon the broad platform of immutable truth.

Travellers upon the same rugged road, it ill becomes us to nourish the seeds of discord and strife, for while it can only tend to embitter the cup of our neighbour, it will destroy, in a far higher degree, the happiness of our own.

> Then " Rise, let us no more contend, nor blame
> "Each other, blamed enough elsewhere; but strive
> " In offices of love, how we may lighten
> " Each other's burden in our share of woe.
>
> PARADISE LOST, B. 10, V. 958.

CHRISTMAS DAY.

Much of the difficulty that is felt in the study of the Scriptures, arises from not understanding the customs of the country in which they were written. Any narrative of events that took place in England would be equally obscure to the inhabitants of Palestine, and it is only by an acquaintance with the modes of expression and the manners of life that are peculiar to certain portions of the globe, that the history of those regions can be clearly comprehended. In this light, a knowledge of the Old Testament is essential to the right interpretation of the New, and those who, in any measure, disregard the former, under the idea that they belong almost entirely to the Jews, are in danger of involving their faith in much uncertainty, and of erring widely in their practice, from the path in which they should tread. And that such must be the case will be more especially evident when we consider that the Old Testament and the New are linked together in the character of type and antitype:—the one being an exact resemblance, or shadow of the other. Some of the most vital doctrines of the Gospel are unintelligible till we refer to the Old Testament as the key; for the Church under one dispensation is but a counterpart of the Church under the other. But in matters of less moment, it is also of great importance to have a just conception of the habits and occupations of the inhabitants of that Country where first the Sun of Righteousness arose upon a benighted world. We have just been to Bethleham to view, by faith, our infant Lord. The place of his nativity is situated on a hill, and the surrounding scenery remains almost precisely as it was when so unspeakably honoured by his glorious presence. And on the top of the hill stands that noble Church, which was erected fifteen hundred years ago, by the English mother of the first Christian Emperor of Rome! Alas, has division entered there? How sad the thought, that three rival Christian communities—the Greek, the Armenian, and the Latin—should exist upon the very spot where first appeared, in human form, that long expected Messiah who was foretold as the Prince of Peace, who broke down the middle wall of partition between Jew and Gentile, and who certainly designed to unite, in one holy, undivided bond of Christian brotherhood, all those who "call on his name." Yes, on this very spot, so great is the jealousy of the professing members of the same spiritual household, that, altho prayers are perpetually offered up, yet one party regularly succeeds the other, in the same building, with its different forms of worship.

But when we read of the birth-place of our Lord as being a *stable*, how erroneous will be our ideas if we are unacquainted with the meaning of the word in Asiatic language. So profound was the veneration of the first Christians for the place, that it has been carefully preserved from generation to generation. There can be no reasonable doubt that the precise spot where the Redeemer was born, may be visited at the present day. It is a cavern or natural grotto, such as stables, in Palestine, almost invariably are; and they are used, by the shepherds, to protect their flocks from the heavy rains, or scorching heat of that land. How thrilling the emotions that must arise in every Christian's breast on entering that sacred retreat! Would not the devout mind feel itself addressed in those words, that once fell upon the ear of Moses:—"put off thy shoes from off thy feet for the place whereon thou standest is holy ground"? But not only has *division* cast her shadows on this hallowed soil, but *superstition* reigns there too. Multitudes are, at the present moment, returning from a pilgrimage of hundreds of miles to that cavern, under the belief that such journeys will benefit their souls! But, however misguided in their devotions, does not their zeal put to shame the cold feelings of numbers amongst us, who are kept from the "House of Prayer," when at their very doors, by any of the trivial circumstances of the domestic arrangement, or any slight inclemency of the season? A religion that depends, in any degree, upon the excitement of the feelings, is, to to say the least, bordering upon a dangerous enthusiasm; but a religion *without* feeling is only infidelity in disguise.

POLAR EXPEDITION.

Much anxiety is experienced at this present time respecting the fate of those of our intrepid Countrymen, who left the shores of their native land many months ago, to make discoveries in the neighbourhood of the North Pole. The difficulties and dangers that, under the most favourable circumstances, must be endured in that distant and unexplored region, may well fill the minds of their friends with alarm at the long period that has now elapsed since any tidings were received of their safety. Nature in those regions wears an aspect of awful majesty and grandeur, unrelieved by the softer and gentler beauties which distinguish her in the South. In the islands of those frozen seas, no meadows ever smile in emerald verdure, no waving corn fields ever gladden the heart of man—the song of birds never ushers in the morning, nor does the hum of insects lull the "parting day."

All is dreary solitude! The death-like silence that pervades the scene, inspires a feeling of involuntary awe, as if the hardy explorer had intruded into a region where he ought not to be. Frost, it is well known, is a powerful antiseptic: animal substances, may be kept in it without decay, for an indefinite period. Thus Captain Parry's crew, when fast locked up in the ice, enjoyed a Christmas dinner of roast beef, in perfect condition, which had been put on board nine months before. That huge, and now unknown animal the Mammoth, a specimen of which was dislodged some little time since, by the falling of a cliff, had been preserved from putrefaction for many hundred years. But deeply affecting instances of this property of cold have been witnessed by the discovery of the bodies of men, who, having died in these icy regions, had lain for years unburied without decay.

About seventy years ago the uncouth form of an apparently deserted ship was met with, strangely encumbered with ice and snow. On boarding her, a solitary man was found in her cabin, his fingers holding a pen, while before him lay the record which that pen had traced twelve years before! No appearance of decay was manifest, save a little greenish mould had accumulated on his forehead. A strange awe crept over the minds of those who thus first broke in upon his loneliness. For twelve years had that ill-fated bark navigated, through sun and storm, the Polar Sea.

Does not the recital of such a fact lead us to contemplate with wonder, that mysterious union of soul and body, which death disolves? Twelve years before had the soul of that lone wanderer passed into its eternal state, while his body remained almost as perfect as if the blood were still circulating in his veins! Can any one forbear to say, "Let me die the death of the righteous, and let my last end be like his?"

ORDINARY TALENTS BETTER THAN
UNCOMMON GIFTS.

Ah! who can tell how *hard* it is to climb,
The steep where Fame's proud temple shines afar!

BEATTIE.

IT is at once allowed, that there are difficulties in the way of intellectual acquirement; but after all they are not the towering mountains, described by affrighted ignorance. The gradual and certain foot of perseverance, makes the upward journey with ease, and contrary to natural facts, objects, which in the distance seem gigantic, wear down to easy trifles on the approach. Resolution, will overcome all the difficulties of the way; and those who faint, or fall short of the Temple of Knowledge, are poltroons.

Literature should not be an aristocracy, but a commonwealth; and it is equally interesting and possible, for thousands of us to enter this brilliant republic; since only that ordinary talent, which is rated at so little value, and which is God's good gift to the greatest number, is, if rightly directed and spurred on by that mighty moral engine perseverance, quite sufficient for the purpose.

Direct me if you please to any one specific science, and I will demonstrate the fact, by naming hosts of men who understand it. Adding link after link to this magic chain, they have surrounded the empire of knowledge, and then gone down in all the spirit of enthusiasm and philosophy, from things in the general, to things in the particular; from the comprehension of worlds, to the analysis of atoms.

And let me tell you, the most of these persons were more remarkable for the virtue of industry, than the gift of intellect. At every step their power both to will and to do, so increased, that no effort however Herculean, no labour however prolonged, no undertaking however onerous, could daunt, much less defy their enterprize. As the arm grows from a puny and flabby member to a nervous and iron limb by long exercise, so the mind's labour only gives an endurance which results in a settled power, next to omnipotent.

Let me not be misunderstood in these assertions, nor deemed a tyro in experience, for although my head has not become grey in the pursuit of science; nor my physical man wan and pale by midnight application; yet I can assure the young of this—all my *peculiar* opportunities of observation, conjoined to my own personal acquaintance with the matter, have gone to establish the conviction—that laziness is the bugbear and lion in the way; and that the Siren sloth has shorn the head, and taken away the strength of scores, who, nevertheless like Adam, grossly and wickedly place the imputation elsewhere, and say—nature was at fault.

The hare and tortoise will be a true and living fable for ever. The plodder, in harmony with the order of nature, makes slow but sure progression; whilst he, who depends upon his intellectual swiftness, and only moves on by impulse, will soon find himself sadly contrasted and infinitely distanced.

I reckon it rather a blessing than not, to have, what is called, *mediocre* talents; and especially, if joined with a fixed habit of industrious thought. It is ten to one, but a person liberally endowed by nature, will rest satisfied with the mere dower : like many others in the world, who take *born-rank* as the only thing wanted; whereas, in each case, the very reverse is true; for both God and the world, expect that this high position, should only be a starting post to higher fame.

The man of uncommon gifts, often becomes like a giant in a caravan, a mere object of exhibition. His great powers are useless here, but vulgar praise keeps him under restraint, until effort is irksome, and labour is impossible. How different is the case of the diffident and diligent. He neither sparkles, nor carries bustle in his career : knowing that his ability depends upon his sustained courage, he is too fearful of himself to become proud ; and the very quiet of his movements, and the fact of his humility, are safeguards against paltry praise, and idle compliment. Like the sun, in the early dawn, he hardly rises above a hillock, and for long seems but a slow traveller; clouds and disadvantages mark his path; till gaining his bright meridian he destroys the force of opposing circumstances, and causes thousands, who once looked down with scorn and enquiry, now to gaze upwards for him, with constrained delight and admiration.

Take twenty boys, of like ages, from the form of any school in the kingdom, and their Preceptor will instantly tell you, that the chief difference in their mental progress is the result of industry; nay more, that, in the majority of cases, the promising boy not only defeats his expectations, but seldom draws an equal trace with his steady fellow; and as rarely reaches his repute for sound and solid acquirement. This constitution of mind is not desirable; as it is mostly the indicator of a restlessness, which can never dig long enough to reach the ore; if it be done at all, it must be by explosion: a sort of mental blast. This restlessness often degenerates into a vague ,and wandering mind, that begs at no door long enough to get gold, and departs satisfied with the merest trifle. It is flighty and changeful; and never sees more of a country, than its first blush of beauty and sunshine; leaving the real possession and true value to be entered upon, and realized by others.

I have said all this, not only to remove a general and erroneous belief, that the precocious and promising are the best subjects for the Educator, and that great things can only be accomplished by great and uncommon gifts; but especially to encourage the diffident, and to offer a guarantee to every order of mind, that the KEY OF INDUSTRY will find its way into all the wards of the lock, that keeps fast the *Treasury of Knowedge.* G.

MORAL REFLECTIONS.

IN all small towns and villages, as well as in cities and large towns, numerous social evils are allowed to exist, whose extinction would greatly improve the condition, and increase the happiness of the inhabitants. No one, therefore, will deny that to endeavour to remove them would be the course of true wisdom and of sound policy; or that the honour which such a course would reflect upon the inhabitants of a place would be equal to the advantage they would derive from it. It is equally obvious, that, as all social evils, whilst they are nourished and extended by the influence of association, originate with individuals, the corrective process must have a similar origination: nor will the most gloomy and cynical observer of human affairs, or the most sceptical enquirer into the mysterious relation between the agency of man and the Providence of the Sovereign Spirit doubt, that the influence which would be put forth by the determined and simultaneous effort of all the individuals concerned, would blend and grow into such a force as would soon expel the evils in question, even though their nature were demoniacal and their name Legion.

These remarks will apply equally to the corresponding forms of positive good, which the inhabitants of every town would do well to unite in securing, with as much ardour and diligence as a colony of bees evince, during the hours of sunshine, in storing their cells with the delicious nectar.

By the epithet *social,* as applied to evil in these remarks, it is intended to designate those forms of it which, originating with individual conduct, become, through association, injurious to the public interests. There is, again, an obvious distinction of such evils into two classes—the secular and the moral; the former including whatever interferes with the well-being of the present life strictly speaking; the latter comprehending whatever affects, on the more general and extended scale, the interests of men considered as accountable and immortal beings. It were easy to perceive, before hand, that these classes of evils would, and to a certain extent in what manner they should, exert a reciprocal influence, tending to promote the growth of each other: the observation of every one will have furnished him with numerous instances of proof that such is the case.

It were, further, obviously difficult to discriminate between private and social evils, in any number of particulars, tending to shew a difference between them intrinsically. They are so blended together as to suggest the course of a great river, from its original diminutiveness as it springs from the mountain side; or they would be more properly represented, in the social form, by the dark and threatning thunder cloud, whose portentous bulk has been composed by the gathering together of the smaller masses, scattered over the heavens.

Evils, of all sorts and proportions, grow and multiply their species with as much rapidity as weeds in a garden, or the baneful couch-grass of the field. With respect to the latter, every one knows that the timely use of the hoe and the plough is requisite to preserve the garden and the field from becoming, not only useless, but unsightly and noxious; and who will question that with regard to the former the application of a suitable and timely check is equally necessary to preserve individuals and society from ruin? And, as a high degree of cultivation is required to render land productive on a large scale; so, private and social happiness will be secured in a degree corresponding to the advancement of the process of moral improvement.

Petty evils, (if indeed anything evil will bear such a designation) often disregarded because they are viewed in that light, grow, if not prevented, into the form and dimensions of great ones; and, not unfrequently, gender still greater ones of another sort. In how many instances has a slight cold, for example, for no other reason than that it was "only a slight cold," been suffered to insinuate its fatal influence, by an imperceptible but certain process, through the constitution, until it had succeeded in poisoning the springs of life, and in sowing the seeds of premature decay. An ominous subsidence of the bloom and vivacity of youth; the irrevocable departure of health and vigour; general emaciation of a robust frame and an untimely death have formed the punishment awarded to the neglect; whereas a due attention to the incipient cause might have prevented the so sad a catastrophe. How often, in the domestic circle, have irritating differences, at first slight and infrequent, grown, through mutual unforbearance, into turbulent disputes and biting recriminations, until, through the frequency and violence of domestic broils, the angel of peace has been banished from what *had been* the abode of happiness and tranquility. Pestilence and death have grown out of the gradual and almost imperceptible accumulation of filth. And the *effect* of abused power, appearing at first in the smothered uneasiness of passive resistance, but diffusing and swelling, like the volcanic element, in proportion to the increased pressure of the external cause, (for tyranny *will* grow, if it be not crushed in the bud, until it has reached the point, at which, by its very excess, its destruction becomes inevitable) has, at length, burst forth with overwhelming violence, in the desolating plague of civil warfare.

There is a characteristic resemblance of principle and modes of operation, in all the forms and degrees of evil. Proceeding from one source and tending to one final issue, it maintains a character of uniformity in all its fearfully diversified and multiplying varieties. The progress of disease in the human frame; of error in the operations of the intellect; and of depravity in the dispositions and sentiments of the heart: the internal discords of states and of their subdivisions in counties, towns, villages, and families display a striking similarity in their principles, modes and results.   S.

Soham.   *To be continued.*

OUR LETTER BOX.

The Editors do not wish to be considered responsible for all the sentiments
of their Correspondents.

VOLUNTARY LABOUR RATE.

To the Editor of the Soham Magazine.

SIR,

AMONGST the various schemes for improving the condition of the Labourers, during a period of the year when there is a dearth of employment, none has appeared to me to be more effectual than a Labour Rate, when it has been judiciously and with fairness carried into effect.

The Act of Parliament which made a labour rate compulsory, if adopted by a majority of three-fourths of the rate payers present at a general vestry meeting, expired in 1834; but the occupiers of land in any parish, have still the opportunity of adopting, if they so please, a valid agreement amongst themselves, so as to bind each party to expend during the winter, a certain sum per week in labour, in proportion to the extent of his occupation.

"Property has its duties as well as its rights," and the substitution of the word "tenancy" for "property" would not impair the justice of the motto, and a Tenant is guilty of injustice to society, if he refuse to take his share of the burden of maintaining the labouring population of his parish, who must otherwise be almost uselessly employed on the roads, or driven to the unwelcome necessity of resorting to the workhouse, an alternative which causes dangerous discontent in the minds of the men, who may justly complain of being placed in the position of paupers, when they are willing to earn bread for themselves and their families, by honest and industrious labour, if employment be afforded to them.

I am aware that it will be asserted that it is impracticable to obtain a general concurrence in a proposition of this kind, and that it would be unjust to impose an additional tax on a few liberal minded men, who are already expending their full quota in labour; but I assert, and I may point to the example of a neighbouring parish to prove, that the difficulty will disappear if it is energetically encountered, and if a meeting of the occupiers is convened for the purpose of considering the propriety of effecting an equitable distribution of the surplus labourers; few persons will be inclined to incur the odium of dissenting from so reasonable a proposition.

A few hints on the practical details of such a plan may not be unacceptable to your readers:—

1st. The rate in fairness should be calculated on the " gross estimated rental " of the parish valuation, and not on the " net annual value," otherwise the occupier of fen lands which generally afford the greater opportunity of profitable employment in claying, &c., would, if the taxes were deducted from his assessment, be exempted from a portion of the expenditure, which the occupier of a similar area of upland of equal quality would be obliged to bear.

2ndly. The amount of weekly rate must of course depend on the circumstances of each parish, but there are many reasons why it should not be fixed too high. An extreme labour rate so as to include the whole of the labouring population, would possibly be objected to by many occupiers whose means would not allow of a large addition to their expenditure, and it would induce the labourers to rely in future, more on the exertions of others, than on their own resources, and there are always a certain number of men in every parish, to whom it is desirable to teach the lesson, that idleness, improvidence and misconduct, can only result in misery and the degradation of the workhouse, and it may also be urged that some farms afford a greater degree of profitable employment than others, so that a rate which would not increase the expenditure of one occupier, might be ruinous in its operation on another occupier, who has no opportunity of expending a large increased amount in labour, with advantage to himself and his family. I am an advocate only of a moderate labour rate, which would oblige each occupier to employ such a portion of regular labour as would be advantageous to all parties, and in the parish to which I have alluded, a rate of 4d. in the pound, per week, on the gross estimated rental, has been found to be sufficient.

3rdly. The smaller occupiers should be permitted to return as labourers their unmarried sons, living with, and employed by them, to the extent of about 10s. in a rental under £50., and 20s. under £100.

4thly. Schedules containing the names, ages, &c. of the labourers employed, should be submitted weekly to the inspection of a committee to be appointed for that purpose, as it would be useless to adopt any measure, unless it were conducted in a proper and business-like manner.

I have submitted these observations to you with great diffidence and not with the object of figuring in your columns as an elegant writer, to which title I am fully aware I have no pretensions; but solely with the view of communicating practical information which I have found useful, and which I hope may prove so to all parties who are inclined to take advantage of it.

I am,
Your obedient Servant.
AGRICOLA.

NATURAL HISTORY.

Under this head we purpose occasionally to to give a little sketch, and sometimes to illustrate the same through the powerful aid of a well-executed engraving. We this month select for our subject the *Thibet Watch Dog*, with an accurate delineation, admirably engraved on wood by MR. JABEZ HARE.

THE THIBET WATCH-DOG.

THESE noble animals are the watch-dogs of the table-land of the Himalaya mountains, about Thibet. Their masters, the Bhoteas, to whom they are most strongly attached, are a singular race, of a ruddy copper colour, indicating the bracing air which they breathe, rather short, but of an excellent disposition. Their clothing is adapted to the cold climate they inhabit, and consists of fur and woollen cloth. The men till the ground and keep sheep, and, at certain seasons, come down to trade, bringing borax, tincal, and musk, for sale. They sometimes penetrate as far as Calcutta. On these occasions the women always remain at home with the dogs, and the encampment is watched by the latter, which have an almost irreconcileable aversion to Europeans, and in general fly ferociously at a white face. A warmer climate relaxes all their energies, and they dwindle even in the valley of Nepaul. Those which were in the Zoological Society's Garden in the Regent's Park died soon after their arrival. They were considered very great rarities, and were brought over to this country by Dr. Wallich. The Hon. Edward Gardner, British resident at the court of the Rajah of Nepal, never heard of any other instance of this variety being domesticated by Europeans.

The Whelps are born blind, and do not see till nine days are fully expired: they sometimes see on the tenth, and sometimes not till the twelfth day. At the fourth month the teeth begin to change, and at two years the growth of the animal is considered complete. A dog is considered old at the expiration of five years, and the limits of his existence rarely exceed twenty years. *Penny Cyclopædia.*

POETRY.

[In Original Poetry, the Name, real or assumed, of the Author, is printed in small Capitals under the title; in Selections it is printed in Italics at the end.]

A VOICE FROM THE TOMB.

DAVID GUNTON.

This is the hour, so calm and still,
We love to spend apart;
When every pure and holy thrill,
Awakes within the heart.

When nature is half-lulled to sleep,
Come then to me—
As twinkling stars begin to peep,
And sombrous tints of darkness creep,
O'er land and sea.

Come to my grave, and there repeat
One word of love;
Mine ear the music will not greet,
Affection's tones, however sweet,
No more shall move.

Yet linger there awhile, and dream
Of life and me;
Of days of bright and sunny gleam,
O'er neighbouring dell and lucid stream,
I spent with thee.

Think of our many playful hours,
When hope was young;
Of home, and its luxuriant flowers,
Where all eve long, amid the bowers,
Some sweet bird sung.

Of winter tale, and summer sport,
And favoured nooks;
Of all our spots of sweet resort:
Of all we ever said or thought,
By tongue or books.

Remember me in health and bloom,
And joy elate;
Ere yet disease had mark'd my doom,
Or set the signet of the tomb,
In changeless fate.

Call up the break of morning gay,
When sleep just fled;
When mother came to hear us pray,
And taught us holy words to say,
And joy-tears shed.

She kissed her boys, and told us when
Few years should glide,
We should be strong and active men;
And oh! if wise and virtuous then,
Her only pride.

Think of these glowing short lived days
Too bright to stay;
Lit only by affection's rays,
For love met love at every gaze,
And hearts were gay.

But sully not a scene so fair
By sorrow's sigh;
Forget my latter hours of care,
When those I loved in mute despair,
Beheld me die.

Hear not again that church-yard knell,
For grief was wild;
And tears of bitter anguish fell,
While fond ones took a last farewell,
Of their lost child.

Beside my coffin bending low,
My mother knelt;
And with a mother's love and woe,
Pressed burning kisses on my brow,
But oh! unfelt.

Then all was still—they bore away,
In solemn tread,
My ashes to their kindred clay,
Till judgement's trump and earth's last
Shall wake the dead.   [day,

Brother, the year is in its spring,
And fair flowers bloom;
High in the air sweet songster's sing,
And hill and vale their raptures ring,
Come to my tomb.

When nature is half lulled to sleep,
Come then to me—
As twinkling stars begin to peep,
And sombrous tints of darkness creep,
O'er land and sea.

REFLECTIONS.

I gazed on the stars which at evening first brighten
  The skies, when o'ershadowed with darkness and gloom :—
And I thought of those friends who our sorrows can lighten,
  And shed e'en a solace o'er death and the tomb.

I opened the vase where the rose leaves were faded,
  But sweet was the incense they breathed from their rest,
And I thought of past joys though by distance long shaded,
  That live in the mind in reality drest.

I saw the sweet flower that the rude foot was pressing,
  How closely it clung, and how fragrant it grew!
And I thought of that love that would perish, caressing
  The hand whose unkindness its happiness slew.

I watched the swoln waves on the green ocean bounding
  How they chased one another, then died on the shore,
And I thought of frail man, with life's tempests surrounding,
  We struggle—we fall—and are heard of no more.

Then I turned to the West, where the sun was reposing,
  And awed by the radiance that mark'd his decline,
I thought of the *Just* with mortality closing,
  And sighed for such peace and such death to be mine !   *O.*

OUR CHILDREN'S PAGE.

FACTS WORTH REMEMBERING.

Twelve honest men form an impartial Jury.
The national debt is 800 millions.
The taxes are about 50 millions.
There are above 100 different languages.
There are above 1000 millions of people on the globe.
Gælic is spoken in Ireland.
Erse in the Scotch Highlands.
Welsh in Wales.
The English Language is a mixture of Welsh, Saxon, Norman-
    French, German, Latin and Greek.
There are three or four times as much sea as land.
The clouds are from a quarter of a mile to 7 miles high.
The highest mountains are 4 or 5 miles high.
The heat of the human body is 98 degrees
Water boils at 212°.
Water freezes at 32°.
Summer heat in England from 60°. to 90°.
Winter heat in England from 40° to 10°.
Water is 830 times heavier than air.
Gold is 19 times heavier than water.
Silver is 10 times heavier.—Iron 7 times heavier.

MISCELLANY AND EXTRACTS.

DONATI found the bottom of the Adriatic to be composed of a compact bed of shells, not less than a hundred feet in thickness; and that a few feet below the surface of the bed, the deposits were converted, by pressure and the action of the chemical laws of nature, into solid marble, and the shells completely petrified.

WE cannot, for a moment, suppose that the first man was ever an infant, or the first oak an acorn. Much less then can we suppose the earth to have been formed in any other way than is mentioned in the first verse of the Bible. " In the beginning God *created* the heaven and the earth."

WHEN the ice breaks up in the polar regions, on the return of summer, immense islands are set afloat, rising high into the air, and sinking a great depth into the sea. The melting process, in most cases, goes on inequally in the water and in the air, and, from the huge mass thus changing form, the stability is lost, and one of the grandest phenomena in nature thus produced. The mountain is suddenly overthrown, with a fearful tumult of the ocean, which is often felt at the distance of many leagues around.

THE advice that Wallace gave, in the 13th century, would be valuable, even now, if it were not too late to adopt it. But stage coaches, steam boats, manufactures, and *a false principle of Education*, which superseding the old-fashioned study of the scriptures as the *all in all*, teaches discontented ambitions rather than honest emulations of "doing their duty in that state of life unto which it has pleased God to call them,"—have all combined to make some of the most distant parts of Scotland, too much like those nearest the British metropolis;—and they need not be described! But there is an effect of this change which Wallace did not forsee,—the tyranny of a multitude, still more formidable than that of a single man, an example which France, the long signal example of luxury and a despotic monarch at last exhibited, in that of a despotic people with "every man's hand against his brother,"—*Scottish Chiefs. P.* 234, *note, Vol.* 2.

THE SCHOOLMASTER.—In Cincinnati, United States, a place which was a wilderness only 60 years since, a single publisher has printed, in six years, 650,000 school-books.

MONTHLY NOTICES.

JANUARY.

1st.—Eau Brink Tax due, must be paid before the end of March.

Padnal and Waterden, and South Level Taxes due, must be paid before the 28th.

5th.—Half-yearly dividends on some of the species of Stock due.

6th.—Isle of Ely Quarter Sessions *at Wisbech.*

8th.—Insurances due at Christmas must be paid on or before this day.

PLAYFORD'S

SOHAM MAGAZINE,

AND

Friendly Monitor.

FEBRUARY, 1847.

THE FORCE OF EXAMPLE.

 T is a maxim, uttered by an inspired apostle, and established by the sad experience of ages, that "evil communications corrupt good manners." Were we to trace to its origin any one vicious habit by which an individual has become enslaved, we should rarely find that it sprung from the innate evil of his heart, without the contagious influence of sinful society. Hence the vital importance, to our present and future interests, of the careful selection of our associates and friends; for however deeply we may have been imbued with right sentiments of religion and virtue, such impressions will seldom long survive in an atmosphere of immorality and vice. How many there are who have travelled far towards the close of a lengthened life, tied and bound by inveterate habits of intemperance, who can trace their early departure from the paths of purity, to the shame or fear that they experienced from the anticipated ridicule of others. The power of conscience, and the influence of education, may, for a while, withstand the shock, but these barriers will be gradually overpowered by the presence of an unceasing temptation. How often has the morning of life, which made promise of a bright and happy day, been overcast by those clouds of darkness and storm which have never been dissipated to its close! And whence arose the evil? The native corruption of the heart has been aroused into fatal energy and life by the pernicious

No. 2. Vol. I. c

influence of companions, whose own career of sin was so much
the less easy while a solitary obstacle could be found to withstand
it.   Lost as to every high and honourable principle themselves,
they sought the gratification of the dark passions of their hearts
in the ruin of their brother.

It becomes, therefore, not more the duty than the interest of
every one who values a good name among mankind, deliberately
and determinately, to shun that society of which he can have
any cause to be ashamed.   Let him beware then, in the first
place, of any familiar intercourse with those who endeavour, in
the slightest degree, to destroy the principles of Christianity—
who treat with levity the scriptures of inspiration—who speak
without reverence of spiritual and eternal realities, or regard
religion with indifference or contempt.   There are many of this
class of every age, and in every station of life—shallow and
conceited persons—affecting a high spirit, and a superiority to
what they are pleased to call the prejudices of others, while, in
reality, they are themselves the prey of ignorance and the dupes
of folly, deserving only the detestation and scorn of every honest
and enlightened mind.   The most abject superstition is more
rational than unbelief, and the poor benighted child of sorrow,
who thinks he sees his god in a stone, may be a far more exalted character than "the fool who says in his heart there is
none."

A second class of those whom it becomes us to avoid, consists of all who have a tendency to destroy in us the true
principles of honesty.   Under this head we may rank the low
and infamous of every profession, and especially gamblers of
every denomination.   Such characters are justly described as
"knaves whose practice it is to invite the unwary to game,
and to cheat them," and despicable indeed must be the man
who would not burn with indignant shame at such a charge.

But the class that commonly proves the most dangerous, especially to the young, is formed of those who make sensual
pleasure the chief object of pursuit.   For however much the
various degrees of it may be deserving of corresponding degrees
of condemnation, yet its invariable tendency is to corrupt the
purity of the mind, to enervate those energies by which alone
we can ever advance ourselves to a position of eminence, or

honour among our fellows, and to destroy, at length, every vestage of that moral feeling which distinguishes man from the brutes, and makes him fit for rational and civilized society.

Besides these three classes, whose "communications" are radically "evil," there are others who come under the denomination of trifling and worthless:—those who follow no useful occupation—who are led by no ideas of improvement—who spend their time in dissipation and folly, and whose highest praise is that they are not openly immoral. "Let no such men be trusted." They are utterly useless as members of the community; and, but for the influence of an all-controling energy from above, they will sink from one degree of senselessness to another, till overtaken by that imbecility of mind, if not by that depravity of the affections, which will render them a burden and a pest to all around.

Resist, therefore, the first encroachments of evil. If you desire to occupy a station that becomes an immortal being, fly from the society of the sensual, the profligate, and the profane. In the eyes of the wise, they can only render you obnoxious to contempt; while the good will regard you as objects of pity in *this* world, and as hastening to ruin in the *next*.

THE SLIDE OF ALPNACH.

THOSE enormous pine trees with which the masts and spars of ships of the line and merchantmen are formed, it is well known, are not among the natural productions of this country. Large quantities of them are procured from the forests of Switzerland, where they grow with luxuriance upon the sides of the rugged Alps. The difficulty of conveying them from the distant spots where they are found, which are often quite unapproachable except on foot, has occasioned the invention of many singular contrivances. Among the most wonderful was the slide of Alpnach, which was a huge trough six feet broad, from three to six feet deep, and eight miles and a half in length, constructed of pine trees with the bark removed. This singular wooden road was carried along the sides of hills, and over vallies and defiles at a height of one hundred and twenty feet from the ground by means of scaffolding, while in several places it passed through the mountains by tunnels; and in others, was hung to the perpendicular face of granite cliffs at a giddy elevation above the torrent that rushed through the dark ravine below.   Down this viaduct pine trees were impelled with such excessive velocity as to appear, in their passage, only a foot or two long, while, in reality, they were perhaps upwards of a hundred.   Along this slide workmen were placed at convenient intervals to carry on the communication from one end to the other. When those at the bottom were ready, the words "let go" were passed from man to man and reached the top, under ordinary circumstances, in about three minutes.   The tree, which had been previously placed in the slide, was then let go, the persons releasing it crying out previously "it comes," when the enormous mass, frequently a hundred feet long, with a proportionable diameter, shot past with the rapidity of lightning, sometimes traversing the whole distance in two minutes and a half, and plunged into the lake of Lucerne.   Some trees were once turned off this slide, by way of experiment, and buried themselves from eighteen to twenty feet in the earth, and one of them having, by accident, struck another in its descent, cleft it through its whole length, as if it had been smitten by a thunder-bolt.

SHIPWRECK AT ALDBORO'.

A few years ago, during a very heavy gale off the Coast of Suffolk, among the many vessels that were standing out to sea to avoid the dangers of a lee shore, one was observed which seemed to have become unmanageable, and which, after buffeting the waves for a considerable time, was gradually drifting towards the Town of Aldboro'.   The moment it became evident that she was in danger, the beach, notwithstanding the extreme violence of the gale, was crowded with spectators, evincing by their gesticulations and countenances the agony of suspense and excitement within.   The certainty of the destruction of the ship became, every moment, more apparent, because she was close upon the outermost of the two steep ridges, or banks, that lie a mile or two to sea, over which it seemed impossible for her to ride.   Suddenly, however, she righted herself for an instant as if by some skilful manœuvre of the crew, and to the intense delight of all on shore, especially of the seamen, she took advantage of a mountain wave and, with one long lurch, heaved over into deep water.   But there was still another danger to be encountered equally formidable with the first, and she was now rushing upon the crest of a foaming wave upon the hidden, and too often fatal sand.   "She must have the best pilot in the world aboard"—cried a weather-beaten Tar,—"if she does not go to the bottom,"—but he had scarcely uttered the words, when, as if in proud defiance of the tempest, she lifted her bows upon the billows, and was once more saved from instantaneous and total ruin.   All hands were now hastening to the spot where it was supposed she would take the ground, prepared to peril their lives amid the breakers to save so gallant a crew when the timbers of their vessel should be scattered on the foam. One huge wave after another overtook the trembling bark, tossing her as if she were a feather in their gigantic arms, till, at last, the whole fury of the storm seemed let loose upon its victim, and one long rush of the maddened waters threw her with a fearful crash upon the shore. As the mountain wave subsided, leaving her so high upon the beach as to be almost in contact with the houses, a number of sailors leaped upon her deck, to lend a hand in any way they could, but, to their utter astonishment, they found not a human being there as her guide. On going below they discovered the whole of her crew in the cabin, petrified with dismay. They were foreigners, who knew nothing of the coast; and having given themselves up for lost, had abandoned the helm, and determined to perish in each others arms.

But who was it that directed that frail vessel through dangers where no mortal arm could steer? It was He whose "wonders are seen in the deep";—without whose permission "not a sparrow falleth to the ground";—and, while by His hand the glittering orbs are launched through the vault of heaven, the humblest of his creatures is sustained from day to day!

MORAL REFLECTIONS.
Continued from Page 10.

The somewhat abrupt manner in which these observations were brought to a pause in the last No. of the Magazine, renders it necessary to supply a link to connect the contribution in that, with what is to follow in this. Let this, then, be the link.

The natural resemblance between the several forms and varieties of evil in some of their most essential features, already slightly glanced at, suggests another obvious reflection, viz., that there must be a resemblance, also, in the modes of getting quit of them. One of the most discouraging circumstances, to the Christian Philanthropist, connected with the numerous forms of social evil by which all communities, down to the smallest village, are afflicted, is, that they have acquired a sort of licence to grow and luxuriate without molestation, whilst the inhabitants seem determined, under an amazing infatuation, that they shall exhibit the property of an immortal existence. At the same time that they are suffering severely from their *natural* effects, and even bitterly lamenting those effects and complaining of them, they persist, in spite of remonstrance and of example, in contributing to perpetuate and swell the causes. In how many instances, in the course of a life-time, will a serious person be astounded and appalled, by the spectacle of a young man in promising circumstances, and (with different dispositions and habits) the subject of a cheering prospect of respectability, comfort and usefulness, pursuing a course which has led thousands to ruin, without appearing in the least degree apprehensive that it will lead *him* also to ruin, even when there are instances of what it has done, staring him full in the face? He cultivates the same habits and becomes, in an equal ratio, the slave of those habits; he visits the same haunts, for similar purposes and with similar results; and addicts himself to the same vicious practices, with the same degree of rapidity and success, in the formation of an abandoned character. The *necessary* consequences—in the entailment of wordly difficulties and the loss of capacity to command and surmount them; in the falling to pieces of a bodily constitution, naturally strong and durable; in the prostration of self-respect and the abandonment of all virtuous principle; and (what is far from being the least distressing circumstance, or the least censurable, in the estimate formed of his conduct by an upright mind) in a total recklessness of the claims of a dependent, but ruined family—thicken around him; yet he puts off the evil day, and with it all *serious* thoughts of amendment, for still the infatuation clings to him which befools him into scepticism, at the least, as to the issue of all this in *his* case, until, with a full consciousness of the fearful reality when it is too late to be of service to him, he finds himself irretrievably lost. But communities, too frequently, display a similar infatuation. True it is, that there are individuals in the social body, and in all its minor divisions, (otherwise society must soon become extinct) whose influence in preserving it from decay and ruin, is similar to what, it might be supposed, would have been the effect, in the individual case, of a sufficient number and force of virtuous principles, to counteract the vicious process and to prevent the final catastrophe. And it would be an infinite mercy, if the number of such persons were indefinitely increased. But let them, in imagination, be abstracted—transferred, say, to happier economy—and what then? Who would venture to predict for the remaining portion, a less disastrous result, than that they would speedily bring down upon themselves wrath to the uttermost?

There is little or no hope of social improvement, but in proportion as society becomes sensible of its own account in the evils which afflict it, and of the connexion between its own agency and their removal; in other words the evils which, like ulcers in its side, or demons in its path, fret and balk and curse a population, large or small, will shew signs of mortality, when that very population shall set its face, as a flint, against them; instead of supplying them with the nutriment which perpetuates their existence and swells their proportions. It is undeniable that a fearfully large proportion of the inhabitants of most places, are, directly or indirectly, the abettors and nursers of the very evils which torment them; and a general awakening to the true posture of affairs will be the omen, so devoutly to be wished, and earnestly to be sought by every lover of his species, of the approach of a happier state of things.

The inhabitants of towns and villages, are, for the most part, prompt and eager enough, in employing the measures requisite to increase their property; and either singly, or, when necessary, in combination to resist the aggression of whatever threatens to deprive them of it: it were a great happiness, if they should be as prompt and diligent in enlarging their store of that property which springs from virtue; and in defending it against those vulture-like despoilers of it,—their own vices.

It is deeply interesting to observe, with what skill and activity, the resources of nature and the discoveries of science are brought to bear, in securing the necessaries of life and in multiplying its comforts; and with what an instantaneous excitement and an immense power of congenial feeling, a beseiged people will throw themselves into the attitude of mutual defence, from the assaults of the invading foe. The reflections suggested by these impressive features of the human character, in the mind of a true Philanthropist, would inevitably converge in some such question as the following :—By what fatality have these people, so easily wrought upon by every other kind of concernment; so actively alive to their social welfare in its subordinate forms—by what fatality have they been beguiled, into so total an indifference, to what is confessedly their supreme interest; in so much that at the same time that they are labouring with untiring diligence, to secure their prosperity in those forms of it which are merely secular and external; and would, to a man, stand up to defend it in those forms, with the utmost readiness and vigour, they yet suffer the little that remains of it, in its true spiritual essence, to be consumed by an internal process, as insidious it may be, but also as certain as that by which the fatal worm at the root of a plant destroys the vital principle, or the dry-rot in a piece of timber, transforms it into dust.   S.

Soham.   *To be continued.*

FESTIVALS, when duly observed, attach men to the civil and religious institutions of their country; it is an evil, therefore, when they fall into disuse. Who is there that does not recollect their effect upon himself in early life?—*Southey.*

ECONOMICAL HINTS.

The following Article, written by a Lady formerly residing at Soham, and addressed to a female domestic on her quitting service, we hope will prove interesting
to some of our readers. The person to whom this kind advice was given had just
married a respectable labouring man; she still resides in this town, and, if we
may judge from the manner in which she has brought up her family, there can
be no doubt but that she has profited by the lessons which it contains.

As my recent and perilous illness, in which you so kindly attended me, prohibits
me the unlimited use of speech, I purpose to employ some of my leisure moments,
when tired of reading and other amusements, in writing out a few rules for economy which may be of service to you in the new mode of life into which you have just
entered. The change to you must be so great a one from having every thing so
amply provided for you without your being the least aware of the expense of such
a provision; and it is so many years since you have left your parents' cottage that
you can scarcely bring yourself to the methods necessary to make your expenditure
answer to the small means your own industry added to that of your husband shall
provide for your support.

The sweet and pleasing reflection, however, that you are now enjoying your own
liberty after having been so many years at the command of others, and that whatever little you possess, is the fruit of your honest labour and provident frugality,
will afford a gratification to your minds, and give a relish to your simple viands,
superior to what any other situation imparts. To preserve this feeling in its most
fervent and primitive glow, which, if once suffered to fade away, is scarcely, if
ever, to be restored, should be your most earnest endeavour, and to assist you in
the accomplishment of so desirable an end as the establishing your future independence on the basis of your own industry and frugality, would be to me an unspeakable satisfaction. To every inhabitant of this happy country, independence ought
to be the first earthly object. By independence, I do not mean a state that exempts
you from being indebted to the assistance of others (for we are *all*, however raised
above want by our rank in life, dependent on each other for a thousand attentions,
as you have so lately had a proof of in myself) but the independence that should
lead us to use our own most strenuous endeavours for our support whilst we are blest
with health and strength, and *then* if those *should* fail, we should feel no hesitation
in applying for the support so liberally provided by our charitable country, for those
who really require it. Of this more hereafter.

To you who have been so fortunate as to have received an education superior to
most in your rank of life, and who have a capacity to understand, and principles
to appreciate my meaning, I shall take a view of economy in a higher light than it
is in general beheld, but in the light in which it has ever appeared to me to be most
necessary to consider it. When I look around me on the vast creation, so beautiful
in all its parts, so wonderful in all its movements! so orderly, so strictly economical
in the most minute particle, that even the clear water which allays my thirst, is
filled with living animals! the clod of earth which I pick up and cast carelessly
from me, is a world to myriads of moving creatures, formed with veins and muscles,
and every thing necessary to life; when I consider that not an atom was made in
vain, but, as Sturm observes, " the smallest particle of the first leaves of the crea-

tion at this moment exist, and fertilize the earth" and that all which it produces returns again to it for that beneficent purpose; when, I repeat, I reflect on all this, I am struck with astonishment, that man, dependent, helpless man, who cannot of himself "add one cubit to his stature," can be so lavish of the gifts of his bountiful Creator, and wantonly squander them away, when a very slight degree of reflection would convince him that even he himself might in a short time be thankful for what he now thoughtlessly destroys. When He, who was Lord of All, and could so easily feed the five thousand with the five loaves and two small fishes, thought it necessary to say "gather up the fragments that remain that *nothing* be lost" shall man presume to disregard, and waste any portion of what he cannot increase by his own means, even in the most minute degree. These reflections have impressed most strongly on my own mind the conviction, that ALL WASTE IS SIN! and when to others I have appeared to be acting from a parsimonious habit, I have been actuated by, I hope and trust, a much higher principle.

It has never surprised me to observe, that servants in a large family, should be regardless of what they either do not know, or at least never reflect on, the value of the article they destroy, but that a poor labouring person, who literally earns the little he possesses "by the sweat of his brow" should not of that little be careful of every atom that may be of service to him, has, I own, often astonished me. It is a frequent remark, that the poor are by no means so economical as the rich; and from the few observations I have been enabled to make, I believe it to be too generally the case. Why it is so, is to me most unaccountable. It might be reasonably supposed that they could not want a more efficient teacher than necessity, to enforce on their minds the advantage of making the most of all that they possess; but if any other is requisite, most desirable would it be to have lectures on that art in the schools instituted for the instruction of the poor, blessed institutions, which cannot be too highly appreciated by those to whom they are appropriated, for by them they are taught the way to everlasting life, not to trifle away their invaluable hours over useless books that at best can but amuse, and too frequently enervate the mind, and unfit it for its proper avocations, (and by doing so, let it ever be remembered, that they are *doubly* losers, as during those hours they might have earned an addition to their little income) not to indulge in speculations incompatible with their situation, is this excellent education given them which they could not otherwise have obtained; but to *learn their duty* in whatever state of life they may be placed, and to *practice it*. This is the grand object of these institutions, and this they must further by their own endeavours, or be doubly reprehensible. Here they are taught from that Book beyond all price, that "if any will not work, neither shall he eat." That we should not be "slothful in business," but "labour, working with our hands," not only for our own support, but that we might have to give to him that needeth" as Paul laboured that he might be "chargeable to no man," and worked at his useful occupation with those of his own profession. Shall any therefore refuse to labour, and to make the *most* of the time allotted them? Shall any who shall read that "the poor man is honoured for his skill" not exercise that skill to the best advantage? All have some talents given them, and for what? to be "laid by in a napkin?" Recollect the fate of the "slothful servant" and risk not the penalty. Most justly does Miss Talbot remark in her excellent Reflections (a work that ought to be in every persons hands who can afford the trifling sum at which it is published) that most *merciful* as well as *just* was the sentence of *perpetual toil* pronounced on man for his first transgression.

To be continued.

ROSLYN CASTLE.

FROM A DRAWING BY L. READ.   ENGRAVED BY MISS HARE.

A few miles to the south of Edinburgh stand the ruins of this once magnificent castle. Its situation is one of extreme beauty and seclusion. Embosomed in a deep glen, amidst the most luxuriant shades, it presents itself to view on a peninsulated rock, accessible only by a bridge of stupendous elevation. It was once the seat of the Sinclairs, one of whom was Oliver, the unfortunate favourite of James V., and the innocent cause of the loss of the battle of Solway Moss, from the stubborn pride of the Scotch nobility, which would not bend to his command. On the height above is the highly decorated Chapel of Roslyn, an edifice of exquisite beauty, founded by William St. Clare, prince of Orkney, in 1446; and, at a short distance, are some very remarkable caves, supposed to have been constructed by the Picts. The brave Alexander Ramsay made these caves his residence for a considerable time, in 1341, where all the gallant youths of Scotland resorted to him, to learn the art of war; and, with him, made frequent excursions to the English borders.

No. 2.   Vol. I.   c2

OUR LETTER BOX.

The Editors do not wish to be considered responsible for all the sentiments
of their Correspondents.

To the Editor of the Soham Magazine.

SIR,

UNDERSTANDING from the prospectus of your Periodical, that it
will have for its principal object the dissemination of truth, in articles
of local interest connected with our town and neighbourhood, I
hail with delight the appearance of such a praiseworthy medium,
a medium long wanted, and one, which if carried out with spirit,
must assuredly do much good; and I trust I shall not be considered as trespassing on your pages, if I can prevail upon you to
insert a few lines in favour of a Society, lately formed in this
place, for the "Diffusion of General and Useful Knowledge amongst
all Classes"

Intellectual improvement, an object worthy the attention of
even the humblest individual, has been much neglected in our town,
and, concerning many subjects, which might be known as sources
of pleasure and profit, and the causes of national advancement,
lamentable ignorance prevails.

In the present age, commercial speculations and business engagements occupy the attention and engross the thoughts of the
greater portion of the community. The merchant and his clerks
are intent upon the acquisition of wealth, the enlargements of
establishments, and the increase of trade. The farmer drives his
plough, harvests his grain, sells his produce, and finds his mind
fully employed in seeking the means most likely to increase his
possessions. The artisan toils in his shop, his head and hands are
completely occupied in the production of articles useful or orna-
mental, or in the more pleasing occupation of waiting upon his
friends and customers. But, amid these various engagements, the
noblest part of humanity is either comparatively inactive, or is
occupied with subjects little calculated to develop its all but unlimited powers.

The great thing that is needed is a habit of inquiry and investigation; a state of mind which is not satisfied with the fact
that a thing *is so*, but which advances a step farther, and asks
WHY it is so? a mind which is disposed to push its researches
until it either gains the desired knowledge, or rests satisfied that
the solution of the problem is beyond the powers of *human* intellect.

The present age affords innumerable facilities for the acquisition of knowledge, both general and useful, and for the advancement of intellectual character. The press, like a perennial spring, is sending forth the streams of literature; books are now within the reach of ALL, not only the trashy sentiments published daily in "cheap editions," but the writings of the *giants* of literature, men of the most profound learning and intellect are brought to us on terms to which the most limited means cannot object. Associations for the diffusion of useful knowledge, Mechanics' Institutions, and Literary Societies are formed; and many a young man, by the application of his winter evenings, has, by returning spring, found himself introduced into a new intellectual world.

Let me persuade such of my townsmen and readers as are at present members of the "Soham Association for the Diffusion of General and Useful Knowledge," to use their efforts to promote its prosperity by inducing *others* to join it. The terms of admission are so low as to render it available to ALL. The long and dreary winter evenings have arrived; a comfortable Reading Room is proprovided, where books of reference and good society may always be found; there is also at present a small Library of useful and entertaining books for general circulation; besides which, Lectures on interesting subjects are occasionally given.

Should the suggestions here thrown out, induce any persons, more especially any of my young friends in Soham and its Neighbourhood, to become members of an Institution, which, in my belief, is calculated to be of lasting benefit to the rising generation, I shall have reason to be thankful for the means you have afforded me of bringing before them this subject.

I am, 'Sir,

Soham.　　　　　　　　　　Your obedient Servant,

S. W.　　

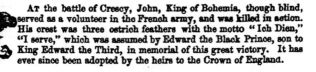

AT the battle of Crescy, John, King of Bohemia, though blind, served as a volunteer in the French army, and was killed in action. His crest was three ostrich feathers with the motto "Ich Dien," "I serve," which was assumed by Edward the Black Prince, son to King Edward the Third, in memorial of this great victory. It has ever since been adopted by the heirs to the Crown of England.

RICHARD the First, of England, defeated the French at Gisors, in the department of Eure and late province of Normandy, in A. D. 1198. This monarch's parole for the day was "Dieu et mon Droit," which has almost ever since continued the motto of the Royal Arms of England.

POETRY.

[In Original Poetry, the Name, real or assumed, of the Author, is printed in small Capitals under the title; in Selections it is printed in Italics at the end.]

THE WOUNDED SOLDIER'S RETURN.

This little Poem was written by JAMES CHAMBERS, who was born at Soham, nearly a century ago; and, when it is considered that, as he himself states, his only attendance at school was for one month, in his childhood, we think our readers will allow it to be a meritorious production.

The sun was just retired, the dews of eve
　Their glow-worm lustre scattered o'er the vale,
The lonely nightingale began to grieve,
　Telling, with many a pause, his tender tale.

No clamours rude disturb'd the peaceful hour,
　And the young moon, yet fearful of the night,
Rear'd her pale crescent o'er the burnish'd tow'r,
　Which caught the parting orb's still ling'ring light.

'Twas then, where peasant footsteps mark'd the way,
　A wounded soldier feebly mov'd along,
Nor aught regarded he the soft'ning ray,
　Nor the expressive bird's melodious song.

On crutches borne his mangled limbs he drew,
　Unsightly remnants of the battle's rage,
While pity in his pallid looks might view
　A helpless prematurity of age.

Then, as by sad contortions, laboring slow,
　He gain'd the summit of his native hill,
And saw the well-known prospect spread below,
　The farm, the cot, the hamlet, and the mill.

In spite of fortitude, one struggling sigh
　Shook the firm texture of his throbing heart,

And from his hollow and dejected eye
　One trembling tear hung ready to depart.

"How chang'd" he cried, "is this fair scene to me!
　Since last across this narrow path I went,
"The soaring lark felt not superior glee,
　"Nor any human breast more true content.

"When the fresh hay was o'er the meadow thrown,
　"Amongst the busy throng I still appeared,
"My prowess too at harvest-time was shewn,
　"When Lucy's carol ev'ry labour cheer'd.

"The scorching sun I scarcely seem'd to feel,
　"If the dear maiden near me chanc'd to rove,
"And if she deign'd to share my frugal meal,
　"It was a rich repast—a feast of love.

"And when at ev'ning, with the rustic's pride,
　"I dar'd the sturdiest wrestlers on the green,
"What joy was mine, to hear her by my side
　"Extol my vigour and my manly mien!

"Alas! no more the sprightly maid shall run
　"To bid me welcome from the sultry plain,
"But her averted eye my sight shall shun,
　"And all my fondest cherish'd hopes be vain.

"And you, my parents, must ye too endure
　"That I should ever damp your homely mirth,
"Exist upon the pittance ye procure,
　"And make you curse the hour that gave me birth!

'Ah! hapless hour, when at a neigbour-
   ing wake,
   "The gaudy sergeant caught my
     wond'ring eye,
"And as his tongue of war and honour
     spake,
   "I felt a wish to conquer or to die.

"Then while he bound the ribbands on
     my brow,
   "He talk'd of Captains kind, and
     Generals good,
"Said a whole nation would my fame
     avow,
   "And bounty call'd the purchase of
     my blood.

"But I refus'd that bounty, I disdain'd
   "To sell my service in a righteous
     cause,
"For so to my dull sense it was ex-
     plain'd,
   "The cause of honor, justice, and the
     laws.

' The rattling drums beat loud, the fifes
     began,
   "My King and Country seem'd to ask
     my aid,
"Through ev'ry vein the thrilling ardor
     ran,
   "I left my homely cot, my village
     maid.

"In loathsome vessels now like slaves
     confin'd,
   "Now call'd to slaughter in the open
     field,
' Now backward driv'n, like chaff before
     the wind,
   "Too weak to stand, and yet asham'd
     to yield.

"'Till oft repeated victories inspir'd
   "With tenfold fury the indignant foe,
"Who closer still advanc'd as we retir'd
   "And laid our proudest boasted honors
     low.

"Through burning deserts now com-
     pell'd to fly,
   "Our bravest legions moulder fast
     away,
"Thousands, of wounds and sickness,
     left to die,
   "While hovering ravens mark'd them
     for their prey.
"Ah! sure remorse their savage hearts
     must rend
   "Whose selfish desperate phrenzy
     could decree,
"That in one mass of murder man should
     blend,
   "Who sent the slave to fight against
     the free.

"Unequal contest! at fair Freedom's call
   "The lowliest hind glows with celes-
     tial fire,
"She rules, directs, pervades, and orders
     all,
   "And armies at her sacred glance ex-
     pire.

"Then be the warfare of this world ac-
     cursed,
   "The son now weeps not o'er his
     father's bier,
"But grey-haired age for nature is re-
     vers'd.
   "Sheds o'er its children's grave an
     icy tear."

Thus having spoke, by varying passions
     tost,
   He reach'd the threshold of his pa-
     rents' shed,
Who knew not of his fate, but mourn'd
     him lost,
   Among the numbers of the un-nam'd
     dead.

Soon as they heard his well-remember'd
     voice,
   A ray of comfort chas'd habitual fear,
Our Henry lives, we may again rejoice,
   And Lucy sweetly blush'd, for she was
     there.

THE SWORD.

'Twas the battle-field, and the cold pale moon
   Look'd down on the dead and dying,
And the wind pass'd o'er with a dirge and a wail
   Where the young and the brave were lying.

With his father's sword in his red right hand,
   And the hostile dead around him,
Lay a youthful Chief; but his bed was the ground
   And the grave's icy sleep had bound him.

A reckless rover, 'mid death and doom,
  Pass'd a soldier, his plunder seeking;
Careless he stept where friend and foe
  Lay alike in their life-blood reeking.

Drawn by the shine of the warrior's sword,
  The soldier paus'd beside it;
He wrench'd the hand with a giant's strength—
  But the grasp of death defied it.

He loos'd his hold, and his English heart
  Took part with the dead before him,
And he honour'd the brave who died sword in hand,
  As, with soften'd brow, he lean't o'er him.

"A soldier's death thou hast boldly died,
  A soldier's grave won by it;
Before I would take that sword from thy hand,
  My own life's blood should dye it.

"Thou shalt not be left for the carrion crow,
  Or the wolf to batten o'er thee;
Or the coward insult the gallant dead,
  Who, in life, had trembled before thee."

Then dug he a grave in the crimson earth
  Where his warrior foe was sleeping;
And he laid him there, in honour and rest,
  With his sword in his own brave keeping.

                                        L. E. L.

---◆---

OUR CHILDREN'S PAGE.

FACTS WORTH REMEMBERING.

The first King of all England was Egbert, in 828.
Ireland was united by Henry II., in 1180
Wales, by Edward I., in 1283.
Scotland, by James I., in 1603.
The Revolution took place in 1688.
America was discovered, by Columbus, in 1492.
Printing was invented about 1440.
Rome was built 753 years before Christ.
David became King 1044 years before Christ.
Moses died 1460 years before Christ.
England and Wales are about 400 miles long, and 250 broad.
Scotland is about 280 miles long, and 100 broad.
Ireland is about 220 miles long, and 160 broad.
England and Wales contain above 13 millions of inhabitants
Scotland, about 3 millions
Ireland above 7 millions.

MISCELLANY AND EXTRACTS.

EXTRACT FROM LORD BROUGHAM'S SPEECH ON THE BEER BILL. — To what purpose is it that the clergy cultivate the morals of the people, by affording them education and information—what is the use of all the education they endeavour to bestow—what is the use of here and there sowing a little of the seeds of knowledge, of plucking out a little of the seeds of ignorance—if all the while the legislature, by means of beer shops, is sowing broad-cast the seeds of what is worse than ignorance, calculated to combine with it the seeds of immorality, and thus terminating in the most frightful produce that was ever yet in a civilized country allowed to grow under the eye, and I am ashamed to add, under the fostering care of Parliament: thus polluting the very soil of the country, casting a dark shade over the minds of the people, and infecting and poisoning the moral atmosphere which the people ought to breathe.

A small mass of gold may be hammered into thin leaf, or drawn into fine wire, or cut into almost invisible parts, or liquified in a crucible, or dissolved in acid, or dissipated by intense heat into vapour, and yet, after any or all of these changes, the atoms can be collected again, and the original gold can be exhibited in its pristine state without the slightest diminution or change. And thus all the substances or elements of which our globe is composed may be cut, torn, bruised, and ground into powder a thousand times, and yet be always recovered to their original perfection.

MORTALITY.—The human race resembles the withering foliage of a wide forest. While the air is calm, we perceive single leaves scattering here and there from the branches; but sometimes a tempest or a whirlwind precipitates thousands in a moment. It is a moderate computation, which supposes a hundred thousand millions to have died since the exit of righteous Abel.—*Foster.*

THE DISTANCE OF AN ECHO.—To produce an echo, says Dr. Albert Haller in his Physiology, requires a distance of 110 feet between the reflecting or echoing body from the ear.

POTATOES.—The origin of the word potato is from *battatas* or *pattatas*, which enunciation is common among the natives of Virginia, in North America. The potato was originally a poisonous plant, but rendered esculent by culture.

NEWTON found by experiment that a ball of glass, or a watch-glass laid upon a flat surface of glass, does not really touch it, and cannot be made to touch it even by a force of a thousand pounds to the inch.

THE Swallow is one of my favourite birds, and a rival of the nightingale, for he cheers my sense of seeing as much as the other does my sense of hearing He is the glad prophet of the year; the harbinger of the best season: he lives a life of enjoyment amongst the loveliest forms of nature—winter is unknown to him; and he leaves the green meadows of England in autumn, for the myrtle and orange groves of Italy, and for the palms of Africa; he has always objects of pursuit, and his success is secure. Even the beings selected for his prey, are poetical, beautiful, and transient. The ephemera are saved, by his means, from a slow and lingering death in the evening, and killed in a moment when they have known nothing but pleasure. He is the constant destroyer of insects, the friend of man, and may be regarded as a sacred bird. This instinct, which gives him his appointed season, and teaches him when and where to move, may be regarded as flowing from a divine source; and he belongs to the oracles of nature, which speak the awful and intelligible language of a present Deity.—*Sir H. Davy.*

CHEAP FUEL.—Take one bushel of small coal or sawdust, two bushels of sand, and one bushel and a half of clay; mix them with water, and shape the mass into balls, or into the form of bricks; pile them in a dry place, and when they are hard, they may be used. A fire cannot be lighted with them; but if put behind a fire, they will keep it up stronger than any common fuel.

DR. Beattie, in the eloquent conclusion of his essay on the Immutability of Truth, speaking of sceptics and deists very forcibly remarks :—Caressed by those who call themselves the great, engrossed by the formalities and fopperies of life, intoxicated with vanity, pampered with adulation, dissipated in the tumult of business, or amidst the vicissitudes of folly, *they* perhaps have little need, and little relish for the consolation of religion. But let them know, in the solitary scenes of life, there is many an honest and tender heart pining with incurable anguish, pierced with the sharpest sting of disappointment, bereft of friends, chilled with poverty, racked with disease, scourged by the oppressor, whom nothing but trust in Providence, and the hope of a future retribution, could save from the agonies of despair. And do *they* with sacrilegious hands, attempt to violate this last refuge of the miserable, and to rob them of the only comfort that had survived the ravages of misfortune, malice, and tyranny? Did it ever happen that the influence of their tenets disturbed the tranquility of virtuous retirement, deepened the gloom of human distress, or aggravated the horrors of the grave? Ye traitors to human kind! ye murderers of the human soul! how can ye answer for it in your own hearts? Surely every spark of your generosity is extinguished for ever, if this conclusion do not awaken in you the keenest remorse.

LONGEVITY OF HARD DRINKERS. Dr. Cheyne, of Dublin, speaks of a gen-tleman who, on one occasion, boasted that he had drank two, three or four bottles of wine every day for fifty years, and that he was as hale and hearty as ever. "Pray" remarked a by-stander, "where are your boon companions?" "Ah" he quickly replied, "that's another affair; if the truth may be told, I have buried three entire generations of them.

THE COW TREE.—When travelling in South America, Humbolt and his companions had an opportunity of satisfying themselves, by ocular examination, respecting the truth of the accounts they had received of the *palo de vacca* or cow tree, the milk of which the negroes were said to consider a wholesome aliment. They found by experience that the virtues of this extraordinary tree had not been exaggerated. The palo de vacca is a handsome tree, resembling the broad-leaved star apple : incisions are made in its trunk ; it yields an abundance of glutinous milk, of an agreeable and balmy smell. This sweet and nourishing fluid flows most abundantly at the rising of the sun. The blacks and natives are then seen hastening from all quarters, furnished with large bowls to receive the milk. M. Humbolt declares that in the whole course of his travels he never met with any object which so strongly affected his imagination as the cow tree.— This inestimable gift seems peculiar to the cordilleras of the coast.—*Youth's Instructer.*

MONTHLY NOTICES.

FEBRUARY.

1st.—Annual Meeting of the Members of the Association for the Prosecution of Felons, &c., at Fordham.

5th.—Annual Meeting of the Members of the Association for the Prosecution of Felons, &c., at Soham.

7th.—Within fourteen days from receipt of Justices' Precepts, Overseers to convene a Parish Meeting to make out a list of a competent number of persons qualified to serve as Constables, under 5 and 6 Vic., c. 109.

PLAYFORD'S

SOHAM MAGAZINE,

AND

Friendly Monitor.

MARCH, 1847.

 HEN we see a country, favoured in an eminent degree with fertility of soil and salubrity of climate, whose inhabitants are gifted with an unusual share of mental vivacity and physical power, presenting, from age to to age, a picture of poverty and degradation before the world; it is natural to enquire into the causes of so strange a phenomenon. The question, with regard to Ireland, has been asked a thousand times, and answered in as many different forms according as a moral, political, or religious bias may have swayed the feelings of the observer.

Perhaps a slight reference to the history of other nations, as well as of our own, may tend, in some degree, to unravel the mystery; for as in the human, so in the political body—altho' there may be certain peculiarities of constitution which may modify or aggravate the symptoms of disease—yet the *causes* of disease remain almost invariably the same. Now, however unusual it may have become to trace any national calamities to the afflictive dispensations of Heaven, it is a *fact*, which the history of England will clearly demonstrate, that, in proportion as the Government has lent a fostering hand to the impostures of Popery, so have the fortunes of the kingdom declined;—and, in proportion as it has maintained its proper attitude of resistance towards this monster evil, so, however much we may have been before depressed, have we again preponderated in the balance of the world.

No. 3. Vol. I.   D

And not only is this true with regard to our naval, military and commercial prosperity; but, it is also singularly true as to that alarming deficiency of the means of support which now so widely prevails in the British dominions.   Two hundred and fifty years ago, the Papists endeavoured to lead the ignorant to believe that peace and plenty had left our land when their own abominable idolatry was cast out.   The answer of the then Bishop of Worcester is directly to our point :—"Touching their pretended plenty when Poperie ruled, wee say it is a Tale, for as great dearth was then as since.   Touching our own Countrey, of which I chiefely speake, let them remember what our Chronicles note in Richard the first his time, how sharpe a scarcitie there was by the space of three or foure yeares.   What a Sommer that was in Edward the third his time, called the deer Sommer.   In Richard the second his time what a dearth, when the people where forced to feed upon fruit to sustaine nature, as that thereby many fell into fluxes and dyed. How the childrens cries were so pittyfull for the want of foode, which their Parents had not to give them, as a stonie heart could not indure to heare.   Of Henry the sixth his time, when people were forced to make bread of Fearne rootes.   And (to goe no further) of Acrone bread in Queene Maries time."

But with regard to other countries let us contemplate, for instance, the effects of Popery among the Cantons of Switzerland. Mr. Brockden, in his excursion to the Alps, says : " It is impossible to notice the filth, the laziness, and beggary of the Roman Catholic Cantons of Switzerland without believing that the religion of the state under which these unfortunate people live is either a direct or the remote cause of their degradation, and that it operates as a powerful check to their advancement in such a state of social comfort and moral worth as their neighbours enjoy, who are less under the influence of the Roman Church."   Indeed almost every traveller has observed that the line of demarcation that separates the Protestant from the Romish Cantons, is not geographical but moral; and that the inseparable ignorance, squalidness and poverty of the Popish districts at once proclaim the withering influences of a perverted christianity.

Let us now narrow our view again to Great Britain, and in this soil, so favoured and blessed, it will be seen that Popery, as soon as it gains the ascendant, can beat back the tide of civilization and social refinement. Look at the moral condition of Scotland, the land of naked mountains and impetuous floods—the land of storm and snow, with almost every disadvantage of soil and climate: notwithstanding the growing degeneracy of her commercial and populous towns, and the spiritual destitution of an overgrown population, we can see in the homes of her peasantry, piety, comparative prosperity and peace; and in the calendars of her courts of justice, a small amount of deep and atrocious crime. Contemplate Ireland, on the other hand, disjoined from Scotland by a narrow arm of the sea, and there you find wretchedness and want, and ignorance in the cabins of the great mass of the people—insubordination and dissatisfaction pervading almost every circle—the minister of peace marked out and murdered in the open day, and the Message of Peace burned in the public streets, amid the shouts of a priest-ridden people; and all this in spite of a lovely clime, a fertile soil, harbours capable of holding the navies of Britain, and rivers admirably fitted to be outlets for mercantile enterprise. Ireland has every physical advantage, Scotland every physical disadvantage, and yet Ireland is awfully unhappy, while Scotland is comparatively the reverse. Moreover Ireland started in the race of social and national prosperity with every thing in her favour; Scotland with every thing against her. The former Country, before the usurpation of Rome, was one of the luminaries of the Western world: the latter, during the influence of Rome, was the most enslaved of the nations of Europe. Ireland received the laws and superstitions of Rome, and, from that hour, has retrograded in morality, knowledge, and prosperity—and is miserable. Scotland broke from her fetters, and, from that hour, has advanced in national wealth, and honour, and strength—and is prosperous.

The solution is forced upon our minds, that Popery is the curse that blights and preys upon the life and strength of every land, over which the shadow of its deadly wings extends.

Our space will not allow us any further to illustrate the temporal influences of Popery, or we might press upon the Priests of Rome our proofs, till we left them no possibility of escape. But, were we even to institute a comparison between one of the sections of Ireland and the other three, we might demonstrate by history, by living witnesses, by the laws and customs, and by the calendars of the Courts of Justice, that Ulster, a Protestant province, is superior to Connaught, Munster, and Leinster, the Popish portions of Ireland, as are Scotland and England. How then can any man shut his eyes to the fact that misery and ignorance, and vice have followed in the footsteps of Popery, like death and barrenness behind the simoon of the desert? How can we get rid of the lesson of a universal experience, that, in countries most favoured by clime, and soil, and situation, Popery and degradation, moral and bodily, have moved athwart them; and that in countries where natural advantages are "few and far between," Protestantism, and piety, and learning, and morality have indissolubly tabernacled together?

No political measure will meliorate the condition and the prospects of a nation, while the monastery, the priest, the confessional, and all the abominations of Popery, are suffered to exert their influences on its people.

Popery would blast the happiness of an Eden; and sweep, as with the besom of desolation, every trace of moral and intellectual improvement from the earth.

WILLIAM, Duke of Normandy, invaded England A. D. 1066, and defeated Harold, the reigning Prince, at the battle of Hastings, in Sussex. In this famous engagement, which lasted from morning till sunset, there fell 15,000 Normans; and the loss on the side of the vanquished, was yet more considerable, besides that of the King and his two brothers. William had three horses slain under him. This put an end to the Saxon monarchy in England, which had continued for more than 600 years.

> The haughty Norman seized at once an Isle
> For which, through many a century, in vain,
> The Roman, Saxon, Dane had toil'd and bled.
> THOMSON.

The conquering despot became a most cruel tyrant to his English subjects. The property and honours were taken from the nobility and gentry, and given to the Normans. The country for above 30 miles was laid waste to make the New Forest in Hampshire, for the king's deer and other game; and no less than 36 churches were destroyed on this occasion: so that, as Pope remarks, he

> Stretch'd o'er the poor, and church his iron rod;
> And serv'd alike his vassals and his God.

THE HAPPY COMMUNITY.

(A VISION)

READER, have you never been so fatigued, either by mental or physical exertion, that your couch has become a rack, your night cap an iron crown, and sleep as difficult to find as the philosopher's stone? Have you never suffered from a peculiar sort of ill health, that gives acute nervous sensibility; and a restlessness of brain that generates an endless series of ideas; making that monotonous state of mind—the sure precursor of somnolency—beyond ready attainment? We have been the martyrs of these combined evils; and when half the world have been sleeping soundly, silence has heard us invoke the dull yet benignant god, in the beautiful words of the bard of Avon.

> Nature's soft nurse, how have I frighted thee,
> That thou no more wilt weigh my eyelids down,
> And steep my senses in forgetfulness.

Wonder not then, that "pleasant dreams and slumbers light," should be in our case a subject of record.

Last night was a notable and blissful one, for I had no sooner placed my head upon the pillow, than I found myself under the opiate of a sleepy lull, that soon put the genius of mental activity into a corner, the world out of my calculation and sight, and as the last idea animated itself into sluggish and undefined existence, I (proh pudor) snored!

In a moment I found myself in a region, whose melodies were more ravishing than ever resounded amongst the hills of Arcadia; whose skies were the truest cerulean; whose verdure was intense yet ever varied; and whose golden sun gave life and colour to flowers, which Zephyrs kissed and soft airs fanned. Nor was I less struck with the dwellers in this second Eden, for the ample mark of mental distinction was written on every forehead, and ignorance was with them only a matter of history, associated with the times, when men who laboured in the splendid cause of Education, were deemed euthusiasts, and left to perish under the burden of their holy toil.

I witnessed bodily industry, always so necessary to health and enjoyment, in all its varieties: the shame of labour was lost in its advantage; and those who worked for hire, wrought under the cheering stimulus of thankful employers and equal gains. The blood-lash of the slave driver, never moved through the gentle current of this atmosphere, nor were its peaceful echoes ever broken by the task master's voice, or the hoarse ediot of the tyrant.

The rustic, only such in pursuit, would make the Faradays of the old world blush, for so freed from hard names, and so simple of development, had that which we call chemistry become, that he tilled the soil on principles of wonderful precision, and earth, as is her wont, in all her bounty, paid back a hundred-fold the pains bestowed; whilst no one, being unfed, repined at Providence, or laid to the charge of heaven, ills, that result too often in the ignorance or avarice of man. The artisan was plying but not pale-faced, for luxury did not demand his health for her satisfaction, nor clothe herself in silks to leave him shirtless. I noticed that simple habits had rendered it needless for men to manufacture gew-gaws, and contrive knick-nacks: all had the necessary, none the useless; and as to fancy and fashion, the reds and yellows, the odd devices of the tailor and milliner, these were no where to be seen. The illness that is the modish loveliness of our time, and the cruel pressure that constitutes the beau ideal in form, are unknown; for nature is left to her own sculpture, and exercise has thrown the tints of full health into all the composition.   The shepherds, as of old, kept their folds, tuned their reeds to pastorals, listened to gurgling brook, to insect hum and high ethereal lay; or turned the eye in rapt wonder to read the book of nature, and to gaze on the hosts of heaven,

> Such caught of yore the glorious song,
>   When sable midnight gleamed with fire;
> And wafting winds conveyed along,
>   The music of a heavenly choir.

Here man is never maddened by intoxication, nor fevered by excess.   Temperance has tuned his mind to sedate calmness, and endowed him with a robust health, that says hearty grace over an anchorite's fare, and finds a piquant zest in the simplest meal.   And when the sweet day of active life goes down, evening throws out her softened shades, and wandering feet of love and meditation, fall to the chant of warbling song bird.   The night is a sacred one, for the stars never watch a prowling thief, nor bear record against the base assassin.   No fiend gropes about with the torch of destruction, to do deeds that devils scarce would dare.   Labour is the lullaby, and peace of mind the anodyne, that subdues the mind with soft and holy influences.

How endless are the leaves of nature; how striking its passages; how moving its appeals.   In this fair · country, such theology was written on every blade, such influence moved on every breeze; but this had not been the prime magnetic mover of their passions, nor the preacher whose sermons had touched their moral sensi-bilities.—The beautiful feet of those who bring glad tidings of good, had travelled down their mountains,—traversed their dales,—Righteousness had covered the earth; and thus they had become—A Happy Community.

The first sun beam dissipated my vision, and brought me back to all the realities of the world, as it IS.   G

MORAL REFLECTIONS.

Continued from Page 22.

The reader is supposed (by a fiction of the imagination if he pleases so to consider it) to retain in memory the substance of the concluding sentence in the last communication.   Should this be the case he will not, now, need to refer to it otherwise than by an easy glance of the mind, to recognise the series of the obser-vations.

This indifference to the supreme interest, as consisting in the practice of virtue, is not confined to any one particular class.   It might be considered a happy circumstance, if it were so confined; for then it might be expected that an earnest and energetic co-operation of the exempted classes, would soon be instrumental in reducing *that one* to the right temper.   The inevitable division of society into subordinate sections, has gendered also a corresponding diversity in the circum-stances attendant upon each; a diversity which extends to almost every particular, leaving scarcely any thing in common amongst them (not excepting the recognition of that brotherhood which is the birthright of every human creature) and presenting the vast family of man as divided, with slight local modifications, into so many castes.   Not only is this diversity obervable in the condition and manner of life; it includes also the intellectual development, the modes of thought, and the habits of feeling; with only here and there a rare and noble exception, in the case of a mind pre-eminently endowed, bursting, by the mere force of its own superior nature, through the restraints which circumstances had imposed, and ascending with astonishing rapidity and apparent ease, through all the intermediate stages, from the lowest to the highest point in gradation ; where, from the elevation, which, in spite of innumerable obstacles, it has attained, it asserts its rights to whatever is worth possessing in each and all of them. It cannot be said that this difference, in almost every thing of importance, so strikingly characteristic of the various classes of society, extends also to the estimate of the supreme interest. The indifference to what, beyond calculation, most of all concerns the great society of the earth, is the common infatuation of all its ramifications. Here, as in the final allotment, the prince and the peasant, the philosopher and the rustic, the rich and the poor meet together. In a former communication, an exception was admitted in the case of what must be designated, most emphatically, *the few*. It might, perhaps, be proper in this place, to recur to it in the way of a specific reference. A sentence or two will suffice. The excepted few will be found to comprise some of each of the classes ; but decreasing in the actual, respective numbers, in a ratio from the lowest to the highest. It will be allowed to be a happy and a merciful circumstance for *the many* that there *is* this exception, even, although the number of the fraternity composing it is comparatively so small. The effect of the combined influence of virtuous example and effort has been to restrain society within those limits, beyond which lie the regions of inevitable destruction. There is observable in the larger portion a gradual, sometimes rapid, movement towards the dark frontiers whose threatening aspect indicates those fatal regions beyond which the smaller portion has been appointed and empowered by the supreme Ruler, instrumentally to check and restrain ! One has not yet to learn, that this style of remark is sure to provoke the laugh of derision in that quarter, where every thing of a serious nature ; like certain substances when brought into contact with other substances charged with the electric matter, meet with an instantaneous repulse ; or is retained, only, as a topic of profane jesting, and that species of despicable ribaldry, not unfrequently mis-named wit. Be that as it may ! so many generations of a depraved race have not passed away, without leaving behind direful examples, that the reduction of this subject to that species of proof, which men of this temper are wont to demand as alone valid in respect to an affair so equivocal, forsooth, as religion and morals, would be a fearful method of convincing even them.

The true notion of virtue, as implied in the nature of the case, and as taught by Revelation, is different altogether from that lax and impalpable system (if indeed it can be called a system) of morals, which combines practical atheism, with the verbal acknowledgement of a supreme Being ; which panders to the most absolute selfishness in the name and guise of benevolence ; and which admits, when convenient, an easy compromise, in any particular, with the corresponding forms of vice. Such a virtue as this latter most men and some philosophers will allow, as a very convenient affair, and a thing proper to be inculcated, with the understanding, of course, that since utility is its sole basis, it may be dispensed with ,whenever circumstances shall be of a nature to shift that basis. But the clear voice of Reason confirms the clearer dictate of Revelation, that the virtue of an intelligent being consists in the fulfilment of all the relations he has been created to sustain. Revelation, with what the enlightened understanding instantly perceives to be an infallible correctness, assigns *love* as the universal substratum, the great principle of virtue ; and describes the various attributes of a virtuous character as so many emanations, or modifications of that principle ; like the colours of the rainbow, which, in each instance, separately, and in the beautiful assemblage, are but modifications of light. The instances are too numerous for specification ; and the recollection of every devout student of the Word of God, will, by presenting examples, render specification unnecessary. The same authority, with characteristic simplicity and comprehensiveness divides the great principle into two branches in respect to the relations of man, as forming the only correct basis and motive of his conduct in reference both to his Maker and to his fellow creatures. " Thou shalt love the Lord thy God with all thine heart, and thy neighbour as thyself: upon these two things hang all the law and the prophets." A character to be perfect in virtue must be in absolute conformity to this standard ; and a truly virtuous character in its very incipiency, involves, as

the necessary conditions of its being such, the desire and aim and process of becoming so conformed.   The ultimate object of the remedial scheme which forms the
grand subject of the evangelic economy, is the restoration of fallen human nature
to this state of absolute conformity ; and each successive step of the process conducted under the auspices of that scheme is a movement directly onwards towards
that object.   Commencing its operation with the elements of character—the springs
and motives of action, and diffusing its renewing influence successively, through all
the ramifications of the moral nature, it advances with a steady and unswerving
purpose until it shall have accomplished the complete transformation.   Then, when
it has rendered its subject perfect in love it will have been successful in elevating
him to a condition of inconceivable purity and happiness.

Soham.   *To be continued.*   S.

ECONOMICAL HINTS TO COTTAGERS.

Continued from Page 24.

Who that sees the rustic returning with cheerfulness from his laborious day's
work, anticipating the comfort of his neat fire-side and wholesome supper, with a
smiling wife and delighted children ready to receive him,—who, that contrasts that
poor man with the rich one, who although surrounded by every blessing that heaven
can bestow, is dull and listless, indifferent to the endearments of his wife, and the
caresses of his children, never cheerful but when some excitement to pleasure
arouses him, who, I repeat, will not pronounce the poor man, by many degrees, the
most happy of the two, although condemned to labour for his daily bread.—What
occasions the difference between these two human beings, who have probably the
very same feelings ? What but that the rich man is not *compelled* to work, and therefore will not exert himself till he finds idleness irksome to him.

But I wander from my subject. As I wish to enforce economy in the most minute
article, you must not be startled at my descending to what may appear too trifling
to require attention, but recollect the universe is composed of atoms, and that God
attends to their distribution in every department,   " Not a hair of your head falls
to the ground but your Heavenly Father knoweth it" says our blessed Saviour.
Are trifles then beneath *our* consideration ? Never let it be said that we differ from
our Creator, or presume to overlook what His providence affords for our gratification
and convenience.   The more capacious our comprehension, the more likely we are
to attend to things high and low. We have but to reflect that the infinitely small,
is, to us, much more astonishing than the infinitely great, in fact, it it past our
comprehension.

I shall begin with what may appear at first sight incompatible with the duties of
a Christian, that is, by recommending you ever to preserve a degree of proper pride ;
I have already alluded to it in respect to independence, but I now speak of it as
it regards the neatness and cleanliness of your habitation.   To have your house
in the neatest possible order, to have, as a Scotch Novelist says ; " every thing in its
proper place ; " to have no litter, no dirty corner or drawer, but all so exactly arranged that you could find every article you want without the assistance of a light—
to be able at any moment to display every part of your house to any accidental
visitor, who, by observing and admiring your neatness and order, might have it in
her power to recommend you in some way that might be beneficial to you—this is
the pride I would wish you to inculcate next to that of being able to provide for your
own support.   Strict cleanliness may not appear to you so very essential a requisite

in life as it really is, but believe me, not half the fevers and other complaints would assail the cottage of the labouring classes, if they attended minutely to this very material and practicable consideration.　Their beds, in particular, are I fear, seldom or ever sufficiently exposed to the atmosphere; they roll the covering off and on again, without even separating them, and they return to their couch with the same bad air enclosed around them, in which they have slept the preceding night.　This is one certain way of producing infection, which you cannot be surprised should attack them under such circumstances.—A poor woman says ; " I have not time to attend to all this trifling," but would it take up more of her time, if, immediately when she arose, she shook out *singly* every article of her bed-clothes over the back of a chair, tossed up her bed, and left it to rise while she kindled the fire ? &c. and by that time, if she took care to open her window, her bed would be sufficiently purified, and she could return to it at night with comfort, and exemption from all injurious effects.　But allowing that it would take her a little more time, would it not be well bestowed, if it kept off the infection it might otherwise have imbibed ? She ought also never to omit mopping under the bed every morning, and removing every particle of dust as quickly as it collects, and, above all things, to avoid laying any spare blanket, or any article of clothing between the bed and the bedstead. This, I fear, is a very common practice amongst people who are confined for room, and I scarcely know a worse one, for by so doing, it is utterly impossible that their beds can ever be sufficiently purified.

If you have any carpets near your bed, never neglect to shake them out *every day ;* half a moment will suffice for this purpose, and as in small dwellings, your bed-room is frequently not far removed from your fire, dust from thence must necessarily be collected.　The only system of economy, I have ever observed in a cottage, has been in respect of firing ; that article no doubt, is found very expensive, and I do not wonder at the endeavour to make it last as long as possible ; but still, an amendment might be made even in *this* respect.　The cottager generally has her grate half filled with ashes, whilst the top of the fire is flaming up the chimney ; whereas, if she would keep the *bottom* of the grate clear with only bright cinders visible, and have the top of the fire *close*, either with small coals, or, if she choose it, the ashes thrown above the cinders, all the heat which the fire produced would be thrown into the room, and not, as it too generally is, suffered to waste itself up the chimney.　This is no small advantage, besides that of the fireside looking so much more neat and comfortable. Except when cooking this might always be the case, and, so far from finding it a more expensive plan than the present one, it would, in fact, be less so, whilst you kept it confined at the top.

I have now come to the chief particular in which I wished to give you a little advice, and that is of making every article of food go as far as it possibly can, and also to improve it.　To combine this must be your chief study ; and a little practice will make it not only easy, but agreeable to you. It is fortunate, that which the cottager is the fondest of, and what to hard-working people is very wholesome, namely pork is the cheapest and most easily procured of any other animal food.　But do they always make the most of this ? On the contrary, how often are you annoyed on passing a cottage, with the smell of bones burning, as well as many other substances This ought never to be the case, for however incredible it may appear to some people, and even ridiculous, bones will digest over and over again, when placed in an iron pan with a little water, covered up close, and set by the side, or on the top of a very slow fire, where it is scarcely suffered to simmer, and produce a soup more nutritious than you could possibly imagine, till experience convinced you.

To be continued.

INCIDENT AT SEA.

ONE fine starlight evening, about half-past Eight o'clock, the officer on deck of a transport ship, homeward bound from Rio Janeiro, came into the cabin, and announced that a ship was hailing. All hands immediately came on deck, and the Captain asked the position of the stranger. At that moment, "Ship ahoy!" was heard, the voice apparently being to windward. A lantern was put over the gang-way, the mainsail was hauled up, and the mainyard backed, to stop the vessel's way. No ship was to be seen. "Silence fore and aft!" ordered the Captain, for the decks were now crowded,—soldiers, sailors, women, children, all were up. "Ship ahoy!" again came over the waves, and "Hilloa!" answers the Captain at the top of his voice. Every one now listened with breathless attention for the next question, expecting that the name of the ship would be demanded, as usual. "Ship ahoy!" again resounded, and several together answered "Hilloa!" louder than before; but no notice was taken of the reply, and no sail was in sight. "Its very strange!" exclaimed the Captain, "where can she be?" One thought she might have passed them; others suggested it might be a pirate-boat about to board. The captain took the hint, put the troops under arms, cleared away the guns ready for action, and double shotted them. Silence being again obtained, "Ship ahoy!" was again heard, and the voice still seemed to come from the windward. The chief mate then suggested the possibility of some persons being on a raft, and volunteered to go in a boat to ascertain. The boat was lowered, and the two mates, with the boats crew, each armed with sword and pistol, rowed at some distance round the ship.

On the officers' return, they reported that they could neither hear nor see any-thing. Silence prevailed while they reported this to the captain, every one being desirous to know the issue of the search. Instantly the same "Ship ahoy!" was heard, though much less audibly, and, apparently, at a greater distance than before. The next moment it was heard much louder and closer. A feeling of intense ex-citement now prevailed in each of the crowd of persons on board the transport. More than an hour had passed since the ship was hove to, every one had repeatedly heard the stranger's hail, coming through the darkness, but nothing had been seen of him, and no further question or answer could be elicited. The screams of the women and children, and the muttering of the men, showed that a superstitious dread of something supernatural and unearthly was creeping over every one. The captain issued orders to shoulder arms, and to make ready the guns.

Just at this crisis, one of the cabin boys, who had been standing near the main-mast, stepped aft, to the chief mate, and said, "Its a fowl in the hen coop, sir, that's a-making that 'ere noise." The officer indignantly bestowed on him a sound box on the ear for his information, but recollecting that he was an intelligent lad, accom-panied him to the hen coop with a lantern; where he saw a fowl lying on its side. He took it out, and placed it on the capstan, and there, in the sight of the whole company, was beheld a poor hen dying of the croup, occasionally emitting a sound "ee-a-aw," which resembled the words "Ship ahoy!" coming from a distance, as closely as any hail that ever was heard.

Naut. Mag. 1842, *p.* 409.

OUR LETTER BOX.

The Editors do not wish to be considered responsible for all the sentiments of their Correspondents.

RAILWAY PROSPECTS.

To the Editor of the Soham Magazine.

DEAR MR. EDITOR,

I do not know whether you are very deeply involved in the issue of the present contest about the different lines of the contemplated Railways through our town; for *my* part I am only anxious that *one*, out of the three, should sweep across the swamps that surround us, and that Soham might thus have some chance of occupying a rather more respectable position in the map of England. Had it not been for the numerous fires for which we have lately acquired so unenviable a notoriety, I am not quite sure whether we should, by this time, have found a place in the Post Office Directory. I hope, therefore, that, after all, the Railway will not prove " *a Soham Job;*" and our present prospect of being brought into direct communication with civilized society, turn out to be " NO GO."

Your obedient Servant,
SPECTATOR.

"HOBSON'S CHOICE: THIS OR NONE."

However familiar this proverbial saying may be to the inhabitants of Cambridgeshire; there are few, perhaps, who are acquainted with its origin. Hobson was a carrier between Cambridge and London, in 1614. Having realized a fortune, he expended a large sum in the construction of the aqueduct, by means of which the unfailing supply of pure water is conveyed to the Conduit in the market place at Cambridge. It might perchance have been a very good thing for the Inhabitants, if " this or none " had been the only alternative as to the beverage to be consumed in that bibacious place; and perhaps the morals of our *own* litle Town would be much improved by a somewhat similar restriction. We venture to assert, that if Hobson had not been himself a man of temperate habits, it would never have been in his power to render so great a service to his native place; nor would he ever have left behind him a "good name" which " is rather to be chosen than great riches."

But Hobson kept, also, a Livery Stable; and, as " a righteous man regardeth the life of his beast," so was he determined that every horse should have an equal share of labour. With this view he would never *let* out one out of its turn; and hence the saying :—" Hobson's choice: this or none".

NATURAL HISTORY.

THE BOA CONSTRICTOR.

ENGRAVED BY MISS M. HARE.

THIS immense animal, the largest of all the serpent tribe, is frequently from thirty to forty feet in length, and of a proportionate thickness. A gentleman, who had some large concerns in America, informs us, that he one day sent out a soldier, with an Indian, to kill some wild fowl, and in pursuing their game, the Indian, who generally went before, sat down on what he supposed to be the fallen trunk of a tree. But the monster beginning to move, the poor fellow perceived what it was that he had thus approached, and dropped down in an agony of fear. The soldier, who at some distance saw what had happened, levelled his piece at the serpent's head, and, by a lucky aim, shot it dead; and, on going up to the relief of his companion, found that *he* was also dead from terror. These monsters have been known to kill and devour a buffalo, crushing its bones and body till it was reduced to one uniform mass, and then swallowing it whole. It is happy for mankind that their rapacity is often their own punishment; for whenever they have gorged themselves in this manner, they become torpid, and may be approached and destroyed with safety.—*Bingley.*

POETRY.

[In Original Poetry, the Name, real or assumed, of the Author, is printed in small Capitals under the title; in Selections it is printed in Italics at the end.].

THE SILENT HOUR.

Where the moon-beam sleeps on the
　　ocean's breast,
Where the sparkling sands invite to be
　　press'd,
Where the sea-bird flies to its cavern to
　　rest,
　　Oh! there let me rove;
When Spirits of light look down from
　　on high,
And no voice is heard but the night-
　　wind's sigh,
　　And hers that I love.

I fly from the crowd and its riotous glee,
The brilliant saloon, and its mintrelsy,
These are for others—they are not for me,
　　Oh! no, let me rove,
Where lips, from the soul, breathe a mu-
　　sic divine,
And eyes that deceive not, are smiling
　　in mine,
　　They are hers that I love.

Soham.

OUR FATHER'S GRAVE.

JOHN HAZLEWOOD.

Brother—twelve years have passed away
　　Since our beloved father died;
Grief rent my bosom on that day,
　　Deep as the ocean's restless tide,
Which bore you far from home and me,
　　Its dark tempestuous surge to brave:—
Sad was the hour I went with thee
　　To visit our dear Father's grave.

Brother,—oh never be forgot
　　The words he uttered ere he died,
" Remember me." How sad our lot
　　To lose him in his manhood's pride.
I would not bear again that woe,
　　For all the wealth the earth e'er gave,
But brother let us once more go
　　And visit our dear Father's grave.

Liverpool.

PARAPHRASE OF THE 3RD PSALM

BY R. M. B.

O Lord the troubles of my youth are fled,
The hosts that girt the mountains now
　　are dead,
Saul and his sons for ever prostrate lie,
From them no more thy servant needs
　　to fly.
As once they sang of thousands put to
　　flight,
Of tens of thousands in Philistia's fight,
So multitudes increase, who risen are
Against their king to bear the ready war
Many there be that taunting greive my
　　soul,
And ask what help in God can yet con-
　　trol
The wrathful malice of the tented foes
Who round about my royal way oppose.
But thou, O Lord, art still a shield to me,
My glory, thou shalt lift my head all free
Above the billowy waste of hottest war,
For still to me is dear thy holy law.
In seasons past, I cried to thee, O Lord,
And found thee gracious, as thy given
　　word ;
Thou heard'st me then, from out thy
　　holy hill,
And all my feeble cries thou did'st fulfil,
I laid me down and slept without a fear,
For thy sustaining hand O Lord was
　　near,
Encourag'd thus by my experience past,
Why should I fear the thick embattled
　　blast,
That tens of thousands threaten 'gainst
　　their king,
Whilst safe beneath thine all-protecting
　　wing :
About though thick beset, thy guardian
　　care
Shall save thy servant, from the treach-
　　'rous snare.
Arise, O Lord, and save me, O my God,
Smitten the cheek, has thy avenging rod,
The ravening teeth, are broken with the
　　stroke,
The ungodly fail as swift departing
　　smoke.
Salvation ever resteth with the Lord,
His blessing still is for his people stor'd.

ISABEL.

MRS. FIELD.

Thou'rt silent, Isabel! tho' ling'ring o'er
Thy lowly couch I bend, thy voice no
    more
  My welcome here will speak;
Thine eyes, that watch'd the ev'ning sun
    decline,
Behold not now its morning beams,
    which shine
  Bright on thy wasted cheek.

That cheek, where often, as my feet drew
    near,
Pleas'd I have seen the sweetest smiles
    appear,
  Now cold and senseless lies;
And the wind that's passing o'er thy
    golden hair,
Thou know'st not, Isabel—is breathing
    there,
  With friendship's parting sighs.

Fortune's bright sun ne'er cheer'd thy
    humble lot
Yet thou wer't happy, for thy hopes
    were not
  Fix'd on earth's fleeting toys;
They higher rose—and, tho' I mourn
    thee dead,
Thou blessed art,—thy gentle spirit's
    fled
  To taste celestial joys.

But who could stand and view, with
    tearless eye,
The sad remains of frail, mortality,
  All I behold of thee:—
The cold, unconscious form,—the pale
    still face
Where death has been, with chilling
    touch t'erase
  Those smiles which shone for me?

Ah! who unmov'd can linger in that
    scene,
Where those, now gone, with us have
    often been,
  Or dwelt for many a day;
Where all around, with some memorial
    fraught,
Speaks of the things they lov'd, the
    works they wrought,
  And whispers—"where are they?"

The summer roses that thy casement
    twine,
Were planted there by these cold hands
    of thine;
  And mem'ry loves to tell

How oft the choicest bloom was cull'd by
    thee,
To deck my home, and yield its sweets
    to me.—
  But now,—poor Isabel!

The dewy leaflets, all unseen, I spread,
To spend their fragrance on thy silent
    bed,
  With thee, to fade and die:
No sable plumes will shade thy lowly
    bier,
But these fresh blossoms, gemm'd with
    friendship's tear,
  Its tribute there shall lie.

Farewell lov'd maiden! I can never see
Thy form again; yet oft I'll think of
    thee:
  And tho' no sculptur'd tomb
Mark thy last home, soft wisp'ring o'er
    thy grave,
The fairest wild flow'rs in the breeze
    will wave,
  And shed a sweet perfume.

There will affection, fondly ling'ring,
    weep,
There faithful mem'ry silent vigils keep,
  And many a village maid
Stay her light step, whene'er she wan-
    ders by,
  Cease her gay song, and say, with
    heart-felt sigh,
  "Here Isabel is laid."

SPEAK NO ILL.

Nay speak no ill! a kindly word
  Can never leave a sting behind,
And oh! to breathe each tale we've heard
  Is far beneath a noble mind.
Full oft a better seed is sown
  By choosing thus a kinder plan:
For if but little good be known,
  Still let us speak the best we can.
Give me the heart that fain would hide,
  Would fain another's fault efface;
How can it pleasure human pride
  To prove humanity but base?
No: let us reach a higher mood,
  A nobler estimate of man,
Be earnest in the search for good
  And speak of all the best we can.
Then speak no ill, but lenient be
  To other's feelings as your own:
If you're the first a fault to see,
  Be not the first to make it known.
For life is but a passing day,
  No lip may tell how brief its span;
Then, oh, the little time we stay
  Let's speak of all the best we can. X

OUR CHILDREN'S PAGE.

FACTS WORTH REMEMBERING.

The atmosphere presses on every square inch of any surface with
a weight of 15 pounds.

England contains 40 Counties.—Wales, 12.—Scotland, 32.—
Ireland, 32 in 4 provinces.

The coldest hour of the 24, is an hour before sunrise.

The warmest is from 2 to 3 in the afternoon.

The mean heat is from half-past 8 to half-past 9.

The 14th of January, on an average of years, is the coldest day in
the year.

Eggs are hatched at 104° of heat.

In air, sound travels from 1130 to 1142 feet per second.

In water, sound passes at the rate of 4708 feet per second.

A bell, sounded under water may be heard under water at 1200 feet
distance.

Sounds are distinct at twice the distance on water that they are on
land.

MISCELLANY AND EXTRACTS.

THE Kingdom of Bohemia is the bottom of one of the great lakes which once covered Europe. It is an amphitheatre formed by ridges of mountains, with but one outlet evidently formed by the action of a running stream, through which now runs the beautiful river Elbe. The lake of Geneva may, by the same cause, become a valley. Although confined by granite rock, it is continually lowering its outlet, and the surface has fallen considerably within the period of accurate observation, and records. Several towns and villages, which were close upon the lake a century ago, are now separated from the shore by fields and gardens.

IN the stillness of night, a steam vessel announces its approach, by the sound of the splashing of its paddles, when fifteen miles from the harbour.

A whole boat's crew of the "Valiant" were once upset in Torbay, near Plymouth, and drowned. On the following day, the Admiral ordered each of the ships of the fleet to fire some guns; and, in about an hour after, as was expected, the whole of the bodies were found floating on the surface

ALMOST every object that attracts our notice has its bright and its dark side. He who habituates himself to look at the displeasing side, will sour his disposition, and consequently impair his happiness: while he who constantly beholds it on the bright side, insensibly meliorates his temper, and in consequence of it, improves his own happiness, and the happiness of all about him.—*Harris.*

It is unworthy of a reasonable being to spend any of the little time alloted us without some tendency, either direct or oblique, to the end of our existence, and though every moment cannot be laid out on the formed and regular improvement of our knowledge, or the stated practice of a moral or religious duty, yet none should be so spent as to exclude wisdom or virtue, or pass without a possibility of qualifying us, more or less, for the better employment of those which are to come. It is scarcely possible to pass an hour in honest conversation, without being able when we rise from it to please ourselves with having given or received some advantages, but a man may shuffle cards from noon till midnight, without tracing any new idea in his mind, or being able to recollect the day by any other token than his gain or loss, and a confused idea of agitated passions, and clamorous altercations.

Rambler, No. 80.

WE are frequently importuned (says Dr. Johnson) by the bacchanalian writers, to lay hold on the present hour; to catch the pleasures within our reach; and remember that futurity is not at our command. But surely these exhortations may, with equal propriety, be applied to better purposes: it may be, at least, inculcated that pleasures are more safely postponed than virtues; and that greater loss is suffered by missing an opportunity of doing good, than an hour of giddy frolic, and noisy merriment.

MONTHLY NOTICES.

MARCH.

Guardians are elected in this month, or within forty days from the 25th of March.

Before the 5th of this month, Overseers of every parish containing a population exceeding 2000, to enter in a book the names and addresses of persons who before the 1st of February have claimed to vote as Owners or Proxies; such book to be open for inspection till the 10th.

On the three first Sundays of this month, the List of persons nominating as Constables must be on Church and Chapel doors.

Burnt Fen Tax, due in October last, must be paid this month.

10th.—On or before this day, Overseers are bound to distinguish in the Rate Book the persons qualified to vote in the forthcoming election of Guardians.

24th.—Last day for Overseers to return Lists of Constables to Justices.

24th.—Between this day and the 9th of April, Justices appoint Constables, and, within fourteen days of appointment, Overseers to publish their names on Church doors.

25th.—Overseers to be appointed this day, or within 14 days after. The accounts of those whose year has expired must be verified by them on oath before a Magistrate within 14 days, and be delivered to their successors.

25th.—Surveyors of the Highways to be appointed for the ensuing year.

PLAYFORD'S

SOHAM MAGAZINE,

AND

ꜰ𝔯𝔦𝔢𝔫𝔡𝔩𝔶 𝔐𝔬𝔫𝔦𝔱𝔬𝔯.

APRIL, 1847.

EN of all classes in society, and of every shade of religious and political sentiment, seem to agree in the opinion that the moral renovation, so much needed in our overgrown population, must begin in the young. The subject, therefore, of comprehensive and universal education, occupies a prominent position in the public mind; and is regarded with more or less of interest and anxiety, as the well-being of the community, and the advancement of social happiness are desired. But while we are looking forward with hope and expectancy to the development of some extensive scheme which is to prove the panacea of all the evils we deplore, what have we already done with the means that are within our reach? Is the mischief which we are so anxious to remedy, really to be traced to any defective system of instruction in our schools; or is it to be attributed to the indifference and neglect of individual members of the community to the moral welfare of those who are immediately within the sphere of their influence? How hopeless must be the efforts of the most zealous friends of intellectual advancement if the rising generation are withdrawn, under every frivolous pretext, from their care! Under what insuperable obstacles must the most perfect form of instruction labour, if the atmosphere of home is infected with the pestilence of vice! What permanent results can be anticipated from stated lessons of virtue and morality, however earnest, however frequently repeated, if so far from being enforced by the precept

No. 4. Vol. I. E

and example of those with whom they habitually associate, they are counteracted and practically reviled !

Education and *Instruction* are words of very different import. The latter, even in its most limited sense, is almost confined to the walls of the school room ; while the former is exerting an almost unceasing influence upon us from the earliest dawn of life.

Among the many existing obstacles to any lasting improvement in the social condition, and moral character, of the labouring classes in our own immediate locality, the unrestricted employment of females in the fields has hitherto had a most deplorable effect ; and, so long as it remains unremoved, it will inevitably thwart the most strenuous exertions that can be made for their benefit.

It may be asserted, without any fear of contradiction, that the good morals of any community will always bear a direct proportion to the purity and retirement of the female character. What, then, is to be expected if we habituate them from early youth to masculine occupations, coarseness of manners, and the violation of that natural modesty which the great Creator has implanted in the breasts of all his creatures ? How unseemly is the picture, so often presented to the eye, of large numbers of females, degraded by male habiliments, not only neglecting their proper duties at home, and occupied in the rude and unfeminine labours of agriculture, but positively displacing their husbands, and brothers, and sons from the station they alone are duly qualified to hold, and throwing them altogether out of employment ! Is not such a state of things an indication of those barbarous habits of life, which must be banished from our land before we can make any real progress in civilization and christian refinement.

But, with regard, more particularly, to the young ;—need we recount the evils that so palpably spring from this fatal source ? What system of instruction can avail if our children are deprived of its influence, and sent to toil in the fields, from day to day, from almost the earliest period of their existence ? What lessons of obedience, of morality, of religion can be expected to impress their hearts with a lasting and active energy, while they are exposed to the baneful effects of vicious example, and thrown into contact with those " whose glory is in their shame ? "

Moral and intellectual depravity must be the infallible result of such a course; and the evidences are before our eyes in the rudeness and licentiousness of the young, whose very language has become so gross as to shock the ears even of those who are most accustomed to the sound.

We would earnestly, therefore, call the attention of all who are concerned for the welfare of the community to this subject. No palliation but necessity can be pleaded for a practice which is fraught with such incalculable evils. We hold those parents who thus, for the sake of gain, crush the best feelings, and blight the best hopes of their female children, to be culpable in the highest degree. The misery and disgrace which they, too often bring upon *themselves*, is only the inevitable result of their unnatural course ; but the cruelty they are guilty of towards their offspring is so deep and so durable, that they must be lost to all parental affection if they allow it to continue.

But let those, also, who offer the inducement for such a ruinous and demoralizing practice reflect upon the responsibility they incur. "Am I my brother's keeper," once said a proud enemy of God and man. We trust there are none who would feel disposed to make a similar reply when appealed to upon the subject we have thus briefly touched, Let us take heed that we do not become our brother's *destroyer* by indirectly nipping the seeds of virtue in the bud, by depriving him of every opportunity of mental improvement, and by exposing him to the unchecked influence of that evil example which will ultimately render him unfit for intercourse with any but the lowest of his species, and a pest to society at large : debased as to all the better feelings of the present life, and utterly regardless of the life which is to come.

POPERY.

In the memorials of Richard earl of Corke, as also in those of Archbishop Usher, and the manuscripts of Sir James Ware, a singular circumstance is narrated tending to show by what apparently trivial means it pleases Divine Providence sometimes to preserve his people from the hands of those who seek their life.

Queen Mary having dealt severely with the protestants in England, about the latter end of her reign signed a commission to take the same course in Ireland. In order to execute it with greater force, she nominated Dr. Cole as one of the commissioners, and sent the commission by him. Upon his reaching Chester, the mayor being also a papist, waited on the doctor, who took the commission out of his box, saying : — "Here is a commission that shall lash the heretics of

Ireland;" calling the protestants by that title.   The good woman! of the house, being well affected to the protestant religion, and having a brother who was a protestant, then residing in Dublin, was much troubled at the doctor's words; and watching the opportunity, whilst the mayor took his leave and the doctor was complimenting him down stairs, she opened the box, took the commission out, and wrapped up in its place a pack of cards in a sheet of paper, with the knave of clubs facing uppermost.

The doctor soon returned to his chamber, and suspecting nothing of what had been done, put up the box as formerly.   The next day, having reached the sea side, and the wind being favourable, he sailed for Ireland, and landed on the 7th of October, 1558, at Dublin,   Upon coming to the Castle, the Lord Fitz-Walters, being lord deputy, sent for him to attend the privy council; when Dr. Cole, having made a speech upon the subject of his mission, presented the box to the lord deputy, who having caused it to be opened that the secretary might read the commission, there was nothing to be seen but the pack of cards with the knave of clubs, face uppermost, on the top.   The lord deputy and the council were much startled at the discovery, the doctor himself being equally amazed, who could only assure them that the commission had been produced by him at Chester, and that he could not conceive what had become of it.   To this the lord deputy answered: "let us have another commission, and we will shuffle the cards in the mean while."   The doctor, much troubled in mind, returned again into England, and coming to the court, immediately obtained another commission; but while he was waiting for a fair wind at the sea side, news was brought that the Queen was dead; and thus her cruel commission fell to the ground, and the lives of the protestants of Ireland were saved.

Queen Elizabeth was so delighted with the circumstance, that she settled a pension of forty pounds a year for life upon Elizabeth Edwards;—the woman who had thus been the instrument of so much good.

ECONOMICAL HINTS TO COTTAGERS.

Continued from Page 41.

Some years back, in the time of scarcity, digesters were invented to make the most of all bones, refuse meat, &c.; but as they might not be to be procured now, I see no reason why a pan, as above described, might not answer the purpose quite as well.   If the rest of the fireside looks neat and clean, a saucepan in the same order would not take from the comfort of it by standing on, or beside the fire.   Let me recommend you to try this plan; collect all your bones, fat, and scraps, that you would otherwise throw away; break the bones as small as you can, which will make them yield better, and put them into a pan with no more water than will cover them; let them simmer all the evening and all night, and in the morning when the soup is cold, remove all the fat from it.   This you may put by in a clean cup, and it will serve to fry pancakes, potatoes, or any other thing you may have to prepare in that manner, than which, nothing can be better.   Drain the soup from the dregs at the bottom, and set it by till you have prepared the following addition.   Tie up a teacup full of pease in a bag, leaving them a little room to increase; they will probably take some time before they are sufficiently softened, then pound them in the bag till they are quite a paste, and put them into your soup with a little onion, pepper, a leaf or two of mint, if you like the taste, and let all boil up well together. If it is not then as good as you could wish, add a spoonfull of made mustard, when you take it off the fire, and have some nice crisp toast cut in small squares in the bason in which you pour it. Your husband when returning cold and hungry from his day's work, if he finds this quite ready on his arrival, will probably make it suffice for his supper with the addition of a little bread and cheese, which would be rather comfortless without it. What a pleasure it would be to you, whilst you sat enjoying your tea comfortably beside him, to think that by a little management you had saved the expence of one meal of animal food, and yet that your husband should not feel its loss. You will be amply repaid by it, for any little trouble you have taken. You will scarcely believe it till you have tried it, how many times the bones of beef, and particularly the head, may be so stewed, and yet afford a tolerable soup with the addition of barley and herbs instead of peas, which last are best with pork only. Whenever you make broth, you should be sure to put nothing into it, at first but the meat and some shelled barley; let it boil an hour or two according to the quantity of your meat; the night before would be still more convenient, that it might have sufficient time to cool, if not set it out in a safe place for an hour or two, till you can take the fat entirely off, which renders the broth more wholesome for yourselves, and saves you the skimmings for other purposes, as I pointed out before; whereas, if you leave it till you put in the herbs, you are obliged to throw it away, or leave it on the broth, when it it is very apt to disagree; besides you lose the flavour of the herbs, which ought never to be added till the last hour. You may put in small pieces of turnip, carrots, onions or chives; a little thyme and majoram, parsley and marigold; not too much of any, but a little of all, these give your broth a good taste. Potatoes are best added when you eat it, if you like these better than bread, which is a saving of the latter. A little piece of beef or mutton, if done very slowly makes a cheap and nice dinner in this way, and coarse pieces are as good as the best when stewed till they are tender. Another dish in which a little meat goes a good way, is an Irish stew, and which, when properly made, is most excellent, either baked or boiled. The best way of preparing it, is to cut your meat, (which ought not to be too fat) in small pieces, then season it a little with pepper, and salt, and place it in layers in your pan or dish, intermixed with layers of potatoes, peeled and sliced, and a little sliced onion to your taste. If baked, put only as much water as will cover it, and have some ready boiling when it comes out of the oven, that you may add to it, if necessary. `Shake some pepper on the top of all, and an hour and a half, or two hours will bake it, according to its size, or the heat of the oven. If you prefer this dish boiled, you may prepare it exactly in the same way, except that you put more water to it, and let it simmer very slowly over a low fire, or it will be very apt to burn, which you must prevent by stirring it often. A pound of sliced lean beef would make a dinner for a large family, prepared in this way. This reminds me of what I have too frequently seen wasted, that is a good piece of onion, which if put by on a small plate and covered close with a teacup or small bason, would keep good for some days, recollect that it is exposure to the air that makes most things spoil, particularly anything that has been peeled; so you should always cover it up, as it might be of use to you another time.

To be continued.

QUAKERS,—BUT NOT FRIENDS.

Nay, let a thousand darts be hurled,
Whate'er be said of dull pretence ;
Slay hydra-headed ignorance,
The curse of Albion and the world.

THERE is generally more of cowardice than prudence in fear, hence long before the nature of any undertaking is well understood, a storm of voices cry out, "It is impossible, do not attempt it." This is the fear, that makes us ever deferring to others, the task we ought ourselves to perform, till under the guise of quaking modesty, we skulk out of the duty of individual responsibility. Be it the formation of a Book Society, the establishment of a Mechanics' Institute, the publication of a Magazine, a civil reform, or a social adjustment; what is manifestly the duty and advantage of all, is frequently and unfortunately left to the few.

Do you sneer upon the beginnings of things, because, though undoubtedly good, they are as certainly small? Do you fear for our success, or tremble, lest in our progress across an evil world, some of its dirt should stick to our heels? Do you take alarm lest we fail to please everybody? "Rome was not built in a day," is a good and wholesome adage, and what we are at first, is a mean ¡index of what we may ultimately become; and whatever result, we take it, that the world of letters like the world of nature, has not the term annihilation in all its vocabulary. The spark, struck here, may fly and blend itself with other fires; yet it is unextinguished. The atom, which is the microcosm of our literary existence, may roll onward, and taking up congenial elements become a globe; yet we are not lost. The stream from the stricken rock, may leap, and gather, and swell into the ocean tide; yet there its identity, not its being is engulphed. Evil may be mingled with our doings as dregs are with our ink; but we will write as limpidly as possible, and rather cease, than pollute our pen with the foul sediment of harm and error. As to pleasing every body, we might as well enact the Old Man and Donkey; or expect that a large family, from the infant to the adult, would all be delighted with the same toy; or that good men and bad, wise and ignorant, had all tastes and ends in common.

But there are other fears more apart from ourselves, and which we may discuss with greater ease.

Of learning. Some persons are as much afraid of learning as of the plague, and do all in their power to keep it up in a corner, and hinder its progress, lest forsooth it should do men an injury, by making them wiser than their betters, and disaffected towards their condition. We wish these monopolists a mental surfeit, or an intellectual apoplexy; but of this we are sure, that pent up knowledge, like confined air, is converted into a curse: and as to their ancient apprehension, we leave common fact to reply.

Of defeat. There is the fear of attempting to do more than one is able, which if yielded to, makes a man just do nothing at all; for if you never face a difficulty that defies you, nor strive to move a weight whose ponderous gravity stretches every sinew, you will never know, either the complexion of your spirit, or the strength of your arm. Take nothing for granted: difficulties vanish as you come at them, as ghosts flee into thin air on inspection. It is time enough to pipe, when the battle is lost; but as we buckle on our armour, let us remember, that every uplifted arm has might in it; that our phalanx is invincible, save where a craven heart, throbs under a coat of mail ;—there alone is the open door for disaster and the herald of defeat.

Of progression. There is a foolish, though more pardonable apprehension, which is found in fathers, when advising their children to "Let well alone." In their times, the stage and bridle way were the sure and slow means of transit, and a dozen miles, an honest day's journey. Wonder not that they tremble at steam boat and railway, and suspect a demon agent in electricity. This is the timidity of an old hen, set upon ducks eggs, who after incubation, sees her young ones break the thin shell, and rush into the nearest pool; while she, forgetting that nature has given them the ability to sail on its surface, clucks out on the bank "You'll all be drowned"

> Cluck, Cluck, Cluck,
> Come out of the water;
> Your chick is a duck,
> And nature has taught her.

Of comparison. This is the fear either of impotency or conceit; for no common man ought to be ashamed that he is not a giant. Would you keep your infant at home until manhood, or the mind in swaddling bands and leading strings, waiting for its maturity? Turn your sons to the winds of heaven and the toils of labour; give your mind its training, set it out with its fellows, try its nerve with competitors. The village contrasted with the city, is not rendered insignificant; on the contrary, its just size is ascertained; and the currency mark of virtuous intellect, will stamp an appreciable value, on the humblest as well as the most exalted effort. The copper farthing, will never blush before the golden sovereign, whilst both have their fixed worth, and indisputable utility.

Of ridicule. From whom? The base and the ignorant! for assuredly none others will act the mountebank. "Their praise is censure, and their censure praise." They may hiss at your heels, but the sibillation of a thousand geese is harmless sound, and should hardly move your anger; much less excite your fear. Every tom fool laughs, when he ought to blush; and he who cannot endure the pointed finger of contumely, is not likely to be a far traveller on the path, either of religion or letters. Beside, this is a *distinction*, which has been more or less common, to all good men, and, which you will neither wish, nor be able to avoid.   G.

MORAL REFLECTIONS.

Continued from Page 22.

Continued from Page 22.

[In excuse of one or two slight verbal and about as many constructional inaccuracies in the last communication, the writer has only to say, that being from home at the time of going to press, he was unable to inspect and correct the proof copy.]

What can be more deeply, pungently, affecting than the reflection, that by far the greater portion of mankind, are, and have been, from the earliest ages, habitually acting, living *so* as to render it notoriously unquestionable that to what incalculably most imperiously concerns them, they are totally, perversely, obstinately insensible? It is the same in effect as if the capacity of forming a just estimate, a distinct conception, of their supreme interest had been blotted out; and the race—a race of intelligent creatures—abandoned to the folly of dissipating amongst trifles the term allotted them for securing their eternal well-being. Anchorism is justly condemned and censured as unworthy, alike, of the man and the christian; but, indeed, the fanaticism of abstracting oneself from the great stage occupied by one's species, and from *them*, and of retiring into voluntary and permanent exile, has, in a multitude of instances, owed its existence to a thousand far less venial follies, combined with a prodigious host of vices—and preeminently to that monster vice, that compound of infatuation and wickedness, the parent of all other vices and follies—*indifference to the supreme interest*. Let a serious person of extreme sensitiveness, whose intellectual and moral nature shall be *but* slightly defective in the reasoning faculty and in the principle of benevolence; and who, in consequence, will be subject in a degree corresponding with that of the excess, in the one case, and of the deficiency, in the other, to the gloomy influence of a morbid imagination; let such a person come unavoidably into frequent contact with mankind as they are in the mass, and it will not be surprising, however much it may be a thing to be deplored, if, overwhelmed with mingled pity and disgust, he should suddenly quit, for ever, a scene where at every turn he had been lacerated by a thousand goads, urging him on to desperation. He had been-accustomed from the examples, included in his earlier associations to regard his fellow-creatures, on the whole, as reasonable beings; to consider them as possessed of the capacity and the disposition to estimate things according to their nature and value, and to direct their conduct, in the main, in accordance with the relative importance of the numerous objects which claim their attention, and solicit their pursuit; that they were, at least, rational, however, unfortunate: and that the numerous ills by which they were afflicted, although originating, for the most part, in their own misconduct, were owing rather to ignorance than to perversity. He, however, had no sooner gone out into the broad daylight of actual life than he discovered with dismay that in judging of the many from the select few he had committed a grievous mistake; that the mental character which this mistake had conspired with other causes in forming for him, was of a description to render it certain, that his continued association with mankind would be attended with a corresponding series of painful impressions, often in a degree amounting to agony; and that solitude was the only condition in which *he* could expect to find repose. Who does not remember to have sometime read, or heard related, the beautiful and touching story of one of the most lovely of youths, one of the most excellent and extraordinary of men? When Europe was about to emerge from the more than Egyptian darkness in which Popery—the most terrible beyond comparison of all the plagues which have been permitted to scourge the human race—had enveloped it for a frightful number of centuries, a young man of extraordinary amiability, remarkable equally for his talents, his erudition and his piety; remarkable for his intellectual and moral elevation, his unearthliness; and more remarkable still for the symmetrical perfection of his character—himself enlightened by Revelation; seeing clearly through the gross absurdities and grosser impieties of the papacy; thinking in his inexperience that nothing more would be requisite to enlighten and liberate mankind than for the truth to be presented in the manner in which he could and would present it; and prompted by that benevolence which will undertake any task however arduous, and confront any difficulty however formidable, to do good—went forth, bent on the reformation of the world. Not long afterward he was heard to sum up the issue of the enterprise in the memorable exclamation " Old Adam was too strong for young Melancthon!" Had the character of Melancthon's mind been of the description above alluded to, would he not, on finding his fellow mortals, inveterately, perversely, wedded, to the very thing which befooled, enslaved, and destroyed them, have quietly, but irrevocably retired into the solitude of his cell.

Ages have passed away, and the earth and its inhabitants have sustained many convulsions and have undergone many and wonderful revolutions since then; yet who does not see, that the same insensibility to that which alone is of sterling and permanent and unchangeable value is still the prevailing epidemic, the universal delusion? Whatever changes it has undergone are only like those of the moon; it may have presented different phases, but its own stubborn, unconquerable, invulnerable nature is still the same. Go where one may there are to be seen indubious indications that it is there.—Amidst the scenes where nature seems to luxuriate in an endless alternation between beauty and sublimity, and every thing is suggestive of the grandeur and resources of that Being by whom all things were made and are sustained, and of the inevitable security and happiness of all who are in subordination to Him; in those regions where nature has done little else than furnish materials for human industry and art, and where, by the absence of every thing calculated to feast the soul of man through the medium of his senses, signifying how utterly barren she *can* be of all but the means of furnishing food for his body as the reward, only, of his patient and laborious industry, when the sovereign Proprietor has interposed his interdict, she admonishes him to cultivate the favour of that Being who can both give and withold; in the crowded city and the most retired and rural retreat; in the mansion of the rich, and the cottage of the poor; in the workshop of the artisan, the mart of commerce, the counting house of the merchantman, the laboratory of the man of science, and in the library of the philosopher—it seems as if it had been inscribed in legible characters, *Every thing receives due attention here but the chief concern.* Nothing can be more affectingly significant that it is *so* than the full, broad, consciousness one feels at the very moment of writing or giving utterance to remarks like these, that they will be read or listened to, as similar remarks have been read and listened to, myriads and millions of times, and will be as many times again, with far less emotion than would be produced by the mawkish incidents of romance, the commonest occurrence of daily life, or the song or tale of yesterday's folly or misfortune. When will it be otherwise? Ah! when? Let the Christian look abroad and say, where are the signs of a general reviviscence from the long spiritual death! It is frightful to think of the multitudes that will pass away in the train of the countless myriads already gone, before then! It seems as if a dark and dreadful cloud had gathered above the horizon and a voice issued, amidst its thunders and its lightenings, pronouncing the terrible words: "They are joined to idols; let them alone." "They are of their father the devil, and the works of their father they *will* do."

Soham.   *To be continued.*   S.

OUR LETTER BOX.

The Editors do not wish to be considered responsible for all the sentiments of their Correspondents.

THE LATE FIRE.
To the Editor of the Soham Magazine.

Sir,—I wish some means could be devised for putting a stop to the horrible incendiarism which disgraces our town. Here is another destructive fire by which seven tenements and three farm yards are consumed, and still no clue to the motive for the diabolical act, and no trace of the malignant perpetrator. These same premises were fired seven months ago, and that, too, before dark; but as you remember, the flame was immediately extinguished. And now, at five o'clock in the morning, they are completely levelled to the ground. This is really a dreadful state of things, and one which needs to be met by the most vigorous efforts of the inhabitants. Surely it is high time that we had the preventive benefit of a few well appointed policemen, who might challenge every one they met at an unusual hour, or in an unfrequented locality! If some decisive and effectual steps are not taken, every thatched building in the place will be destroyed, and all who can, will seek a more reputable neighbourhood. I understand one of the principal farmers already talks of leaving. And no wonder; for he can never go to bed in comfort and safety so long as these depraved and determined miscreants prowl at large about our streets.

         I am, Sir,
         Your obedient Servant,
Soham, March 16th.   AN INHABITANT.

P.S. there are more evils than one that a Police force could remedy. I hope to see a notice of them, in due time, in your Magazine.

PERILOUS ADVENTURERS.

MANY of the islands which stud the sea around the north and west coasts of Scotland, are remarkable for the stern grandeur of their precipitous cliffs. One might almost imagine that the surges of the mighty Atlantic, dashing against them for ages with unbroken fury, had underminded their solid foundations, and worn for themselves numerous passages, leaving only columnar rocks of vast height, detached from one another, though of similar formation and construction. Such a rock is the Holm of Noss, apparently severed from the Isle of Noss, from which it is about a hundred feet distant. Both the cliffs are of stupendous height, and far below in the narrow gorge, the raging sea boils and foams, so that the beholder can scarcely look down without horror. But stern necessity compels men to enterprises, from which the boldest would otherwise shrink. To obtain a scanty supply of coarse food for himself and family, the hardy inhabitant of the Orkneys dares even the terrors of the Holm of Noss. In a small boat, with a companion or two, he seeks the base of the cliff, and leaving them below, he fearlessly climbs the precipice, and gains the summit.

A thin stratum of earth is found on the top, into which he drives some strong stakes; and having decended and performed the same operation on the opposite cliff, he stretches a rope from one to the other, and tightly fastens it. On this rope a sort of basket, called a cradle, is made to traverse; and the adventurous islander now commits himself to the frail car, and, suspended between sea and sky, hauls himself backward and forward by means of a line. And do you ask what prize can tempt man to incur such fearful hazard, lavish of his life? It is the eggs and young of a sea-bird called the Gannet, countless myriads of which lay their eggs and rear their progeny, wherever the surface presents a ledge sufficiently broad to hold them.

In some other situations the fowlers have recourse to a still more hazardous mode of procedure. The cliffs are sometimes twelve huudred feet in height, and fearfully over-hanging. If it is determined to proceed from above, the adventurer prepares a rope, made either of straw or hogs' bristles; because these materials are less liable to be cut through by the sharpe edge of the rock. Having fastened the end of the rope round his body, he is lowered down by a few comrades at the top, to the depth of five or six hundred feet. He carries a large bag affixed to his waist, and a pole in his hand, and wears on his head a thick cap as a protection against the fragments of rock which the friction of the rope perpetually loosens: large masses, however, occasionally fall, and dash him to pieces.

Having arrived at the region of birds, he proceeds with the utmost coolness and address, placing his feet against a ledge, he will occasionally dart out many fathoms over the water, to obtain a better view of the crannies in which the birds are nestling, take in all the details at a glance, and again swing back into their haunts. He takes only the eggs and young, the old birds being too tough to be eaten. Caverns often occur in the perpendicular face of the rock, which are favourite resorts of the fowls; but the only way of getting at such situations is by disengaging himself from the rope, and either holding the end in his hand, while he collects his booty, or fastening it round some projecting corner. One of these daring men was accustomed to go alone on these expeditions; supplying the want of confederates by firmly planting a stout iron bar in the earth, from which he lowered himself. One day, having found a cavern, he imprudently disengaged the rope from his body, and entered the cave with the end of it in his hand. In the eagerness of collecting, however, he slipped his hold of the rope, which immediately swung out several yards beyond his reach. The poor man was struck with horror! No soul was within hearing, nor was it possible' to make his voice heard in such a position. Death seemed inevitable, for he felt his situation to be hopeless. He remained many hours in a state bordering on stupefaction, but at length he resolved to make one effort, which, if unsuccessful, must be fatal. The rope was swinging in the breeze, and altogether beyond his reach. Having however commended himself to the protection of Divine Providence, he rushed to the edge of the cave, and sprang with all his might into the air:—he grasped the pendulous rope, and was saved!

BLACK GANG CHINE.

FROM A DRAWING BY S. READ, AND ENGRAVED BY MISS R. W. HARE.

WHO would suppose that the beautiful spot represented by Miss R. W. Hare's highly-finished and elaborate engraving above, was to be found in the dark recesses of the celebrated Black Gang Chine! This chine, or chasm is in the Isle of Wight, and is said to have received its name from being the resort of a notorious band of pirates called the "Black Gang;" and it certainly seems well adapted for the strong-hold of such desperate adventurers. It is, altogether, a place which inspires the mind with horror. The sides of the chasm, which are little short of five hundred feet high, rise abruptly from their base, overhung in many places with trees and shrubs, presenting an awe-inspiring, but most romantic spectacle, not easily conceived by those who have never roved beyond the gentle undulations of this eastern quarter of England.

On the summit rises a spring of medicinal quality. When the water is first poured into a bottle, it is as clear as crystal; but after some time, it deposits a considerable sediment, which contains particles of iron-ore, and emits a sulphureous exhalation.

Ships have frequently experienced the destructive effects of the rocks that line Chale Bay. They lie just beneath the surface of the water, and in conjunction with the cape of Rocken-end, occasion in some states of the winds, very heavy swells. Not many years ago, during one tempestuous night, no fewer than fourteen sail were lost in this dangerous bay; and scarcely a winter passes without some such melancholy accidents.

POETRY.

[In Original Poetry, the Name, real or assumed, of the Author, is printed in small Capitals under the title; in Selections it is printed in Italics at the end.]

POLAND.

On, on to the rescue, to succour—to save
  The valiant who struggle in liberty's
    cause,
Can Britain be deaf to the cries of the
  brave?
  When tyranny threatens, can Albion
    pause?
Let Albion blush, and blush Gallia too,
  (Ever rivals in power, as rivals in fame)
Say, shall the cold-blooded northern undo
  That which Vienna saw done in thy
    name?
Shall treaties be made to be broken at
  will?
  Oh! where is your boasted security
    then,
Yes, as it hath ever been, so is it still,
  What the sword can achieve is not
    stay'd by the pen.
Kosciusko,—thy ashes are cold in the
  grave,
  But oh! could thy spirit revive them
    again,
Again should the 'white flag' of liberty
  wave,
  The cannon be heard on thy mountain
    and plain,
Brave Poland hath fallen! and hist'ry
  alone
  The deeds and the day of her glory
    recalls,
Warsaw hath wept the decline of her sun,
  The last 'shriek of freedom' 1 was heard
    on her walls.
Tho it slumber awhile, yet its spirit ne'er
  dies,
  Nor shackles can bind it, nor tyranny
    bow,
And Poland, thy star shall hereafter arise
  More bright from the clouds that o'er-
    shadow it now.
And Cracow—thy towers, if destin'd to
  stand.
  Shall stand a memento of Austria's
    shame,
One spark is sufficient to kindle the
  brand
  When lighted—then let her beware of
    the flame.

1 Freedom shriek'd when Kosciusko fell.
                 CAMPBELL.

And thou, too, O! Prussia, for freedom
  who fought,
  Say, must thy 2 sabre its lustre forego?
That lesson to tyrants thine own Blucher
  taught!—
  Be remembered no more—and forgot
    Waterloo?
Soham.

2. Bright is the blade that for liberty strikes,
  But where is its lustre—for slavery drawn?
             ANDREAS HOFFER.

To THOUGHT.

BY THE LATE MRS. MOODY.

Passing shadow of the mind,
Boundless rover unconfin'd,
Tyrant of imperious reign,
Lord of Pleasure, Grief, and Pain,
Teacher of the erring heart,
Wisdom's ray to me impart:
Come with her enlighten'd power,
Renovate life's drooping hour!
Pure and of celestial kind,
Let me thee an angel find,
Ever guarded be thy sway,
Ever mindful of that day,
When by awful Heav'ns decree
I must give account of thee.
Yet in temper'd colours drest,
Fashion'd like a rainbow vest;
Blended tints of grave and gay,
Cheer my spirit on its way,
Come and wander with the Muse,
Free her airy path to choose,
Free with her to rise or fall,
Soar to skies at fancy's call;
Cling to sublunary things,
Or above expand thy wings.
Yet, oh yet! my soul pursue
In thy garb of rosy hue;
Chase the fear that hints the sorrow;
Bring the hope that crowns the morrow;
Bring Religion, Heaven-born child,
Smiling like a Cherub mild;
Bring the faith that meets the skies;
Vision blest that peace supplies,
When her bright unclouded mien
Penetrates the closing scene.

LINES

Written upon reviewing Soham Church
after a long absence.

CHARLES HASSELL.

With awe I gaz'd on that old church tower
  Upraising its noble head;
Standing alone as a giant power,
  'Mid the silent homes of the dead !

And a thousand thoughts through my
    mind flew fast
  As I look'd on that tower so grey:—
Of the days which, alas! are for ever past
  When my childish heart was gay.

I look'd around on the churchyard green,
  Where once I lov'd to play ;
But, time had now chang'd the happy
    scene,
  My playmates, where are they ?

Though youthful forms still met my sight
  They were all to me unknown :—
Yet I felt a glow of strange delight,
  As I wandered there alone.

Dim are the eyes that once were bright,
  And furrow'd many a brow ;
And many a heart that then was light,
  Lies cold and silent now !

The playmates dear of my early days,
  Were scatter'd far away ;
And all seem'd strange to my wand'ring
    gaze,
  But that stately tower so grey.

But wisdom whispers "murmer not,
  At the changes that here befall ;
For thine, alas ! is the common lot,—
  Such changes are seen by all."

She bids us loose each earthly tie,
  And check each grov'ling fear,
And upward look at the things on high,
  Of a pure and holier sphere,

Let grief ne'er sadden the youthful heart,
  When friendship's ties are riv'n
But hope, through grace, that we only
    part
  To meet again in heaven.

OUR CHILDREN'S PAGE.

FACTS WORTH REMEMBERING.

Gold leaf can be reduced to the 300-thousandth part of an inch,
  and gilding to the ten millionth.

Silver leaf to the 170-thousandth part of an inch.

Lace gilding is the millionth of an inch thick ; gold leaf the 200-
  thousandth.

One grain of gold will cover $7\frac{1}{2}$ inches each way ; or 52 square
  inches ; or be 1500 times thinner than writing paper.

The earth is 24,869 miles in circumference ; its diameter is 7,916
  miles ; its mean distance from the sun is 95 millions of
  miles ; from the moon, 240,000 miles.

880,000 miles, the diameter of the sun.

2,180 miles, the diameter of the moon.

In a square foot there are 144 square inches.

In an acre of ground there are 4840 square yards.

MISCELLANY AND EXTRACTS.

I remember to have read in an old book, written by an Italian, a very singular matter relative to the laws of Athens, of which the Romans asked for a copy; and as I know of no other author who has spoken of it but him, I shall lay it before my readers as a curiosity.

He says, that the Roman Ambassadors being arrived at Athens, and having explained the subject of their deputation, the grand council assembled to deliberate whether they should agree with the request. After having examined the proposition, the judges resolved to send to Rome a wise and sensible man, to know whether the Romans were by their wisdom worthy of receiving the laws, which Solon had given to the people of Greece; but if the ambassador found them rude and ignorant, he was to bring them back without communicating them to the Romans.

This resolution of the grand council of Athens could not be so concealed, but that the Romans got knowledge of it. The senate found themselves very much embarrassed, as at that time Rome was not provided with philosophers capable of arguing with one of the wise men of Greece. The matter therefore to be considered, was by what means they should get over this difficulty. The senate could think of no better method than to oppose a madman to the Greek philosopher; and with this view, that if the madman should happen by chance to prevail, the honour of Rome would be so much the more glorious, as a mad Roman would in that case confound a Grecian philosopher; and, if the latter should triumph, Athens would derive but little honour in boasting of having closed the mouth of a madman at Rome.

The Athenian ambassador being arrived at Rome, he was let immediately to the capitol, and introduced into an apartment richly furnished, where was seated, in an elbow chair, a madman dressed in the habit of a senator, whom they had expressly ordered not to speak a word. At the same time, the Grecian philosopher was told that the senator was very learned, but that he was a man of few words.

The Athenian was then introduced and without speaking a word, lifted up one finger of his hand. The madman, supposing this was a threatning signal to to pull out one of his eyes, and remembering that he was ordered not to speak, lifted up three of his fingers, wishing to signify thereby, that if the Grecian should put out one of his eyes, he would put out both his, and strangle him with the third finger. The philosopher, in lifting up one of his fingers, wished to be understood, that there was but one Supreme Being, who directed everything; and believed that the three fingers the madman had lifted up implied, that with God the past, present, and future, were the same thing, and from thence concluded that he, who in fact was only a madman, was a great philosopher.

The Grecian sage then held his hand opened to the innocent man, meaning thereby, that nothing is concealed from God; but the madman, supposing this to be a sign that he meant to give him a slap on the face, clinched his fist fast, and shook it at the philosopher, wishing him thereby to understand, that, if he executed his threats, he would meet with a resolute opposition, the Greek being already prepossessed in favour of the madman, conceived the meaning in a very different light, and concluded in himself, that the Romans meant, by a clinched fist, that God comprises all the universe in his hand. Judging from thence of the profound wisdom of the Romans, he granted them without any further enquiry the laws of Solon, according to their request.

BOAST not thyself of tomorrow, for thou knowest not what a day may bring forth. For the same reason, despair not of to-morrow; it may bring forth good as well as evil. Vex not thyself with imaginary fears. The impending cloud which is regarded with so much dread, may pass by harmless; or though it should discharge the storm, yet before it breaks, thou mayst be lodged in that lowly mansion which no storms ever touch.

THE velocity of the rays of light amounts to nearly two hundred thousand miles in a second of time, which is about a million times greater than the velocity of a cannon ball.

SICKNESS, when sanctified, teaches us four things : the vanity of the world, the vileness of sin, the helplessness of man, and the preciousness of Christ.

CONTENTMENT AND GRATITUDE.—

I have somewhat of the best things; I will thankfully enjoy them, and will want the rest with contentment.—*Bishop Hall.*

FROM many circumstances it appears that the atoms even of the most solid bodies, are not in actual contact with each other, but are retained in their respective places by a balance between attraction and repulsion. Thus, a solid body dilates or contracts, according as heat is added to, or taken away from it. A rod of iron becomes shorter or longer according as a weight is lodged upon its end, or is suspended from it: the rod in both cases, returning to its former length as soon as the weight is removed. Tin and copper melted together to form bronze, occupy less space by one fifth-teenth than they do when separate : proving that the atoms of one, are partially received into what were vacant spaces in the other. And so also a hundred pints of air may be compressed into a pint vessel, as in the chamber of an air gun; and if the pressure be still increased, the atoms of air at last collapse and form an oily liquid. The heat which was contained in the air, and gave it its form, is forced out in the operation, and becomes perceptible in every thing around.

THE great Albatross, with wings extending fourteen feet or more, is seen in the stormy solitude of the southern ocean, accompanying ships for whole days without ever resting on the waves.

A man ought never to be ashamed to own he has been in the wrong; which is but saying, in other words, that he is wiser to day than he was yesterday.

SWIFT.

DETRACTION is among those vices which the most languid virtue has sufficient force to present, because by detraction *that* is not gained which is taken away. "He who filches from me my good name" says Shakespeare "enriches not himself, but makes me poor indeed." As nothing, therefore, degrades human nature more than detraction, nothing more disgraces conversation. The detractor, as he is the lowest moral character, reflects greater dishonour on his company than the hangman ; and he whose disposition is a scandal to his species, should be more diligently avoided than his who is scandalous only by his office.—*Rambler.*

I cannot but regard it, both as the interest and duty of persons of taste, and sentiment, and knowledge, to take every opportunity of discountenancing a species of fashionable amusement, that of card playing : which is only adapted to the propagation and perpetuation of ignorance ; which occasions a shameful waste of that time which might be more beneficially as well as agreeably employed ; which is equally useless both to the body and to the mind; and which is best calculated to please those persons of both sexes, who are most devoid of genius, and the most insignificant and frivolous. *History of Philip Waldegrave, Vol.* 1, *pp* 32, 33.

SLAVE AUCTON-SCENE IN AMERICA.

IN the winters of 1840 and 1841, having business in Western Virgina, where this particular institution flourishes in its mildest form, (be it remembered, I was at this time opposed to anti-slavery principles,) December 28th, I found myself at Martinsburg, the county seat of Berkley. About ten of the aforesaid day I observed a crowd congregated in the public square, in frout of a superior looking building, which had very much the appearance of a jail, as it proved to be.

On enquiring of my landlord the cause of the meeting, he said it was "a hiring" in other words, a Negro sale, as I afterwards found that a number were hired for life. I walked down to the market; and, to obtain a better view, I mounted a large waggon in the street, directly opposite to the stand of the auctioneer, who had commenced his work. He was a large man, dressed in aristocratic style with a profusion of ruffles, gold finger-rings, watch seals, and last, and not least a large whip, called by the the the drivers a "loaded whip." The hiring I understood to be a number of slaves of a certain estate, who were hired out, from year to year, to the highest bidder, for the benefit of the heirs. These sales take place between Christmas and new year, (the holidays,) quite a recreation for the slaves who are to change masters.

After a number had been disposed of in this way, the crier announced that he would offer for sale six slaves. He then put up two, father and son. The old man was near sixty years of age, a cripple; the son was about twenty-three, a perfect specimen of man. There were two Georgian soul-drivers, who bid eight hundred dollars for both. When the crier remarked it was a small bid for both the Georgian replied, he would give eight hundred without the old man, as he was of no account. The young man gave the bidder a look that could not be well mistaken: the old man wept bitterly. The son sold on the bid; and the father was sold for sixty dollars to an old farmer, who had never kept a slave in his life. Thus the father and son were separated. The next case was that of a girl, fifteen years of age. (These slaves had been hired out to different individuals the past year.) She was brought crying upon the stand. With an oath he bid her to stop her "blubbering," and then proceeded with the sale. She was sold for one hundred and fifty dollars.

THE next case was that of a young white women, sixteen years old, with a young child. I say white woman, because the auctioneer said she was only one-eighth black; and I have seen many of the women of Ohio who could not boast of as fair complexion, or as good figure or features. She came upon the stand with her infant in her arms, in the deepest misery. A gentleman, who had taken his seat beside me, observing that I was much interested, remarked, he thought I was a stranger in that country. I answered that I was. "These things look odd to you." "They do." Said he, "You see that man in the crowd," pointing to one within a few paces of the stand: "that is Dr. C——. He hired that girl last year, and that child is his!" The Georgian bid 300 dollars; some one bid 400; the Georgian bid 450; the girl cast a piercing glance at the crowd; her eye rested on Dr. C——, who instantly averted his face. She gazed one moment, then burst into a torrent of tears. She was knocked off to the Georgian. Thus the fiend saw his child and its mother sold into southern bondage. oh horror! thought I, is it possible? I was cured of my pro-slavery principles.—*Cincinatti Herald.*

MONTHLY NOTICES.

APRIL.

5th.—Dividends on several species of Stock become due.

Assessed Tax Returns made soon after this, by which persons rate themselves for articles, liable, kept or used by them between 5th of April, 1846, and this day.

7th.—Isle of Ely Quarter Sessions, *at Ely.*

8th.—Insurances, due at Lady-day, must be paid on or before this day.

21st.—Bedford Level Corporation Meeting, at Ely.

The Hundred-feet Wash Tax is laid on the second Wednesday in April, (or at an adjournment) payable one month afterwards, and one month more allowed for payment.

The liv	in	g fount, the li	f	e, the wa	y	e, I know,
And but	to	thee	O!	whither	s	hould I go?
All 9	th	er helps a	r	e vain, giv	e	thine to me,
For by th	y	cross my	s	aving hea	l	th must be.
O! hear	K	en, then, wh	a	t I with	f	aith implore,
Lest s	in	and death sin	k	me for	e	vermore
O Lord, my	G	od! thou m	e	direct	a	nd keep,
In death	d	efe	n	d, that from thee I	n	e'er slip;
And at the do	om	let	m	e be raise	d	then,
To liv	e	with the	e.	Sweet Jes	us,	say Amen.

Explanation.

IN deciphering this page, let it first be read through in continuous lines, without regard to the spaces, the points, or the figures of the crosses. The first line will thus be, "My God! My God! in rivers of my tears." The fifth line will be "Let not my God! my God! my faults, tho' great." The eighth line will be "Thou, Lord, rememberest thine if thou be sought." &c. Then let the crosses be read from top to bottom, and they will give the words of our Lord, and of the two thieves, respectively. The letters I. N. R. I. at the top of the centre cross, are the initials of the Latin words JESUS NAZARENUS REX JUDÆORUM. Jesus of Nazareth the King of the Jews.

SOFAM; PRINTED and PUBLISHED by WILLIAM PLAYFORD, for the "EOBAM MAGAZINE," May 1, 1847

PLAYFORD'S

SOHAM MAGAZINE,

AND

Friendly Monitor.

MAY, 1847.

T a time when Popery is making such vigorous and rapid strides to recover once more her usurped supremacy in our land, it is well to bring her proud pretensions to the touchstone of truth. The reiterated assertion of a falsehood, causes it, too frequently, at last to be believed : and it is by these means that some of the worst impostures of this crafty and ambitious system have been palmed upon the world. The very prevalent opinion that the Church of England originated in a separation from the Church of Rome, is an error which the most moderate acquaintance with ecclesiastical history would serve to correct. For though the notices of such matters in ancient writers, are not very frequent or copious, yet they are fully sufficient to show that the christianity of England was derived from a far purer source. Add to which, when the whole christian community of a kingdom throws off, with one irresistible effort, the rule of an Italian Bishop, against which it has protested in every age, it is the greatest possible abuse of terms to call it a separation, as if the Church had never had a previous and independent existence. If in the first ages of Christianity we held communion with the churches of the East, how can this connect us, in any way, with Popery, which is only a gross corruption of Christianity altogether? For "where is the fair daughter of heaven, who, appearing in the hired lodging of Saul of Tarsus, and making her way into Cæsar's household, shone so long

No. 5. Vol. 1.   F

with simple beauty in imperial Rome? She retains indeed the name of Christian, and usurps the name of Catholic; but alas! how grievously is she defiled! Her native purity is gone: and abomination, yea, Mother of Abominations is written upon her forehead."

It appears that the Papal authority was first attempted to be introduced into these islands by the monk Austin, in the year 596. Now, taking only a few notices from ancient history, as we are compelled to do from the necessary brevity of this article, we learn from Gibbon, the infidel, that the council held at Arminium or Rimini, in the year 359, "was composed of about 400 Bishops of Italy, Africa, Spain, Gaul, BRITAIN, and Illyricum." Du Pin tells us that the Western Bishops assembled, from all parts, to this council; and that "the Emperor had sent his letters mandatory for them, and provided for them public carriage, and money for their journey; but the Bishops of France and BRITAIN thought it below them, and chose rather to travel at their own expense." This took place 237 years before Austin set foot upon our shores; while we are expressly informed that, about 45 years earlier still, there were present at the great council held at Arles, in the reign of the Emperor Constantine, "THREE BISHOPS, ONE PRIEST, AND ONE DEACON, FROM BRITAIN."

From these references, then, it appears that in the years 314 and 359 there were Christian Bishops in Britain, who were acknowledged to be such by the Emperor Constantine, and by the Bishops of the whole western Catholic Church.

"Austin first preached in England, says a late writer on this subject, in the year 596; and although I think better of him than Jortin seems to have thought, who says that "the christianity which this pretended Apostle, and sanctified ruffian taught us, seemed to consist principally in two things,—to keep Easter upon a proper day, and to be slaves to our Sovereign Lord God the Pope, and to Austin his deputy vicegerent," yet certainly he burned with zeal for the extension of his master's authority, and the elevation of himself. Now it is a matter of historical fact, that Austin found certain Bishops at the head of well-defined, and, as far as possible in those times, well regulated dioceses. They impeded his ambitious career. And could he, or his powerful master the Pope, have proved them to be not true Bishops, it is impossible to doubt what course they would have taken. These Bishops had a meeting with Austin, which Camden refers to in the following words :—" There is a place whose situation is not exactly known in this county (Worcestershire) called Austin's Oak, where Augustine, the Apostle of the English, and the BRITISH BISHOPS met, and, after some squabbling about the observance of Easter, the preaching of the gospel, and the administration of Baptism according to the Romish Church, separated with as little agreement as before."

Du Pin further tells us, that, in the commencement of his work, Austin sent a series of questions to Pope Gregory, for his direction and counsel. Amongst others, he asked :—" After what manner he should deal with the Bishops of Gaul, and of BRITAIN, He was informed that he was to have no power over the Gallic Bishops, but as to *the British Bishops, Gregory gave full authority over them.*" Now this was to give Austin what Gregory had no power to grant, and therefore the pretended jurisdiction of the Pope was vigorously opposed by the British Bishops and Monks, who refused to receive any Romish customs different from those of their own Church.

From these early Bishops, and not from the Bishop of Rome, does the Church of England derive the commission of her ministers.

A few more notices, and we must conclude. Gildas, our oldest native historian says, A.D. 38, that Joseph of Arimathea, who took down Christ from the cross, being sent here by Philip the Apostle, out of France, began first to preach the Gospel in this Realm, in the time of Tiberias the Emperor. Nicephorus says, that Simon Zelotes came, about the same time, into this Island, and did the same. Theodoretus says, that St. Paul, immediately after his first delivery in Rome, under the Emperor Nero, preached the Gospel in this island, and in other countries of the west. Tertullian, A.D. 230, says that the island of Britain was subject unto Christ in his time. Origen, A.D. 240, says the same ; in whose time Lucius, the English King, was baptized, and received the Gospel : and Bishop Jewel tells us that " Helena, being an English woman, wife unto Constantius the Emperor, and mother unto Constantinus, is notably praised for her faith and religion, by St. Ambrose, by Eusebius, by Sozomenus, and others."

Lucius wrote to Eleutherius, the Bishop of Rome, to inquire how he should order his Church and Kingdom. The answer he received was not that which would be given in the present day :—" Ye have received in the kingdom of Britain, by God's mercy, both the law and faith of Christ. Ye have both the New Testament and the Old. Out of the same, through God's grace, by the advice of your Realm, take a law, and by the same, through God's sufferance, rule you your Kingdom of Britain. For in that kingdom you are God's Vicar."

We tell the Papists, then, that whatever power the Bishop of Rome may, at any time, have obtained in England, it was a usurpation; and that he used it for purposes of tyranny, extortion, and fraud : that 300 years ago, our forefathers died at the stake to emancipate their children from so grievous a yoke ; and that we trust the day may never arrive when superstition so gross, and authority so cruel as theirs, will again spread darkness and death over our land.

MAY DAY.

Come lads with your bills,
To the wood we'll away ;
We'll gather the boughs,
And we'll celebrate May.

We'll bring our load home,
As we've oft done before ;
And leave a green bough
At each good neighbour's door.

THE MAYERS' CALL.

The rejoicing of the heart at the return of Summer, bounteous with gaieties and cheering influences, must have been coeval with the first created beings—with the first revolving year ; and all nations and people of whom we have any trace or history seem to have agreed to mark the annual coming of this season with peculiar homage.

The Druids—the first priests of our own land—celebrated it by a rural sacrifice, (called *beltein* from the fires which were used in the ceremonial) to propitiate divine protection for their flocks. Some few remains of this rite may even yet be traced in the wilds of Scotland, among the Cheviots, and in some parts of our own border land—the beautiful Cumberland.*

The Romans marked this season by games in honor of Flora, the goddess of flowers—hence termed *Floralia*—which continued during the last four days of April and on the first of May ; thus going forth to a distance, as it were, to meet the beautiful *Maia*, and conduct her to her place among the months with the warmth of young hearts rejoicing. It is from these *Floralia* that our old May Day ceremonies descended ; and it is not without regret that we witness them, year by

* Pennant's "Tour in Scotland" vol. i. p. 111. contains a particular description of the ceremony.

year, giving way to the cold tyranny of those business habits which are creeping over every thing, and blighting all the simple and gentle feelings bequeathed us by our more rustic and more happy forefathers.

> "The world is too much with us; late and soon,
> Getting and spending, we lay waste our powers:
> Little we see in nature that is ours;
> We have given our hearts away—a sordid boon!"

In former days all ranks of Englishmen went "a-maying" early on the first morn of the month, but now, the maying—where it is not wholly extinct—is chiefly confined to the mechanics and artisans of large towns (honoured be they for it!) who are glad to retain the privilege of throwing off for one day the shackles of occupation—of turning their backs on their confined and too often cheerless abodes—and of going forth, with free and bounding thoughts, into the garden of nature.

> "Farewell, cities! who could bear
> All their smoke, and all their care,
> All their pomp, when wooed away
> By the azure hours of May?"

Monarchs went a-maying. The sensual tyrant Henry the Eighth, we are told, rode a-maying with his Queen Katharine, accompanied by many lords and ladies, going from his favorite palace at Greenwich to Shooter's Hill, then as in after times a chosen resort of the citizens of London. The poets were all votaries of the gay and perfumed *Maia*. Chaucer, our earliest English poet, has delightfully celebrated the beauteous freshness of the season, and pictured the roaming of the Mayers in the grove in search of boughs; and our own sweet Shakspere, in that rich store-house of poetic beauties, "Midsummer Night's Dream," speaks of doing "observance to a morn of May." Even old chroniclers—plodders in musty records, and matter-of-fact philosophers—in those days yielded to the influence of the "laughing season,"—left their studies—brushed off the dust of antiquity, and sought in early morn those simple flowers which have obtained their name from the month with whose birth their own is contemporaneous. Honest, kind-hearted, hard-working John Stowe tells us that "EVERY MAN, except impediment, would walk into the sweet meadows and green woods, there to rejoice their spirits with the beauty and savour of sweet flowers, and with the harmony of birds praising God in their kind." Herrick, whose muse sings of many of our national customs, confirms—if such confirmation can be needed—the universality of the "observance of a morn of May" in a beautiful little poem, "Corinna's going a-maying." Alas! Corinna was a laggard, and her swain enforces his invitation to "go a-maying" by declaring

> "There's not a budding boy or girl, this day
> But is got up, and gone to bring in May."

So desirous were they in some parts of our country—in the north and in the west, to catch the first delicious breath of May—"like the sweet South, that breathes upon a bank of violets, stealing and giving odour"—that the younger part of both sexes were wont to arise at midnight, and in procession, with music, go to the woods, gather branches of trees and deck them with coronals of flowers and nosegays; and on their return to the village bedeck the pillars of the church, the doors and windows of their houses, and their may-pole, with the arbour by for the Lady of the May, with the flowery spoil.

> "Come, my Corinna, come, and coming mark
> How each field turns a street, each street a park,
> Made green and trimmed with trees; see how
> Devotion gives each house a bough,
> Or branch; each porch, each door, ere this,
> An ark, a tabernacle is,
> Made up of white-thorne, neatly interwove."

Alas! where now shall we find the merry making MAY-POLE that used to stand in every city, town, and village, year after year, a thing sacred to every heart, young or old, gentle or simple—never suffering violation or pollution ; but on every anniversary receiving its new adorning, and giving the glow of health and happiness to all who

> " Hither, from village sweet and hamlet fair,
> From bordering cot and distant glen, repair ; "

and who round it—

> " With heel so nimble wear the springing grass
> To shrilling bagpipe, or to tinkling brass ;
> Or foot it to the reed. "

In places where the May-pole was not a fixture, the ceremony of " bringing it home," as it was termed, was an important feature in the morning's occupation. It has been thus described by the puritan Stubbes, a bitter hater of all pastimes and sports : " They have twentie or fourtie yoke of oxen, every oxe having a sweete nosegay of flowers tyed on the tippe of his hornes, and these oxen drawe home this Maie-pole, which is covered all over with flowers and hearbes, bounde rounde aboute with stringes, from the top to the bottome, and sometyme painted with variable colours, with twoo or three hundred men, women, and children following it with greate devotion. And thus beyng reared up, with handkerchiefes and flagges streamyng on the toppe, they strawe the grounde aboute, binde greene boughes about it, sett up sommer haules, bowers, and arbours hard by it. And then fall they to banquet and feast, to leape and daunce aboute it as the heathen people did at the dedication of their idolles, whereof this is a perfect patterne, or rather the thyng itself."

The prevalence of this feeling against the innocent May-pole led to its disuse ; but it required the authority and power of a special ordinance of " Lords and Commons" to pull down so universal a favourite of the people. A fine of " 5s. weekly till the said May-pole be taken down," to which all churchwardens and constables were subject, effectually removed the " gay tree" from the land ; but the restoration of Charles the Second was the signal for its revival. On the very first May-day afterwards, one was raised in the Strand of such wondrous height, being 134 feet, and size as to require the superintendence of the royal Lord High Admiral (afterwards James the Second), and the exertions of a portion of his chosen crew to plant in its place. A rare tract, entitled " Cities Loyalty Displayed," gives an interestingly minute account of the raising.

" The May-pole" says the writer, " being joyned together, and hoopt about with " bands of iron, the crown and cane with the King's arms richly gilded, was placed " on the head of it a large top, like a balcony, was about the middle of it. This " being done, the trumpets did sound, and, in four hours' space it was advanced " upright, after which, being established fast in the ground, six drums did beat, " and the trumpets did sound ; again great shouts and acclamations the people give, " that it did ring throughout all the Strand. After that came a morice dance, finely " deckt, with purple scarfs in their half-shirts, with a tabor and pipe, the ancient " musick, and danced round about the May-pole, and after that danced the rounds of " their liberty. Upon the top of this famous standard is likewise set up a royal pur- " ple streamer, about the middle of it is placed four crowns more, with the King's " arms likewise, there is also a garland set upon it of various colours of delicate rich " favours, under which is to be placed three great lanthorns. It is far more glorious, " bigger, and higher than ever any one that stood before it, and the seamen themselves " doe confess that it could not be built higher, nor is there not such a one in Europe " beside, which highly doth please his Majesty and the illustrious Prince Duke of " York ; little children did much rejoice, and ancient people did clap their " hands, saying golden days begin to appear. I question not but 'twill ring like me- " lodious musick throughout every county in England when they read this story."

This glory of May-poles afterwards came to be used to support the then largest telescope in the world, that of the illustrious Newton, at Wanstead, in Essex.

Among the latest used May-poles was that at Kennington, a suburb of the Metropolis, which remained till near the beginning of the present century, and was an especial favourite with the Milk-maids ; and among the latest patrons of the sports in connection with the May-pole was Dr. Parr, the great Grecian scholar and political writer, who was always the first of the throng to assemble round the May-pole in his village of Hatton, and to promote the dance around it, himself cordially joining in.*

The love of the May-pole was not confined to our own happy isles. In France and other parts of the Continent it formed a principal feature in the universal homage to the day; and even in Upper India, we are told by Archer, the rude natives, erect a pole decorated with garlands and festoons in honour of the season, and with strings of flowers around their heads give themselves up to the joyousness of the time.

The Milk-maids have been incidentally mentioned. Of them a goodly paper might be pen'd. They were till within the memory of ancient people living diligent observers of May-day. Their bright new gowns, caps, and aprons—their clean and polished pails—their choice garland of plate—a magnificent silver pile set off with the greatest taste by delicious bouquets—gladdened for a while the streets and squares of "the work-a-day world;" but that has passed away.

The poor Sweeps, too, made lords and ladies of themselves for the nonce; and tired themselves around the "Jack-in-the-green" to pleasure the citizens and gather a few pence. But they have gone by—the annual dinner given to the remnant of them by the masters instead of this holiday has proved too much for this relic of by-gone mirth, and the "Jack-in-the-green" has fallen into the hands of the idle and dissolute, who are deservedly discouraged. In some country towns the attempt is however still made to trick out the dingy person of poor sooty with a few gay coloured rags and flowers, but the performance is so miserable, and there is so little heart for such things now, that he has scarcely a sympathiser (the kind-hearted Elia and his pleasant friend Jem White, alas! are gone) in his merry making.

The "May-lord" and his "lady" are not yet quite forgotten personages; at least in our own county; for in some parts it is still, we believe, customary for the young people of the farms to go a-maying and return in procession with a "May-lord" and "May-lady," decorated with flowers and many-coloured ribbons. They go through the village singing a song, more lengthy than poetical, but partaking of a religious feeling (for our simple-minded ancestors in all their pastimes never forgot to whom all things were owing;) and receiving money from the inhabitants, terminate the joyous day with a feast of plumcake and tea.

PHILO-MAIA.

* In some parts of England, a May-pole is even now, occasionally raised, and a long string of men and women, hand in hand, after encircling it a few times, in a species of dance, rush with noisy merriment, through all the streets of the town. ED.

MORAL REFLECTIONS.

Continued from Page 57.

If an inhabitant of one of those bright and blessed worlds where sin is unknown, or known only by report, as having blasted the happiness of an obscure and remote part of the dominions of God, should sojourn for a brief space among mortals, he would instantly perceive, by unequivocal indications, that this was one of the lapsed provinces. He would be assailed by a number of singularly novel emotions on finding himself in the very heart of a rebellious community; whilst he would exult in his own consciousness of rectitude and in his power to abstract himself, at pleasure, from all contact and communication with the polluted and guilty race. His pure and lofty sentiments would be often outraged, by observing the debasement and selfishness of the species, the innumerable forms and modes of hideous deformity in which sin, as the ruling power, presents itself in their actions, and the almost demoniacal facility which men of all ranks have acquired in the commission of crime. All this would appear to him an enormous mass of evil, over which an angel might weep.   But on his becoming acquainted with the history of man's revolt; of the consequences which have continued, through so many ages, and in so many forms of direful calamity, to afflict the race; and of the economy of divine mercy, instituted for his recovery through the mediation of the Son of God, the utter indifference to the whole subject, which he would speedily have discovered to be almost universal, would strike him as a strange anomaly.   The reflections of such a being, in relation to this subject, would, not improbably, take some such form as the following—" The Supreme Ruler might, justly, have abandoned a race of intelligent creatures, in revolt, to the inevitable consequences of their rebellion, There would have been no difficulty, in that case, in perceiving the principles, or the equity of the procedure. " The heavens would have declared His righteousness for God is judge himself." But that mercy should have triumphed over judgment; that a free pardon, and full restoration to virtue and happiness, should have been offered to the human race, on terms so gracious, and involving so vast a sacrifice as the incarnation and death of the Son of God; that, although this all important topic has been urged upon the attention of the successive generations of men, in every possible form of earnest and persuasive representation, the great mass of them should have continued, to this day, to exhibit the most absolute immobility and unconcern; and that, notwithstanding, the Divine forbearance should continue the race in a probationary condition, form, together, a grand phenomenon in the universe—a mystery which, probably, none but the Infinite Mind can fully comprehend. It is not unreasonable to imagine that such a being would feel a strong, impulsive, curiosity to identify the causes whose combined action has produced in the human species this anomalous apathy to the highest interest. In making his analysis with this view he would begin with what should appear to be the immediate cause—the last agent in the production of so strange and dismal an effect. From that he would descend to the rest, individualizing them, one by one, until he should reach the most remote. He would soon perceive that a vast and complicated machinery was at work in human nature,—a mighty array of powerful agencies, all co-operating, with never-failing fidelity, in the production of this effect. His surprise at the prevailing insensibility, would gradually lessen, as he became acquainted with the nature, power, and activity, of the causes conspiring to produce it, and as he perceived that men yield themselves, without resistance, to the influence of these causes, until like the fated ship in a dead calm, they become incapable of motion, though the question at issue be one of life and death. His wonder would now turn upon the circumstance, that men *do* so yield in relation to a subject whose importance and urgency demand a resistance so prompt, determined, and unyielding, that it would not rest, until the last vestige of the hostile influences should have been exterminated.

Of the causes, whose discovery would be the result of the supposed analysis, probably, the following would be specified as amongst the chief. Perhaps the almost universal neglect of the mind and things pertaining to it, observable amongst men, would be noted as uppermost in the series. The heavenly visitant, in making his observations on human character, from the very commencement of its formation, would discover, that, with few exceptions, that formation was conducted on a scale utterly exclusive of all reference to the mind and its interests, in the sense in which those expressions are to be understood, as implying the *true mental character* of the species. He would perceive that mankind are not taught, inured and trained to think in the direction of the highest concerns. That they were taught to think, indeed, and that circumstances were of a nature to oblige them to think; but that the whole mental operation had an exclusive reference to sublunary objects and interests, rather than to those objects and interests which form the true element of *mind* in all its grades. That the process of mental developement and culture so far as it goes, is of a nature to place the mind in a situation of mere passive subordination to that power which inspiration emphatically denominates *the flesh*, as an instrument to be employed for the sole purpose of securing *its* gratification; rather than to raise it to its true position, as a sublime spiritual agent whose grand business it is, to subordinate every thing in working out its eternal well-being.

Soham.   *To be continued.*   S.

ECONOMICAL HINTS TO COTTAGERS.

Continued from Page 53.

Another cheap dish, which I am surprised I do not hear of oftener in this part of the country, is beef tripe; few things go further, and it seems to me a sad pity it should be given to dogs, when so many people would be so thankful for it, if they did but know its value. Any poor woman who was cleanly might make a very comfortable livlihood in dressing tripe. The art is very easily acquired, although certainly a troublesome one, but experience would soon teach you the best and easiest method. It is merely done by scalding and scraping very well till all the dark part is removed, having the water a proper heat, and often rincing it well, and when thoroughly cleansed par-boiled. I have no doubt the dresser might make treble her expenses by selling it out in dinners for 3d. or 4d. and what she could not sell would keep well in a little sour milk and water, or salt and water. This is always done in large towns, and most people are very fond of it, either fried with onions till nicely brown, or boiled with milk and water, served in a deep dish, with some of the liquid, and eaten with onion sauce. You seem, also, here, to be unacquainted with what hundreds live upon in many places, and are most thankful to get, that is, salt herring. I do not mean red ones, which are much dearer, but those that are prepared in barrels in strong pickle, and sent abroad. As those barrels contain a great many, no private family could consume them while they were good, but I am surprised that the shopkeepers do, not sell them here, as you are not so very distant from Yarmouth, where they are cured. At any time when fresh herrings are plentiful, and you can afford to purchase more than you want for present use, you may easily preserve them in the following manner : clean the insides well, removing the gills, &c., then put a little salt over and within them, and let them stand all night singly on a dish, which will purify them of all offensive matter, then clean off the salt quite well, and fill the insides quite full of fresh salt, and lay them in rows in a dish, or deep oval earthen pan, such as they usually cure tongues in ; sprinkling the bottom well with salt, and putting a layer of salt between every layer of herrings, and covering the whole well with the same, which ought to make sufficient pickle to cover them, by which means they will keep good a long time ; some months if you wish it. They must also have a dish or some close cover over them, to exclude the air. They will go further in this state than when fresh, and you may cook them by boiling them by themselves, or with your potatoes, to which they give a flavour: observing to put them in the pan just as the potatoes boil, and they will all be done at the same time. If at any time, you happen to have nothing but cold meat for your dinner, you may improve it very much, and make it go further by making it into potatoe-patties. It is only putting on your potatoes an hour or two before you want them, and when boiled enough, mash them very fine with a little milk, a very small piece of butter, and a little salt to your taste, then make them up into the shape of small raised round pies, working them with a little flour to make them keep together better, fill the hollow which you make in them, with your cold meat minced very small and seasoned with a little pepper and salt, shred onion and a little water. Put them before the fire in a tin oven or cheese-toaster and turn them till they are nicely browned all round. If you have any gravy of the bones, (which you can readily make while the patties are baking,) you

you can serve it up in a sauce boat, which will be a great addition if prepared properly.   If you have to send your husband his dinner out, you will find this dish a
great comfort, as it will keep a long time warm, wrapped up close in a clean napkin,
and covered in a basket.   Undressed meat goes a long way when made into small
raised pies, and nicely seasoned.   You may work up your flour with a little nice
dripping, or skimmings melted and poured amongst it with a little salt, and made
into the most convenient size for your oven.   A short time will bake them, and they
also keep hot a good while, if well covered from the very first.   I may here take
notice of a defect I have frequently observed in people who are not regular bakers,
in regard to their ovens.   In the first place, they never clear their ashes well out
but leave them to stick to the bottom of the loaf, which is not only disgusting, but
unwholesome, and might so easily be avoided by having a wooden hoe made rather
wide, and scraping the oven quite clean but with it, which is much better than a broom.
To be continued.

OUR LETTER BOX.

The Editors do not wish to be considered responsible for all the sentiments
of their Correspondents.

To the Editor of the Soham Magazine.

*Sir,—The suggestions of your correspondent, concerning the Police, in the April
number of this magazine, though very à propos,—will, I fear, be entirely lost upon
"our Town," if no one should be found sufficiently patriotic to consider it his duty to
call the attention of the inhabitants publicly to this subject, by which means, a meeting might be convened, to take into consideration, whether the advantages attending
the establishment of a body of Rural Police, would counterbalance the expense
naturally resulting therefrom.*

*There are many other points for consideration which a friendly challenge to those
of your readers and correspondents, who have it in their power to furnish facts, and
statistical accounts, might enable you to bring forward, through the medium of your
valuable magazine, preliminary to this meeting. Hoping, my wishes for the well-
fare of my native place, may be considered ample apology for trespassing on your
pages.*

I remain, Sir,
Your obliged and humble Servant,

Soham, April 17, 1847.   L. P. J.

We willingly insert this letter of our friend L. P. J. with the hope that it may lead to some decisive
steps upon so important a subject. Taking it in a merly MORAL point of view, there cannot be a
question as to its expediency.   There is not a respectable inhabitant of the Town, who does not
feel that the condition of our streets, particularly on Sunday Evenings, is in the highest degree
disgraceful.   ED.

SOHAM.

SOHAM presents a somewhat striking and picturesque appearance to a stranger at this season of the year, from the number and extent of its orchards, with their fruit trees in full bloom. The approach to the Town through the Moat Closes, of which we give a well engraved view above, is perhaps the best; and we very much wish that the walk were laid out, with more regard to the convenience and recreation of the inhabitants. The proportions of the fine perpendicular tower of the very handsome Church, are seen with great advantage from this spot, and we cannot but regret that a Town once distinguished as a Bishop's See, should have so long stood still amid the general advancement, and even now manifest so little of the spirit and enterprise of the age in which we live. Great improvements have, however, taken place within the last few years, and we believe that a feeling has already been awakend amongst us, which will ultimately lead to a better and happier condition.

The interior of the church exhibits some very beautiful specimens of transition Norman architecture; the arch that divides the transepts from the nave being particularly fine, and the sculpture of a very uncommon character. There was formerly a tower over it, which, from what cause we know not, has been taken down. The transepts are in the early English style, with inserted windows, and the chancel has been converted, from the early English into the decorated. Like most other churches, however, it is dreadfully disfigured by galleries, and unsightly pews. To make way for these selfish intruders, the finely carved oak benches have been cut away without remorse, and the breadth, and harmonious design of the sacred fabric, have been entirely destroyed. In the gable at the west-end of the chapel in the Hamlet of Barway, is a window which appears to be of older date than any portion of the parish church. Not many years since, this secluded spot was frequently accessible only by water, while its ancient sanctuary fell into decay, and became " a couching place for flocks." It is now, however, happily restored to its original purposes, and the voice of thanksgiving may be heard every sabbath within those walls that echoed with the sound eight hundred years ago.

POETRY.

[In Original Poetry, the Name, real or assumed, of the Author, is printed in small Capitals under the title; in Selections it is printed in Italics at the end.]

FADING AWAY.

MRS. FIELD.

Where'er with musing steps I go,
All nature round me tends to show,
How fleeting all things are below,
    What changing hues they wear:
Yes, if I upwards raise my eye,
The clouds which sail along the sky,
Say, tho' they move in silence by,
    They are but trav'llers there.

I wander'd by yon streamlet's side,
Beheld its waters swiftly glide,
A sound came from the murm'ring tide,
    Which told it pass'd away.
I sought the groves green solitude,
With many a summer blossom strew'd,
A breeze swept by e'en while I view'd,
    Gone were those flowers gay.

And when the western sky look'd bright,
With rosy beams and golden light,
Those tints soon faded from my sight,
    Touch'd by the wing of time:—
I saw the gentle moon arise,
She staid not in the cloudless skies,
But wander'd slowly from my eyes,
    To seek another clime.

I pac'd the garden's gay partere
Gaz'd on some beauteous flower there,
Which trembling whisper'd "frail as fair,
    "We must ere morn decay."
And then I went, alone, to tread,
The bloomless garden of the dead.
A voice was there, which plainly said,
    Thus man too fades away.

I saw a with'ring yew tree wave,
O'er many a dark and silent grave,
Its sear leaves to the wind it gave,
    And strew'd the turf below.
While as the night breeze pass'd me by,
I list'ned to its mournful sigh,
It seem'd to say, "thus thou must lie,"
    How soon, ah! none can know.

And then soft breathing on my ear,
A small, still voice in accents clear,
Said learn a useful lesson here
    Give not to earth thy love:
If all things there must fade or flee,
Earth is no resting place for thee,
O let thy first, best wish then be,
    To seek a home above!

LINES IN AN ALBUM.

Dear Fanny, should this simple page,
When I am far away engage
A moments thought from you,
You'll find a wish recorded here,
A seraph's dream not more sincere,
Nor Holy Writ more true.

Thy mind, dear girl, is yet secure,
From folly's trace, and passions lure,
And Heaven preserve it so;
May pleasure's cup, no drop contain,
Its purity to taint or stain,
And never cease to flow.

And when thy pilgrimage is past,
And all aside of earth is cast,
And all of Heaven in view;
Fear not the darkness of the tomb,
Thy faith shall dissipate its gloom,
And light thy passage through.
    Soham.

ON THE ASCENT OF A BALLOON.

From the manuscript of the late Mr. T. W. Gunton, of University College, London.

O gorgeus globe, how glorious there
Thou ridest through the balmy air!
So swift thy course, our aching sight,
Scarce follows through the flood of light.
Far, far on high thy flight sublime
Outtop where Alpine Chamois climb.
While eagle's eyes, with wild amaze
Upon thy daring orbit gaze.
All radiant in the solar beams,
Instinct with life thy motion seems;
As thou would'st there for ever stay
Rejoicing in eternal day.
Through liquid æther, ne'er before
Approach'd by mortal, dost thou soar.
The genius of the storm looks on,
And stays his bolt till thou art gone.
On whirlwinds riding, fast and far,
Mid sleeping thunder, speeds thy car!
Intrepid aeronaut! no fear
Assails thee in thy dread career.
With calm delight dost thou look down
On forest, silver stream, and town;
Till through the clouds, thy flight now past,
All ocean bounds the prospect vast.

NOT FOR EVER.

Those who have lov'd alone, can tell
The pangs that wring the heart at parting
When fix'd as by some magic spell,
The pulse has ceas'd, and tears are star-
        ting,
Yet when that painful hour arrives,
When, soul from kindred soul must sever,
Amid' the heart-wreck hope still lives,
And sweetly whispers, " not for ever !"
Soham.

ADVICE.

Whene'er you speak of those who are
        away.
Suppose them listening to all you say ;
And if you cannot well with truth com-
        mend,
By silence prove yourself to be their
        friend ;
Nor, for the sake of starting something
        new,
Say what you would not like once said of
        you.

THE LOST SHIP.

Deep in the silent waters,
    A thousand fathoms low,
A gallant ship lies perishing,
    That foundered long ago.

There are pale sea flowers wreathing
    Around her port holes now,
And spars and shining coral,
    Encrust her gallant prow.

Upon the old deck bleaching,
    White bones unburied shine,
And in the deep hold hidden,
    Are casks of ruby wine.

There are pistol, sword, and carbine,
    Hung on the cabin wall,
And many a curious dagger,
    But rust has spoiled them all.

And can this be the vessel,
    That went so boldly forth,
With the red flag of old England,
    To brave the stormy north.

There were blessings poured upon her
    When from the port sailed she,
And prayers and anxious weeping,
    Went with her on the sea.

And once she sent home letters,
    And joyous ones were they,
Dashed with fond remembrance,
    Of friends so far away.

How little those who read them,
    Deemed far below the wave,
The child, and sire, and lover,
    Had found a seaman's grave.

But how that brave ship perished,
    None knew, save Him on high,
No Island heard her cannon,
    No other bark was nigh.

We only know from England,
    She sailed far o'er the main,
We only know, to England
    She never came again.

And eyes grew dim with watching,
    That yet refused to weep,
And years were spent in hoping,
    For tidings from the deep.

It grew an old man's story,
    Upon their native shore,
God rest those souls in Heaven,
    Who meet on earth no more.

                                    L. E. L.

OUR CHILDREN'S PAGE.

FACTS WORTH REMEMBERING.

A Man 5ft. 6in. high on the Sea shore, or on level ground, can see
    about 3 miles distant.

The hexagonal cells of Bees present the greatest space with the
    least labour.

The first iron railroad was laid at Colebrook Dale, in 1786.

The first railway coach was from Stockton to Darlington, with one
    horse, 12 miles in one hour and a quarter.

MISCELLANY AND EXTRACTS.

Inscription on the Monument of Sir Isaac Thornton, in Snailwell Church,
May 1, 1669.

Hereunder (waiting till the dead shall rise,)
The body of Sir Isaac Thornton lies,
Left by the soul, which knowing its high birth,
With joy, for heaven, did forsake this earth ;
And leaving to the world a spotless name,
Returned to God from whom at first it came.
But though the body of this blessed mind
Be here to a cold bed of earth resign'd,
'Tis not to sleep forgotten in the dust;
The time will come when once again it must
Arise, and to the soul united be,
Ne'er more to part unto eternity :
And this, which, for a time, death triumphs o'er,
Shall live when time and death shall be no more.

THE odious fashion of card playing (says Dr. Johnson) was produced by a conspiracy of the old, the ugly, and the ignorant, against the young and beautiful, the witty and the gay ; as a contrivance to level all distinctions of nature and art ; to confound the world in a chaos of folly ; to take from those who could outshine them, all the advantages of mind and body ; to withhold youth from its natural pleasures, to deprive wit of its influence, and beauty of its charms ; to sink life into a tedious uniformity, and to allow it no other hopes or fears but those of robbing or being robbed.

Rambler, No. 15.

RAINS in England are often introduced by a south-east wind. Vapour brought to us by such a wind must have been generated in countries to the south and south-east of our island. It is therefore, probably, in the extensive valleys watered by the Meuse, the Moselle, and the Rhine, if not from the more distant Elbe, with the Oder, and the Weser, that the water rises from the earth in the midst of sunshine, which is soon after to form our clouds, and pour down our thunder showers.

IT has been found by experiment that charcoal, which was supposed to be only half as heavy as its bulk of water, is on the contrary, seven times heavier. The discovery tends to confirm the opinion that charcoal and the diamond are identical. Pumice stone consists, likewise, of matter heavier than granite or marble.

I wish I could see in religious professors more of the winning kindness that distinguished our only perfect Exemplar. How constrained has many an ingenuous and well-disposed person been made to feel, by the manner which can speak as plainly as words, in saying, you are not to be admitted to familiar intercourse with us, for you are not an initiated person ! Where is the love and condescension of our blessed Lord, who loved the young ruler, although he could not consent to make the sacrifice that Christ required, and follow Him.

How ought we to esteem those who have all the amiable qualities of that young man, and are also ready to give up all for their Lord, but who are, alas ! ignorant or inexperienced in the outward expression of the faith of Christ.

Records of a Good Man's Life.

THE mast of the Tilbury man-of-war, which was burnt at Jamaica, was thrown, by the current, on the western coast of Ireland.

KING JAMES the 1st, wrote a treatise against the use of Tobacco, and, among other things, says it is a custom loathsome to the eye, hateful to the brain, and dangerous to the lungs.

THE lowliness of the Christian is utterly different from the mean and grovelling lowness of those who live in the indulgence of any base or sordid gratification. It is a lowliness born of glorious parentage, growing, not like a sickly weed at the bottom of some dark and filthy dungeon, but rather like some fresh unnoticed herb upon a mountain's brow, cherished by the sunbeams and the free airs of heaven, and the pure and shining dew. It has no enjoyment in low and degrading attachments, but it delights to lean meekly and confidently upon His love, who " dwelleth not only in the high and holy place, but with him also that is of a contrite and humble spirit, to revive the spirit of the humble, and to revive the heart of the contrite ones."

Records of a Good Man's Life.

WALKING in the country on an autumnal day is like conversing with a friend whom we are about to lose, whose death we know to be near. Every falling leaf is like the last words of those who will soon speak to us no more.

Ibid.

IF air, saturated with moisture approaches a mountain ridge to rise over it,—a phenomenon which may be continually observed in the mountainous districts of our island,—for every foot which it rises it escapes from a degree of pressure which it bore while lower down, and while thus dilating, it becomes colder, and lets fall a part of its moisture. It is this that causes the periodical overflow of the Ganges, and the Nile, with other large rivers of the east.

EDEN HOLE, in the Peak of Derbyshire, is a tremendous yawning gulf, said to be bottomless, which opens its wide mouth on the side of a hill. The noise of stones, or any other body thrown into it, gradually, and as at a distance, dies away. Nothing has ever been heard of again, that has fallen into it. All is inscrutable to man. Many trials have been made, with respect to its depth; but all in vain. A line, with plummet attached, two thousand six hundred and fifty-two feet long, did not reach the bottom. Many stories are told of accidents that have happened at this dreadful place. But nothing can be more horrible than the acknowledgement made by a wretched man upon the scaffold; that a traveller, having once entrusted himself to his guidance over the mountain, was first robbed by him, and then precipitated down this awful abyss. Another instance of an untimely fate happened to a poor man who engaged, for a sum of money, to go to the bottom. He lost his senses in the attempt, and expired raving mad, in a few days.

A large breed of spiders abound in the palace of Hampton Court. They are called there " cardinals," in honour, I suppose, of cardinal Wolsey. They are full an inch in length, and many of them of the thickness of a finger. Their legs are about two inches long, and their bodies covered with a thick hair. They feed chiefly on moths, as appears from the wings of that insect being found in great abundance under and amongst their webs. In running across the carpet in an evening, when the light of a lamp or candle has cast a shade from their large bodies, they have been mistaken for mice, and have occasioned no little alarm to some of the more nervous inhabitants of the palace. A doubt has even been raised whether the name of " cardinal" has not been given to this creature from an ancient belief that the ghost of Wolsey haunts the place of his former glory, under this shape. At all events, the spider is considered as a curiosity and Hampton Court is the only place in which I have met with it.—*Jesse's Gleanings in Natural History.*

THE LAPWING.— When this bird wants to procure food it seeks for a worm's nest, and stamps the ground by the side of it with its feet, after the manner of boys in order to procure worms for fishing. After doing this for a short time the bird waits the issue of the worm from the hole, which, alarmed at the shaking of the ground, endeavours to make its escape, when it is immediately seized and becomes the prey of this ingenious bird.

GOOD PAY.—In Aberdeen the streets are swept every day, at an annual cost of £1,400, and the refuse brings in £2000 a-year. In Perth the scavenging costs £1,300 per annum, and the manure sells for £1,730. Here, then, is a gain of sterling gold—a premium for saving immortal life.

A SABBATH IN NEW ZEALAND.— A small bell was struck outside the building, and it was an interesting sight to watch the effect it had upon the dwellers of the pah; one by one, they came out of their houses, or crossed the little stiles dividing one court yard from another, and, wrapping their mats and blankets around them, slowly and silently wended their way to the place of worship On entering, each individual squatted upon the ground, which was strewn with reeds, and, with their faces buried in their blankets, they appeared to be engaged in prayer; and they opened their Maori Testaments, and a native teacher commenced the sacred service. It would have been a lesson to some of our thoughtless and fashionable congregations, to witness the devout demeanour of these tattooed men, who without the assistance of a European, were performing Christian worship with decorous simplicity and reverential feeling.—*Angas's Savage Life and Scenes.*

PUNCTUALITY.—If you desire to enjoy life, avoid unpunctual people. They impede business and poison pleasure. Make it your own rule, not only to be punctual, but a little before hand. Such a habit secures a composure which is essential to happiness; for want of it many people live in a constant fever, and put all about them in a fever too.

LONGEVITY OF THE TORTOISE.—In the library of Lambeth Palace is the shell of a tortoise, brought there in 1623. It lived till 1730, and was then accidentally killed. Another, in the palace at Fulham, procured by Bishop Laud in 1628, died in 1759. Tortoises are proverbial for longevity; one at Peterborough lived 220 years.
Sir Richard Phillips.

CONTENT.—I knew a man that had wealth and riches, and several houses, all beautifully and ready furnished, and who would often trouble himself and family by removing from one house to another. Being asked by a friend why he removed so often, he replied, it was to find content in some one of them. "Content," said the friend, "ever dwells in a meek and quiet soul."
Walton.

HE that enlarges his curiosity after the works of Nature multiplies the inlets to happiness; and therefore I call upon the younger part of my readers to make use, at once, of the spring of the year, and the spring of life, to acquire, while their minds may yet be impressed with new images, a love of innocent pleasures and an ardour for useful knowledge, and to remember that a blighted spring makes a barren year, and that the vernal flowers, however beautiful and gay, are only intended by Nature as preparatives to autumnal fruits.   *Dr. Johnson.*

IT has been demonstrated that it would require from one million, to three millions of some active animalculæ to form the bulk of a single grain of sand.

MONTHLY NOTICES.

MAY.

9. Soham Stock Fair.
12. County Court for the Recovery of Small Debts, to be held, for the first time, at Soham.
20. Half-yearly Interest on Savings' Bank deposits due.

PLAYFORD'S

SOHAM MAGAZINE,

AND

Friendly Monitor.

JUNE, 1847.

T is observed by an eminent writer upon practical Christianity, that, " if we were under the hands of a wise and good physician, that could not mistake or do any thing to us, but what certainly tended to our benefit; it would not be enough to be patient, and abstain from murmurings against such a physician; but it would be as great a breach of duty and gratitude to him not to be pleased and thankful for what he did, as it would be to murmur at him.

Now this is our true state with relation to God: we cannot be said so much as to *believe* in Him, unless we believe Him to be of infinite wisdom. Every argument, therefore, for patience under His disposal of us, is as strong an argument for approbation and thankfulness for every thing that He does.

Whoso murmurs at the course of the world, murmurs at God who governs it. Whoso repines at seasons and weather, repines at the Lord and Governor of them. It sounds indeed much better to murmur at the course of the world, or the state of things, than to murmur at providence ;—to complain of the seasons and weather than to complain of God ;—but if these have no other cause but God and His providence, it is a poor distinction to say, that you are only angry at the things, but not at the Cause and Director of them."

Now as these remarks are consistent with reason and Revelation, it would be well to bear them in mind under the scarcity and want that now afflict so large a portion of the world.

No 6. Vol. 1.   G

There is a growing expectation of an abundant harvest, and a consequent hope that these times of dearth, may be succeeded by " plenty and cheapness." But if it should please God to afflict us still further, and again to blight the fruits of the earth, are we prepared to submit to His dispensations with humility and resignation ? Is our condition as a nation such as would lead us to anticipate mercies or judgments ? True it is that pure and undefiled religion still distinguishes our Land from every other quarter of the globe. But, at the same time, are not heresy, superstition, profaneness, and deadly sins, prevalent amongst us in an awful degree ; and is it not consistent with all that we know of God's moral government of the world, to " visit for these things," and to " be avenged on such a nation as this ?"

Far-sighted statesmen can, at present, discover nothing but clouds in the political horizon, while every devout student of the Sacred Scriptures is led to the conclusion, that times of trouble and distress may be near at hand, preparatory to the dawn of that glorious period when the Church shall be completely delivered out of the hands of all her enemies, and those hideous forms of infidelity and vice that now stalk abroad at noon-day, be overwhelmed in darkness for ever.

* * *

POPERY.

WE cannot look without the most serious apprehension at the retrograde steps we have lately made as a Protestant nation, and at the rapid development of the powers and pretensions of the Papal Antichrist. If any thing could, humanly speaking, provoke God to withdraw the sunshine of his favour from us, it must surely be these overtures of " peace with Rome." Nothing but ignorance of the real nature of Popery, or a judicial blindness, could lead men to tamper with a system whose aims are so utterly subversive of corporeal and intellectual freedom, and adverse to the best interests, and dearest rights of mankind. Popery is only another name for despotism of the most absolute order. Wherever it reigns, slavery the most abject hangs upon the necks of the people.

" It has often been asserted (says the late learned Bishop of Salisbury) that religion has nothing to do with the question of granting political power to the subjects of the Pope in this country.

On the contrary, we may affirm that religion embraces *the whole* of the question. For why does a Papist acknowledge the ecclesiastical supremacy of the Pope? and refuse to acknowledge that of the King? He does so on account of his religion. And however Christian charity may tolerate the idolatry, blasphemies, and superstitions of conscientious dissidents from the Established Church, yet Christianity is intimately concerned in resisting the grant of political power, which must inevitably be employed for the advancement of antichristian doctrines and worship, and for the overthrow of the Protestant faith."

How alarming then is the consideration, even in a political point of view, that Popery, by means, more especially, of its reckless agent Jesuitism, is, at this moment, undermining in every direction the British Constitution, and openly avowing its determination to bring once more this land of liberty beneath its feet! England has always been the great barrier to its absolute dominion, and therefore England has always been the object of its envy and its hate. Even at this moment, when every class in society in England is submitting to privations in order to relieve the wants of our suffering fellow subjects in Ireland, what is the language with which we are hourly assailed? What is the return which we receive for our efforts of self-denying charity? Popish Prelates, unable to restrain the rancour of their hostility, overwhelm us with the grossest abuse; and while, with the one hand, they grasp the millions that are poured out to save their vassals from starvation, with the other, were it in their power, they would plunge the dagger to the heart of our national existence.

But Popery (cries some deluded political economist) is no longer what it once was. In ruder times it might have partaken too much of the character of the age. In this more enlightened period, it breathes nothing but the spirit of peace and gentleness.

For the benefit of such we will transcribe one of the awful forms of excommunication, used in the Church of Rome, omitting only such portions of it as are quite unfit for publication. Let the reader ponder it well, for it is right he should know the nature of a curse which, if he be a Protestant, hangs over his own devoted head.

" By the authority of God Almighty, the Father, Son, and Holy Ghost, and of the Holy Canons, and the undefiled Virgin Mary, Mother of God, and of the Heavenly Virtues, Angels, Archangels, Thrones, Dominions, Powers, Cherubims and Seraphims, and of all the Holy Patriarchs, Prophets, and of all the Apostles, and Evangelists, and of the Holy Innocents, who, in the sight of the Holy Lamb are found worthy to sing the new song of the Holy Martyrs, and the Holy Confessors, and all the Holy Virgins, and of all the Saints, together with the Holy and elect of God—we excommunicate and anathematize him; and from the threshold of the Holy Church of God Almighty, we sequester him, that he may be tormented, disposed, and delivered over with Dathan and Abiram, and with those who say unto the Lord God, depart from us, we desire none of thy ways. And as fire is quenched with water, so let the light of him be put out for evermore, unless he shall repent, and make satisfaction. Amen.

May the Father, who created man, curse him! May the Son who suffered for us, curse him! May the Holy Ghost, who was given to us in baptism, curse him! May the Holy Cross, which Christ, for our salvation triumphing over his enemies ascended, curse him!

May the holy and eternal Virgin, Mother of God, curse him! May St. Michael, the advocate of holy souls, curse him! May all the Angels and Archangels, principalities and powers, and all the Heavenly Armies, curse him!

May St. John the Beloved, and St. John the Baptist, and St. Peter, and St. Paul, and St. Andrew, and all other of Christ's Apostles together, curse him! And may the rest of his Disciples, and the four Evangelists, who by their preaching converted the universal world, and may the holy and wonderful company of Martyrs, and Confessors, who by their holy works are found pleasing to God Almighty, curse him! May the holy choir of the Holy Virgins, who for the honour of Christ have despised the things of the world, damn him! May all the Saints, who from the beginning of the world to everlasting ages, are found to be beloved of God, damn him! May the heavens and earth, and all the holy things contained therein, damn him!

May he be damned wherever he shall be, whether in the house or in the field, in way or in the path, in the wood or in the water, or in the church! May he be cursed in living, dying, eating, drinking; in being hungry, in being thirsty; in fasting, sleeping, slumbering, watching, walking, sitting, lying, working, resting.

May he be cursed in all the faculties of his body!

May he be cursed inwardly and outwardly! May he be cursed in the hair of his head! May he be cursed in his brains, and in the crown of his head; in his temples, in his forehead, in his ears, in his eyebrows, in his cheeks, in his jaw bones, in his nostrils, in his fore teeth and grinders: in his lips, in his throat, in his shoulders, in his wrists, in his arms, in his fingers.

May he be damned in his mouth, in his breast, and in all his inward parts, down to his very stomach! May he be cursed in his veins, in his hips, in his knees, in his legs, in his feet and toe-nails! May he be cursed in all the joints and articulations of his members; from the crown of his head to the sole of his foot may there be no soundness in him!

May the Son of the living God, with all the glory of his Majesty, curse him! And may heaven, with all the powers which rejoice therein, rise up against him to damn him, unless he repent and make satisfaction. Amen. So be it. So be it. So be it. Amen.

Such is the language which can be solemnly used by those who claim to be considered as alone the ministers of the gospel of peace!

THE MISER.

" Qui totum vult, totum perdit. "

AND what shall we say of the Miser? The Latins have indeed afforded us this term which is expressive of his real character,—miserable, abject, pitiful, mean. And who, after gazing upon man, noble man, in all the fulness of his moral and intellectual dignity, despite the past and primeval wreck of his heavenly character, still bearing impress of the fingers of divine workmanship; who can turn from man the dispenser of blessing, the contriver of a thousand schemes of melioration, and the delighted agent in carrying them out;—who I ask, after gazing upon such a personification of excellence, and feeling himself however humble and unworthy, enlisted in the same phalanx, and aiming at the accomplishment of the same and kindred purposes, who can revert to the contemplation of the drivilling Miser without a generous blush of shame, that a being so unworthy assumes to himself our own common nature.

Love is the first thought of our life, benevolence the earliest emotion of our existence. We are nurtured under the glancing eye of maternal tenderness, and the pure stream of affection, rising with the youngest gush of being, would run on and increase, deepenning and widening with our years, and throwing out its streams of fertilizing blessings as means might be furnished. Men must cast in many obstacles to prevent its swelling tide, and now and then when we think the sluice gate is barred and closed, the impulses of this heavenly passion defy all resistance, carry off every contending disposition, and men become liberal in spite of themselves. To be a true Miser, the soul, so to speak, must have been warped and straitened, served like the foot of a Chinese lady, put into a mould to contract its size, hinder its growth, and prevent its developement. The Miser's heart has been so compressed by some iron-like and unnatural process, commencing one would even think with the first warm flood from life's fountain, that no further full and irrigating streams have ensued. Now and then it may have been aroused to feeble activity, but the narrowed streamlets have refused to become its agents, until more minified and bound, the mind has been left to sterility and barrenness. I look at the Miser's soul as a St. Helena—a lonely unvegetative rock. It cannot produce. You cannot graft on it—the branch dies. You can produce no sympathy or feeling, by all the galvanism of stern argument, or the seduction of soft persuasion. You speak to a soulless creature, and it is reasonable that you should find no communion. His utmost, very utmost skill is cunning, evidenced in the employment of covetous designs and fraudulent intentions. Of all the vocabulary, there is but one favorite word—MONEY! This is the tripping easy dissyllable, the beginning and end of all his harangues, the spirit of all his designs. This Plutus is his god by day, his fearful, though invoked guardian-spirit by night, filling his brain with torturing and avaricious desire,—the posts of his bed into midnight assassins, and the tick of his watch into a robber demanding admission at his door.

But lest you deem us guilty of hanging without evidence, and condemning without an impartial hearing, we will take the anatomy of his character, and judge the wretch according to his desert.

Here he comes! Stand aside.—A nervous, fearful man, prematurely old, misery throws out all her horrid ecstacies in his features, and self-imposed starvation, would, if he invited their aid, bother all the tailors in the empire to produce a *fit*. His hose are full a world too wide, and the vinegar aspect and hatchet visage, cry loud enough wherever he goes " make way." So much for his poor penance begone *trunk*,—but what of his mind? Mark his doings! The chill region of his heart like

Lapland, has not warmth enough in it for the vegetation of the least virtue, and his vices having aggregated around his loved pelf, the gulf of avarice is a dead sea of corruption. You will say that it is no ill thing to become rich, neither is it; but it is the *manner* into which we must enquire as well as the *object.* The silly Miser imposes as much self infliction as the worshipper of Juggernaut. He wrings gold from his back and belly; finds it by lessening all the circumstances of domestic comfort; adds to it by imprisoning himself from his own kind; saves it by making his door the shunned of the alms seeker and petitioner; makes it by knavery and extortion; robs to it by acts of low theft, too contemptible to come under the cognizance of the law, and too dirty to be named. Now he is the soul and body grinder of a helpless class of tenants from whom he bleeds his weekly rentals, anon the keen-eyed usurer seizing or inveighling the unfortunate borrower, who by a high taxed loan thinks to redeem credit elswhere, then the sneaking pilferer, a sort of man scavenger, picking and carrying off with unnatural glee, remnants and refuse, which the very dogs revolt at. He is the owl, the bat of humankind, he walks when other evil spirits stir, and as his thin ominous form flits across the angles of by streets, and unfrequented lanes, safety seems lessened by his presence, and perfect loneliness is an enviable blessing.

But did you ever follow your true Miser to his horrid home? It is a door seldom passed by any other, and the echo of your first step as it falls upon the cold floor, gives back the bristling idea of the phantom and sepulchre. Here is the sordid possessor of thousands in a state of abjectness,—scant furniture so oddly assorted, that they might well represent the History of England, vacant and cheerless walls, a window through which the sun has long ceased to blink, and a hearth wide enough to roast a stalled ox, airiously baulked by a stolen stick or turf, engaged in frizzling a tiny trafficked herring. * * * It is night, there is no candle, yet now and then a crackling thorn throws on the wall a profile of his demon visage, whilst he restlessly peers into the dying embers which for lack of heat, and love of pelf, he is ready to snatch between his bony fingers—beautiful and bright illusions of the first glitter of his strong box, over which with gloating eyes he will soon offer up the sacrifice of a farthing candle. He goes,—what furtive glances, pauses and misgivings! Is no one near, am I alone? In mercy to his restless conscience and quickened fears, let the laughing gusts be hushed, the wind cease, even Zephyr hold its breath, and the flitting owl and raven take some other course, for now is the consummation of his bliss.

He crept into his bed, or rather stretched himself on yon pallet, darkly obscure and desparately hard, and fitfully started, slept, and watched for morning.

Society is as needful for happiness, as sun light for colour, and he who estranges himself from the world, will soon be bereft of its sympathies, and wander a lonely vagabond from social life, as palpably marked and set apart as even Cain of old.

Heaven mostly spares the Miser to a long life of wearing and sordid anxiety, and again and again he passes before the expectant eye of his heir, who is far removed from relationship by blood, and utterly untouched toward him by affection, and he can but read the withering wish for his dissolution,

'Twill be a jolly day, turned to a holiday,
Who can bewail for the useless and bad,
Coffers are broken, and doors are all open,
One is QUITE happy and nobody's sad.

Did you ever see this being go out of the world? None but scanty hirelings are his attendants. There is no hand of love and tenderness to make his couch, or cool his brow. No voice cries out " God bless him," and when the bright sun sinks into the west, and the ebon shade of night makes the world a living sepulchre, the Miser's soul flees to the Judgment.   G.

ECONOMICAL HINTS TO COTTAGERS.

Continued from Page 74.

Another fault is, that, however fierce their oven is, they put their bread immediately into it, and often burn the top quite black, while the bottom is soft and colourless, instead of what I call striking the oven by shutting it up quite close as soon as the ashes are out, for five minutes at least, or while they are making up their bread

If they would but observe to do this, the oven would get regularly heated, and the bread much better baked; they should also heap it up close together when it first comes out, and cover it with a clean cloth, and something thicker over it, by which means the bread would be much more moist and mellow ; when their yeast is flat, a little boiled potatoes, added either to that, or put in the bread, is a great improvement to the rising.—How often have I wished that some clean woman would take up the business of making tea-cakes : they are very nice when made light, and might assist in procuring a comfortable livelihood.   It requires little more than good management to make them, setting the dough very light with a little milk and an egg or two, and a very few carraway seeds.   They should be baked in a very quick oven, and for a very short time.   Formerly they used to colour them occasionally, with a spoonful of saffron tea, which made them look nice ; but this must not be too freely used, as too strong a preparation of it is *poisonous*.—If you could but establish a reputation for making these; the little mutton or beef pies I have already mentioned, which you might have prepared for the hour they are most likely to be required ; some well-made sausages, or any other saleable article, you might earn a little money without much trouble—but one thing you must observe if you do so, that is always to appear as neat and clean as possible, not only in your house, but in your person, in your basket in your napkin, &c., for cleanliness always goes a great way in such matters, for however tempting they otherwise might look, if these appendages were not neat, no one would choose to buy them.—If you do not already know, you might soon learn to make sausages ; a few pounds of the small pieces of what is left in cutting up a pig, are easily procured if you have none of your own, you must shred it *very fine*, picking out all the skins and stringy parts, and mixing the fat and lean in nearly equal proportions, rather more of the latter, then add a sufficient quantity of pepper and salt, and have ready some well-dried and finely-powdered sage leaves, of which you must shake in a little, but not too much, you could easily procure the skins to put them in from any person who is not using them themselves.   Tie them up the usual size and make them look as clean and neat as possible.   In short, there are many ways that an industrious woman could make a comfortable addition to her husband's earnings ; but for you who are so competent, I certainly think you should lose no time in commencing a little school, —God may have sent you the early friends who had you so well-educated, for this very purpose, as I have already observed the parable of the Talents and the fate of the servant who hid *his* in a napkin.   Follow not his example, but endeavour to impart to others the knowledge you have so happily acquired.   Then will you feel the *delight* of being useful, of doing all the good that is in your power, than which nothing can be more gratifying, for we then first find that we are imitating Him who *went about doing good*.   How comfortable would be your reflections at your last hour, how great your reward hereafter, if, by your means, one infant mind has been trained to virtue and religion.   Recollect, that *doing good* is our *bounden duty*.   Besides which you have no incumbrances ; it would take off the loneliness of the many hours your husband must necessarily be absent, and then how delightful, at the week's end, to present him with the fruits of your own exertions.   You are also capable of instructing children, what, in their station of life, is still more useful to them than the reading or arithmetic ; that is, to work well with their needle, and to acquire habits of industry.   Never let them sit idle one moment, if they are not studying their lessons, let them be close at their work, figuring on their slates, or at any other avocation that would occupy their minds.   It will not only give them a habit of attention, but it will make the time appear short which would otherwise hang heavy on their hands, and keep them from counting the moments which elapse, till they shall escape from this irksome confinement.   If they are old enough and capable of it, teach them to cut out every thing to the best advantage. Let the smallest quantity that is possible of the material serve for the purpose.   Lay your pattern in all directions till you find out where it answers most economically. A little consideration is well bestowed in these cases ; if you have a small quantity, you must make the most of it ; and if abundance, you will have some left to repair the article another time.—This is a rule I would recommend you to attend to yourself, and also, of looking over every night, what you are to wear the next day, and see that no repair is wanting.—Recollect the old proverb of " a stitch in *time* saves nine," and practise it more rigidly.

To. be continued.

—◆—

AQUATIC AMUSEMENTS IN THE BAY OF NAPLES

There are certain aquatic amusements practised by the Neapolitans in the Bay, which are peculiar to that locality.   As I do not remember having seen such exhibitions elsewhere described, I may shortly allude to them.   One of them is a tournament, in which the rival forces consist of twelve boats on each side, respectively painted red and blue ; they are very small—probably about ten feet long— and each manned by two men.   One pulls the boat, the other—the champion— stands upon a platform raised flush with the sides of the boat at its stern ; these are armed with very long wooden lances, on the end of which is a leathern ball.   At a signal given, a boat from each of the opposing ranks pulls out, and, meeting midway, the two warriors level their lances, and coming in direct collision, one, and sometimes both, are precipitated into the sea ; the boats immediately pull back again into position, leaving the discomfitted knight to pick up his lance and follow at his leisure.   In this way, the fight continues, till one side (or colour of boat) has every man immersed.   Victory, then, as to the colour, is decided.   It sometimes happens, however, that two of one colour are left, and these again contend for the individual prize.   These, being the most dexterous, often sustain each other's shocks six or seven times, till at length one is precipitated into the sea, and so ends the fight.

Another species of amusement consists in placing a purse of money at the outer end of the bowsprit of a ship—the said bowsprit being well greased, and considerably inclined upwards.   The purse becomes the property of the first man who can take it,   The individuals who make the attempt run up the bowsprit in all variety of ways.   Some of them set out as fast as they can—others, warily and slowly ; but as long as I looked on, none succeeded in reaching the purse—they invariably fell into the sea, and, swimming to the ship, ascended its side, and were again ready for another attempt. The bowsprit is, of course, disencumbered of all its cordage for the occasion. The only risk an individual runs in practising this amusement is, in not being able to get away before his next follower tumbles above him, in which case, as the height is considerable, the parties coming in contact are sometimes very much hurt; and the keenness exhibited is so great, that there are often two individuals on the beam at the same time. There is no fear of drowning. All round the Bay of Naples, the natives, in their youth, live more in the water than on the land; indeed, they spend the whole day lying naked on the shore, and sporting in the sea; they are perfectly amphibious, and the only way to drown a Neapolitan would be to tie a twenty pound shot to his neck.

Burn Murdock's " Notes."

THOUGHTS OF ABSENT HOME.

How delightful and improving are the recollections of one about to visit the place of his nativity, after an absence of many years in a distant portion of the empire. Actions once thoughtlessly or deliberately committed; words once hastily or calmly uttered; purposes once rashly or wisely formed; thoughts once fondly indulged; associations once hopefully cemented; friendships once warmly cherished—are vividly portrayed to the mind, and cause the long forgotten past to be as present, as if passing in panoramic view before our eyes at the moment.

The home of our youth, and scenes of our happiest hours, cause the way-worn pilgrim for a while to forget the cares and toils of his earthly lot, and not unfrequently, lighten up his grief-worn furrowed, countenance with the cheerful smile of youth. Yet, alas! how often does reflection on the past fill the mind with keenest sorrow? Few exist who have not reason to wish some portion of past life were to spend again, that they might avoid those evils into which they allowed themselves to be allured,—or shut their eyes and walk speedily by those scenes of folly into which they deliberately plunged themselves. But no compunction however deep and sincere, will atone for the past; our duty, after having sought and obtained mercy from all-gracious Heaven for the thoughtless follies and crimes of our early days,—is to act more wisely for the future.

Home, loved Home! Where we shared the caresses and endearments of parents whose loved ashes have long since mingled with the dust of our native soil,—parents who led us by the hand to the sacred edifice where Zion's pilgrims congregate to adore and worship Zion's King, our common Father in heaven; and how often while moving thither, have our youthful bosoms swelled with delight at the chime of the church-going bells,—sounds seldom heard in the northern land in which we have long found a lodgement, as we proceed to Kirk where the blessed truths of the gospel of salvation, are so faithfully and affectionately declared. Imagination would sometimes almost make us believe we felt the pressure of the maternal hand while entering the sacred house of prayer, warning the heedless stripling to doff his cap or bonnet before treading on consecrated ground;—or when the pealing organ, harmonious assistant to the united melodious voices of the choir and congregation, has, by its sweet sounds, forced the reluctant tear into the before sparkling eye, which, for very shame, has been concealed or hastily wiped from the cheek with the sleeve of the frock or jacket;—or with what solemnity we have united in the responses of the devotions of the solemn place;—or attentively listened to the venerable preacher's instructions and exhortations;—or how anxiously we watched for the closing of the sacred volume, and listened to the parting benediction. These are some of the scenes of home and youth which are recalled to the mind while wistfully contemplating a return thither.

We also remember the gratification experienced whilst carrying a portion of the kind bounties of Providence from the well-stored family table to grandmother or some aged, imfirm neighbour every Sabbath noon ; and the exquisite happiness felt while among the bushes of the garden, and inhaling the fragrance of the innumerable flowers which bedecked its numerous avenues ; and those only are capable of appreciating the enjoyments thus afforded, who in after life are entirely debarred of them.

Who, from the group of our youthful companions, will welcome us on stepping over the bridge across the lovely stream which separates our native place from the rural districts surrounding it ? Alas ! he who sits on "the white horse" has conquered the major part of them, and those remaining are so changed by the revolutions of time, as to have assumed the aspect of strangers. Nor is time the only agency at work in altering the state of affairs. The house where we first saw the light of day is rebuilt, and the garden converted into a bleaching-ground; the places of resort for our boyish gambols are stances for the habitations of unknown emigrants ; the old mill on the green is removed, and a modern superstructure stands in its place ; the chapel is converted into a dwelling house ; and the meeting house found in another locality, and the school-room metamorphosed into a warehouse. Places where dear friends resided are degraded into shops and gin-palaces ; the very place of sepulture is repeopled, and the tomb-stones of former generations fast disappearing or crumbling with age.

Another reflection which naturally arises in the prospect of revisiting home is one of infinite importance,—Has the improved state of the place, effected by such an expenditure of labour and wealth, led to increased exertions for the moral, mental and physical improvement of the inhabitants? Are they more religious ? The question is not do they attend to the external duties of religion, but are they pious ? Do they serve and love Jehovah with hearts sincere? Is their gratitude for his unmerited daily favours, national, relative, social,—influential ? Does it lead them to sympathize and kindly assist those around them in times of perplexity and distress ! Are means adopted for the moral elevation of the masses of the population ? Is the Sabbath universally kept as a day of rest from all secular business, of grateful commemoration, of holy employment, of benevolent activity ? Or are its hallowed hours desecrated by scenes of mirth and immorality ? Can the devout pass to the house of prayer on that day without having reason to blush at the ridicule or obscenity of the loitering ungodly hords ?

Oh England ! fairest garden of Europe ! how different art thou from "the land of the mountain and the flood," where, at all times, character is revered, and fellow-feelings respected,—where the sarcastic gibe, and insulting sneer of the lowly peasant or meanest mechanic are unknown; and where the hours of sacred rest are rightly appreciated, and duly improved.

Edinburgh.   JAMES PALMER.

—◆—

Rise, light thy candle, see thy task begun,
Ere redd'ning streaks proclaim the distant sun.

ELY CATHEDRAL.

AMONG the many Norman buildings which still remain to adorn our Land, and bear testimony to the zeal and munificence of by-gone years, Ely Cathedral occupies a very conspicuous position. We pity the man who can gaze upon so noble a pile without emotion, or enter its sacred precincts without feelings of devotion and delight.

The engraving which is given above, represents the west front of the Cathedral. The Isle of Ely was formerly a portion of East Anglia. Soon after the introduction of Christianity into that kingdom, Ethelbert, persuaded by Augustine, founded a Church at Cratendune, now called Cratenden Field, about a mile from the present site. The foundation of the present magnificent structure was laid by Simeon, Abbot of Ely, about the year, 1081. It is dedicated to St. Peter and St. Etheldreda. Its interior dimensions are as follows: viz., whole length from east to west 517 feet, length of transept, from north to south 179 feet 6 inches; height of the vaulting of the choir 70 feet. The height of the great tower is now 215 feet, having been reduced about 60 years ago, by the demolition of an unsightly spire, which crowned its summit. The building is undergoing a thorough repair, and is likely to be completely restored, and redecorated, according to its original plan.

It would be impossible to give any thing like a satisfactory description of this magnificent structure in our Magazine. Our readers may pass a happy and not unprofitable day in contemplating its wondrous proportions; meditating among its solemn recesses, and gorgeous tombs; and joining in those soul-inspiring services which have sanctified it from age to age.

For a more lengthy description of this Noble Building, we would refer our readers to the various Illustrated Works, published by Mr. T. A. Hills, Bookseller, Ely, to whom we are indebted for the loan of the above Engraving.

ICEBERGS IN THE ATLANTIC.

ONE morning, earlier than the usual time of rising, the steward awakened us with the news that icebergs were close at hand. This was charming intelligence, for, so late in the season, they are but rarely met with. We were all soon on deck, and for a worthy object. One was a grand fellow with two great domes, each as large as that of St. Paul's; the lower part was like frosted silver. Where the heat of the sun had melted the surface, and it had frozen again, in its gradual decay it had assumed all sorts of angular and fantastic shapes, reflecting from its green, transparent mass, thousands of prismatic colours, while, below, the gentle swell dallied with its cliff-like sides, The action of the waves had worn away a great portion of the base over the water into deep nooks and caves, destroying the balance of the mass. While we were passing, the crisis of this tedious process chanced to arrive; the huge white rock tottered for a moment, then fell into the calm sea with a sound like the roar of a thousand cannon, the spray rose to a great height into the air, and large waves rolled round, spreading their wide circles over the ocean, each ring diminishing till at length they sank to rest. When the spray had fallen again, the glittering domes had vanished, and a long, low island of rough ice and snow lay on the surface of the water. There is something impressive and dismal in the fate of these cold and lonely wanderers of the deep. They break loose by some great effort of nature, from the shores and rivers of the unknown regions of the north, where for centuries, perhaps they have been accumulating, and commence their dreary voyage, which has no end but annihilation. For years they may wander in the Polar Sea, till some strong gale or current bears them past its iron limits; then, by the predominance of winds and waters to the south, they float past the desolate coasts of Newfoundland. Already the summer sun makes sad havoc in their strength, melting their lofty heights, but each night's frost binds up what is left, and still on, on glides the great mass, slowly solemnly. You cannot perceive that it stirs; the greatest storm does not rock it, the keenest eye cannot discover a motion; but moment by moment, day by day, it passes to the south, where it wastes away and vanishes at last.

In June and July they are most numerous in these seas, and there is often much danger from their neighbourhood in the dark, moonless nights; but the thermometer, if consulted, will always indicate their approach; it fell eight degrees when we neared the iceberg which I have now described, and the cold was sensibly felt.— "*England in the New World.*"

OUR LETTER BOX.

The Editors do not wish to be considered responsible for all the sentiments of their Correspondents.

To the Editor of the Soham Magazine.

Sir,

As your periodical is intended for the diffusion of useful information, I beg to suggest through its pages, that, during the present scarcity and high price of flour, it would be well if all your readers would follow the example of the first personage in the Realm, and exercise the greatest economy. There are two very simple ways in which this may be done, first by eating stale bread; and secondly by mixing rice with the flour in making it. The proportions, as given by a Northamptonshire Clergyman, are as follows :—"half-a-pound of rice, boiled in three pints of water, till the whole becomes thick and pulpy : add six pounds of flour and yeast for the dough, and it will make as much good, serviceable bread as eight pounds of flour would produce alone."

Your obedient Servant,

AN ECONOMIST.

POETRY.

In Original Poetry, the Name, real or assumed, of the Author, is printed in small Capitals under the title; in Selections it is printed in Italics at the end.]

SONG OF THE HAYMAKERS.

The noontide is hot, and our foreheads are brown.
　　Our palms are all shining and hard;
Right close is our work with the wain and the fork,
　　And but poor is our daily reward.
But there's joy in the sunshine, and mirth in the lark,
　　That skims whistling away over head;
Our spirits are light, though our skins may be dark,
　　And there's peace with our meal of brown bread.
We dwell in the meadows, we toil on the sod,
　　Far away from the city's dull gloom;
And more jolly are we, though in rags we may be,
　　Than the pale faces over the loom.
Then a song and a cheer for the bonnie green stack
　　Climbing up to the sun wide and high;
For the pitchers, and rakers, and merry haymakers,
　　And the beautiful Midsummer sky.

Come forth, gentle ladies—come forth, dainty sirs,
　　And lend us your presence awhile;
Your garments will gather no stain from the burs,
　　And a freckle won't tarnish your smile.
Our carpet's more soft for your delicate feet
　　Than the pile of your velveted floor;
And the air of our balm-swarth is surely as sweet
　　As the perfume of Araby's shore,.
Come forth, noble masters, come forth to the field,
　　Where freshness and health may be found;
Where the wind-rows are spread for the butterfly's bed,
　　And the clover-bloom falleth around.
Then a song and a cheer for the bonnie green stack,
　　Climbing up to the sun wide and high;
For the pitchers, and rakers, and merry haymakers,
　　And the beautiful Midsummer sky.

"Hold fast!" cries the waggoner, loudly and quick,
　　And then comes the hearty "Gee-wo!"
While the cunning old team-horses manage to pick
　　A sweet mouthful to munch as they go.
The tawny-faced children come round us to play,
　　And bravely they scatter the heap:
Till the tiniest one, all outspent with the fun,
　　Is curled up with the sheep-dog, asleep.
Old age sitteth down on the haycock's fair crown,
　　At the close of our labouring day;
And wishes his life, like the grass at his feet,
　　May be pure at its "passing away."
Then a song and a cheer for the bonnie green stack
　　Climbing up to the sun wide and high;
For the pitchers, and rakers, and merry haymakers
　　And the beautiful Midsummer sky.　　　　　　　*Eliza Cook.*

THE SWALLOW.

I am fond of the swallow—I learn from her flight,
    Had I skill to improve it, a lesson of love:
How seldom on earth do we see her alight!
    She dwells in the skies, she is ever above.

It is on the wing that she takes her repose,
    Suspended and poised in regions of air.
'Tis not in our fields that her sustenance grows,
    It is winged like herself, 'tis ethereal fare.

She comes in the spring, all the summer she stays,
    And dreading the cold, still follows the sun—
So, true to our love, we should covet his rays,
    And the place where he shines not, immediately shun.

Our light should be love, and our nourishment prayer;
    It is dangerous food that we find upon earth;
The fruit of this world is beset with a snare,
    In itself it is hurtful, as vile in its birth.

'Tis rarely if ever she settles below,
    But when for her young she is building a nest;
Were it not for her brood, she would never bestow
    A thought on a place not designed for her rest.

Let us leave it ourselves—'tis a mortal abode—
    To bask every moment in infinite love;
Let us fly the dark winter, and follow the road,
    That leads to the day-spring appearing above. *Madame Guion.*

THE VIOLET.

There is a modest simple flower
Of fragrance rare—and bright of hue,
More pleas'd to grace the lonely bower,
It shrinks abash'd from public view.
Secure it blooms beneath the shade,
Screen'd from the Sun's too parching ray
Expos'd,—the beauteous flower would
    fade,
Melting like rainbow tints away.
I value less the gaudier rose,
Luxurant in the gay parterre;
Yes,—give to me the flower that blows,
Without a thorn to wound me there.

I've seen the Violet chang'd with dew,
Like woman's eye—it then appears,
Kiss'd by a passing Zephyr,—how
It smiles and sparkles through its tears.
Now, is not beauty too, a flower,
Ordain'd awhile to bloom and fade;
Fated to live its little hour—
Soon in its kindred dust 'tis laid.
Oh! Lady, when thy hour shall come,
How will the soul of pity mourn?
Affection's tears, bedew thy tomb—
May friendship's hand, inscribe thy urn.
Soham.

OUR CHILDREN'S PAGE.

FACTS WORTH REMEMBERING

A league is 3 miles or the 20th of a degree.

From full moon to full moon is 29 days 12¾ hours.

The Steam Engine was invented by the Marquis of Worcester in the reign of Charles 2nd.

The first idea of Steam Navigation was set forth in a patent obtained in 1736, by Jonathan Hulls, for a machine for carrying vessels against wind and tide, or in a calm.

MISCELLANY AND EXTRACTS.

DESIRE is the life of prayer; and if you indeed desire what you pray for, you will also labour for what you desire; and if you find it otherwise with yourselves, your coming to church is but like the Pharisees going up to the temple to pray. If your heart be not present, neither will God; and then there is a sound of men and women between a pair of dead walls, from whence, because neither God nor your souls are present, you must needs go home without a blessing. *Bishop Taylor.*

BY the unhappy excess of irregular pleasures in youth, how many amiable dispositions are corrupted or destroyed! How many rising capacities and powers are suppressed! How many flattering hopes of parents and friends are totally extinguished. Who but must drop a tear over human nature when he beholds that morning, which arose so bright, over-cast with such untimely darkness; that good humour, which once captivated all hearts, that vivacity which sparkled in every company, those abilities which were fitted for adorning the highest stations,—all sacrificed at the shrine of low sensuality; and one who was formed for running the fair career of life in the midst of public esteem, cut off by his vices at the the beginning of his course; or sunk for the whole of it into insignificancy and contempt! These O sinful pleasure, are thy trophies! It is thus that co-operating with the foe of God and man, thou degradedest human honour, and blastest the opening prospects of human felicity. *Blair.*

LET it be impressed upon your minds (says Junius) let it be instilled into your children, that the liberty of the Press is the palladium of all civil, political and religious rights of Englishmen.

ERATOSTRATUS set fire to the temple of Diana, at Ephesus, on the night of Alexander's nativity, 356 years before the Christian era. He confessed on the rack, that the sole motive which had prompted him to destroy so magnificent an edifice, was the desire of transmitting his name to posterity.

A deep crevice in a rock, filled by a shower, is frequently the cause of the rock being torn asunder.

ENCKE's Comet has probably no more solidity or coherence than a cloud of dust, or a wreath of smoke, and consequently would lose its velocity very easily in a resisting medium. From the time of its first discovery to the present, the time of its revolution has diminished by about two days, and it is ten days in advance of the place which it would have reached if it had met with no resistance. It was first seen by Mechain and Messier in 1787. Again by Miss Herschel in 1795. In 1805 it was again seen as well as in 1819. This comet, according to observations already made, would require 23,000 years to reduce its velocity to one-half its present value.

OAK NECESSARY TO BUILD ONE SHIP By the report of the Commissioners of Land Revenue, it appears that a 74 gun ship contains about 2,000 tons, which at the rate of a load and a half a ton, would give 3,000 loads of timber, and would require 2,000 trees of 75 years' growth. It has also been calculated that, as not more than 40 oaks, containing a load and a half of timber in each, can stand upon one acre, fifty acres are required to produce the oaks necessary for every 74 gun ship. *Railway Magazine.*

As he that lives longest lives but a little while, every man may be certain that he has no time to waste. The duties of life are commensurate to its duration, and every day brings its task, which if neglected is doubled on the morrow. But he that has already trifled away those months and years in which he should have laboured, must remember that he has now only a part of that of which the whole is a little, and that since the few moments remaining are to be considered as the last trusts of heaven, not one is to be lost. *Dr. Johnson.*

THE little bird called the Stormy Petrel lives chiefly on the waves in the midst of the Atlantic Ocean.

PRIDE is the greatest enemy to reason, and discretion the greatest opposite to pride. For whilst wisdom makes art the ape of nature, pride makes nature the ape of art. The wise man shapes his apparel to his body, the proud man shapes his body by his apparel. 'Tis no marvel, then, if he know not himself, when he is not to day like him he was yesterday; and less marvel, if good men will not know him, when he forgets himself, and all goodness. I should fear, whilst I thus changed my shape lest my Maker changed his opinion; and finding me not like him he made me, reject me as none of his making. I would any day put off the old cause of my apparel, but not every day put on new fashioned apparel. I see great reason to be ashmed of my pride, but no reason to be proud of my shame.

THE note of the cuckoo, though uniform, always gives pleasure, because we feel that summer is coming; but this pleasure is mixed with melancholy because we reflect that it will soon be going again. This is the consideration which embitters all sublunary enjoyments. Let the delight of my heart then be in thee O Lord and creator of all things, with whom is no variableness, neither shadow of changing.

Bishop Horne.

WHAT man should learn is, to reject all that is useless in remembrance, and to retain with cheerfulness, all that can profit and amend. Forget not thy sins, that thou mayest sorrow and repent; remember death, that thou mayest sin no more; remember the judgement of God, that thou mayest justly fear; and never forget His mercy, that thou mayest never be led to despair. *Petrarch.*

I SHOULD marvel that the covetous man can still be poor, when the rich man is still covetous, but that I see a poor man can be content, when the contented man is only rich: the one wanting in his store, whilst the other is stored in his wants. I see, then, we are not rich or poor, by what we possess, but by what we desire. For he is not rich that hath much, but he that hath enough: nor he poor that hath but little, but he that wants more. If God then make me rich by store, I will not impoverished myself by covetousness: but but if he make me poor by want, I will enrich myself by content.

WHOSOEVER is not persuaded by reason, will not be convinced by authority.

Feyjoo.

GOOD example is a language and an argument which everybody understands.

MONTHLY NOTICES.

JUNE.

16th.—County Court for the Recovery of Small Debts, at Soham.

20th.—Overseers to fix on Church Doors and also on Doors of Dissenting Chapels, notices to persons qualified to vote for Counties to make claim. N.B. Persons on the Register need not make a new claim, unless they have changed their qualifications or residence.

21st.—Soham Feast.

24th.—Middle Fen, Fen Tax due, see Advertisements in Newspapers.

30th.—Isle of Ely Quarter Sessions *at Wisbech.*

PLAYFORD'S

SOHAM MAGAZINE,

AND

Friendly Monitor.

JULY, 1847.

The diffusion of publications unfavourable to religion and morality, is one of the worst evils of the age. If left to develop its fearful proportions, the social ruin that must follow will be complete. All the horrors of the French Revolution grew up from this hidden root; and the same desolation must eventually overspread our favoured land, without a speedy and vigorous resistance.

It is a truth which, every day's experience tends to confirm, that man, if left to the bias of his natural propensities, whatever advancement he may make in intellectual attainments, will err with regard to eternal things. And if there be but one volume that can guide him to a right knowledge of himself, and of his duty, how awful must be the consequence of making that volume the subject of systematic ridicule and scorn! Such, however, is unhappily the case, and it has been asserted that in the Metropolis alone there is a continual issue of works of an infidel and immoral character, far exceeding in number those of an opposite tendency.

Now the rejection of the truths of revelation must proceed either from a confirmed dislike to their purity, or from an insufficient examination of the grounds upon which they stand.

In the former case it is not the *understanding*, but the *affections* that are concerned. "For every one that doeth evil hateth the light, neither cometh to the light, lest his deeds should be reproved."

No. 7. Vol. I. H

The objections that such a man conceives against the Gospel arise simply from the fact of his loving sin more than holiness ; the indulgence of his own sensual inclinations more than the service of God.   To argue with him is therefore like casting pearls before swine.   Like Felix, he may tremble when he hears of " righteousness, temperance, and judgment to come," but all his passions are enlisted against the truth, nor " would he be persuaded though one rose from the dead."

But it is a lamentable fact that very few of the believers in Revelation are proof against the sneers of the scorner, from not having examined with sufficient care either the external or internal evidences of Christianity.   Their faith depends too much upon the authority of others, rather than upon the solid ground of a rational conviction. They are therefore continually staggered and perplexed by the plausible objections which are so artfully presented to their minds ; and while unwilling to think that the Bible is a fable, they are still unable to prove that it is not.

Now the truth of Christianity is capable of the clearest demonstration.   It can be proved in a manner so convincing and satisfactory, that the mind which can reject such evidence, must evince a total perversity of reason.   No bygone events are more certain than those recorded in the Scriptures, and if they are to be regarded with any other than implicit faith, every authentic record must be reduced to a state of doubt and uncertainty.

It must be allowed, however, that the many learned works that have been written in defence of Revelation, are, for the most part, beyond the reach of ordinary readers.   Their style, moreover, and method of proof, require a degree of intelligence, and the exercise of more patient thought, than belong to the great mass of mankind. For such, therefore, we require an argument both short and decisive :—one that may be retained in the memory with ease, and applied with unerring certainty as the occasion may arise ;—one that while it establishes the truth in defiance of all the cavils of the sceptic, carries at the same time, all his false positions by storm, and hurls his proud ensigns of blasphemy to the earth.

The brief test first proposed in the year 1697 by the Rev. Charles Leslie, is all that we require for such an end.   It was written at the request of the first Duke of Leeds, who said, that although he was a believer in the truth of the Christan Religion, he was not satisfied with the common methods of proving it; that the argument was long and complicated; so that some had neither leisure nor patience to follow it, and others were not able to comprehend it: that as it was the nature of all truth to be plain and simple, if Christianity were a truth, there must be some short way of showing it to be so, and he wished Mr. Leslie would think of it. In the space of three days this accomplished divine produced a rough draught of what was afterwards published under the title of "A Short and Easy Method with the Deists." This he presented to the Duke; who after perusing it, said to the Author, " I thought I was a Christian before, but now I am *sure* of it."

Mr. Leslie first assumes that the truth of the doctrines of Christianity will be sufficiently proved, if the matters of fact recorded in the Gospels be true;—if the miracles be true, the doctrines in support of which they were wrought must be also true.

The same may be said as to Moses. If he brought the Children of Israel through the Red Sea in that miraculous manner which is related in Exodus, and did such other wonderful things as are there told of him, it must necessarily follow, that he was sent from God. Every Deist would acknowledge it, if he saw such things with his own eyes. The great desideratum therefore is the discovery of such a Canon as shall distinguish between facts and fiction; so that, whenever applied, it shall invariably harmonize with truth, and refuse all adaptation to falsehood.

The Canon is this : 1st. That the matter of fact be such, as that mens' outward senses, their eyes and ears may be judges of it. 2nd. that it be done publicly in the face of the world. 3rd. That not only public monuments be kept up in memory of it, but that some outward actions be performed. 4th. That such monuments, and such actions and observances be instituted, and do commence from the time that the matter of fact was done.

The first two rules make it impossible for any such matter of fact to be imposed upon men, *at the time* when such matter of fact was said to be done, because every man's senses would contradict it; and the last two rules make it impossible for any such matter of fact to be imposed upon men *after* such matter of fact was said to be done, because every man's senses would again contradict it.

All these four rules may be applied to the matters of fact related of Moses, and of his antitype; but one or more of them will be found to contradict the pretended miracles of Mahomet, or what is reported of the heathen deities; and *no imposture can have them all.*

Let us take an example from the Old Testament. It is stated that Moses led six hundred thousand men out of Egypt, through the Red Sea, and fed them forty years without bread in the wilderness. The two first rules may be applied to this fact, for it was *such as mens' senses could perceive,* and it was *done publicly in the face of the world.* But in memory of this great event the Feast of the Passover was instituted *at the very time,* and has been observed by the whole nation of the Jews *ever since*; and this circumstance will bear the application of the two last rules, for mens' senses have discerned the truth of the matter every year, from the very day that the miracle was performed, through the space of three thousand three hundred and thirty-eight years, to the present hour.

In the present unhappy increase of sceptical opinion we would, therefore urge our readers to procure this brief, but conclusive and unanswerable work of Mr Leslie's. It may be obtained for a very small sum, and will render them invulnerable to all those envenomed shafts of infidelity, which, if left to rankle in the breast, will destroy their peace for time, and for eternity!

Lord Rochester's dying testimony to the truth of the Christian Religion, in his letter to the Bishop of Salisbury.

MY most honoured Dr. Burnet:—

My spirit and body decay equally together; but weak as I am in person, I shall write you a letter. If God be yet pleased to spare me longer in this world, I hope, by your conversation, to be exalted to such a degree of piety, that the world may see how much I abhor what I so long loved; and how much I glory in repentance, and in God's service. Bestow your prayers upon me, that God would spare me, if it be his good will, to show a true repentance and amendment of life for the time to come; or else, if the Lord please soon to put an end to my worldly being, that he would mercifully accept of my death-bed repentance; and perform that promise He has been pleased to make, that at what time soever a sinner doth repent, He would receive him. Put up these prayers, most dear Doctor, to Almighty God, for your most obedient languishing servant. ROCHESTER.

For the benefit of all those, whom I may have drawn into sin, by example and encouragement, I leave to the world this my last declaration, which I deliver in the presence of the great God, who knows the secrets of all hearts, and before whom I am preparing to be judged, that, from the bottom of my soul, I detest and abhor the whole course of my former wicked life; that I think I can never sufficiently admire the goodness of God, who has given me a true sense of my pernicious opinions and vile practices; by which I have hitherto lived without hope, and without God in the world; have been an open enemy to Jesus Christ, doing the utmost despite to the Holy Spirit of grace; and that the greatest testimony of my charity to such is, to warn them in the name of God, and as they regard the welfare of their immortal souls, no more to deny His being or His providence, or despise His goodness, no more to make a mock of sin, or contemn the pure and excellent religion of my ever-blessed Redeemer, through whose merits alone, I, one of the greatest of sinners, do yet hope for mercy and forgiveness. Amen. ROCHESTER.

AN ADDRESS TO THE TEACHERS IN A NATIONAL OR SUNDAY SCHOOL.

BY DAVID GUNTON.

MY YOUNG FRIENDS,

It would be utterly in vain to advise a man of my temperament, to enter upon the consideration of so splendid a subject as Education, in any of its ramifications, with coolness and even feeling. Peter the hermit, never preached up the Crusades in a fit of purer phrensy; nor did Alexander, or Cyrus, or Napoleon, look upon the glories of military exploit, with greater complacency; nor have poets' brains been rapt in dreams of holier imagination,—for our topic is of all others, most calculated to arouse and excite those sentiments, which sanctify the heart and dignify the man.

Nor is this subject fraught with less reality than heavenly brightness, and whilst I become a worshipper at the shrine of Minerva, I cannot lose sight of the practical blessings, and solid good, that follow in her train.—Tell me not then of higher ambition, of loftier pursuits, than those belonging to the Educator.—The king's power is brute force, his influence an army, his argument the bullet, where there is no Schoolmaster.—Senators are only privileged makers of tyrannical laws, and magistrates policemen, where there is no Schoolmaster.—Prisons are churches, and the lock-up and cage, chapels, and society at large, human only in appearance, where there is no Schoolmaster.

I tell you plainly the office has no superior, and its effects have no contrast. When nature can boast of a fairer light than yon kingly orb, and evening rejoice in a sweeter brightness than Luna can bestow, then, and only then, shall the universe of mind disfavour and disown the galaxy of intelligence, thrown down upon it by the constellation of the Schoolmaster.

Look at the majesty of science, the blessings of civilization, and the grace of morals.—Think of the gradual development of agencies next to miraculous,—the perfection of schemes, which our fathers would have denounced as utterly impracticable,—and you will see amidst all their intricacies and springs, the talismanic hand of the Schoolmaster. Knowledge is written upon our commonest comforts, engraven on our habitations, pillared and sculptured on our halls and palaces, and hymned and praised, by the myriad tongues of our happy favoured land.

Nor let any one suppose that I am following airy steps, and acting the devotee to a glittering vision, for I mean by knowledge, the fear of God, which is truly the beginning of wisdom,—letters and religion are so interlaced and intertwined in my definition of Education, that they can never be separated.—Learning is moonlight without religion,—it has not upon it the water-mark, the stamp of currency, save as it bears the deep impression of God's truth.—Learning, true learning, clings around the oak of revelation, and when torn away from its support, is only a weak and beautiful weed.

Nor do I lose sight of the truth, that in an army, whilst all have one object to accomplish, one aim in view, and all share in the common glory, there are differences of office and position,—I look therefore upon every teacher, yes every Sunday School teacher especially, as being a valorous and valuable agent in the combat against ignorance, and especially that which is moral. You, if rightly apprehending your duties, are performing a part which shall result in the highest benefit. Not in senate or religious niche may your honours be recorded. Nor in history or in song your name be inscribed,—but it will be if you are only faithful, that God shall smile, that angels shall applaud, that the book of life shall testify, that heaven itself shall witness, the triumphs of your holy and devoted labour.

May I ask you whether you entertain these noble and inspiring views, then you labour with zeal, and fortify yourselves with patience, run on the impulses of affection,—and conscience, being the interpreter of your duty,—you lose no opportunity of sustaining your office with competency and effect.

Now let me call you back to the common fact, that magnificent results mostly depend upon a series of simple and ordinary causes. Nor in our eulogy of Education, let us for a moment forget, that all its results rest upon the diligence of its agents, and the amount of knowledge which they possess.

Your mere pop-gun teachers, will never kill a single stripling under the banner of ignorance. The mere bubble instructor, will direct the mind only a few steps upwards. The vulgar truth is this,—know something well yourself,—know it in all its bearings and aspects, in all its varieties and interpretations, in all its parts and entierty. Let every piece of knowledge, to be communicated, be before your mental eye as a map, over every line of which you can pass your finger,—as a model whose pieces you can unloose and replace, demonstrating their mutual dependency and pointing out their individual need, in carrying out the design. Become builders up and breakers down,—composers and analyzers, for unless you thus understand the thing you affect to teach, you mislead and blunder, and become the instrument of a quackery, more desperate than Morrison, and audacious than Holoway.

Your great and noble text book is the Bible, and whilst you make yourself perfectly skilled in the letter and morals of this, remember that to comprehend its relation, to see the relavency of its parts, you must rise into little chronologers, and historians, understand geography physically and civilly, know somewhat of human mind and manners, and the phases which nations put on, as they feel the influences of enlightenment and religion.—Nor shall I need to urge you to this task, for the conscientious man, who feels his lack, will soon supply it, and whilst the inefficient and ignorant, who want the best incitements, fall out of your ranks, they will only make room for better hands, who wait but the roll of the drum, and the hoisting of the ensign, to join your fine and victorious band.

So much for knowledge.—But you will say, that every clever man is not a good teacher, and this we will allow in an instant. A man may have read with a Magliabecehi, and may possess the genius and research of a Newton, and yet be a poor teacher. To learn is one thing, and to teach is another. Whilst without information, no one can communicate knowledge, it is at the same time not less true, that he may know *what* to teach, whilst he is grossly ignorant *how* to teach. There is the art of teaching, as well as surgery or watchmaking, for the practice of which, the Educator must undergo a course of training, ere he can perform efficiently, the functions of his important and honourable office.

But there are attributes of character, and gifts of God's grace that must be attained, or a man, with all his head skill, will be as awkward as a bear in a quadrille, or a bumpkin at the cut and thrust of the short sword.

Now in what I should call the ethics of teaching, I would particularly dwell upon *patience, and control of temper.* Nothing makes a man so brute-like as hot violent outbreaks of anger. It at once takes him down from the pinnacle of manhood, and classes him with the wild beast, whose wish is propounded by a roar, and whose purpose is accomplished by a pounce of savagery. The blustering threat and cracking downfall of the stick, will certainly make you feared, and perhaps hated, but as you have a moral end in view, you will soon perceive that these are not the agents of its accomplishment. If the world is to be converted by harsh measures, then the Gospel is wrong, and we had better substitute in its stead lynch law, and an army of military marauders, instead of a standing ministry. If your children and youths are to be cuffed and fisted into knowledge, their teachers should be members of the prize ring, and versed in the art of boxing. I tell you then to break up the stick system, and learn, that self possession, and a calm equanimity of deportment, will give you a far better tutelary power over your pupils; while the want of it will communicate itself back again to the children, and produce new sources of irritation without end. I don't say that there is no difficult self-conflict to be endured, knowing that your office requires even the patience of Job.

Yet I repeat the fact, that hard as is the attainment of this state of mind, it is worth all its cost, and will not only add, but be the main auxiliary, in the successful discharge of your duty. *Let there be affection and candour*, rather than sternness and affected distance, for the more a teacher can feel himself as the Latins say, *in loco parentis*, the nearer he brings the instructed to himself, and places him under a spell, that will make the task of acquirement light, and the duty of obedience a pleasure. In a mass of boys gathered from the highways and hedges, I am aware that certain dispositions will be manifested, that make a child very unlovely; but this will the more excite both your pity and diligence, and after all, I can aver from my own experience, that snow is not less easily melted by the sun, nor iron by intense heat, than the most untoward and obstinate boy, by affectionate and prayerful remonstrance.—But suppose you have a remarkable case of wickedness, that yields not to regular treatment, I would recommend you to take the child aside to your vestry, or class room, and there kneel down with him before the broad eye of God, beseeching Him, that His spirit may break down his heart, and reward you openly, by sending him back to his fellows, contrite and amended.

Soham.   *To be continued.*

ECONOMICAL HINTS TO COTTAGERS.

Continued from Page 88.

A button, a string, or any little thing wanting to your dress, not only makes you feel uncomfortable, but gives you an untidy look, which is so prejudicial to your appearance. Do not lull your conscience; if you feel no inclination to take that trouble, by saying " I shall only burn more candle than my work is worth," but recollect how many hours of candle-light you so often waste by the careless trick of letting it burn so low as to heat the candlestick before you raise it up. You will be startled when I tell you that I have *no doubt* but at the very least one *eighth* part of every candle is so wasted; and by too close snuffing, which always makes it run over, and consequently last a shorter time, whereas, if you would but attend to it while burning, and avoid these wasteful methods, and that of carrying it round the house without ever guarding it from the air by your hand, you would find at the end of the week, a greater difference in your expenditure of that article than you could suppose. If you did but save as much as would purchase you a tea-cake for your Sunday evening repast, you would have a peculiar pleasure in enjoying this fruit of a little economy.

Another wasteful habit I have too frequently witnessed, is that of leaving Soap in water till too soft to be used. Whilst washing linen it may be of some use in softening the water, but surely none whilst washing your hands, &c. Again in the article of Cotton balls, what havock do you often observe, instead of making every needle-full go as far as it can, and keeping yourselves from running to the shops so much, more frequently than you would otherwise have occasion to do, if your work box was well arranged, and all your pieces carefully laid up, how often would you find the advantage of it, when repairing your apparel. What you think useless pieces, should on no account be flung away or burnt (the too general practice,) *but always bear in mind* that *every atom is of use,* and have a bag at hand to receive what those who collect for paper makers will gladly give you pins or many little necessary articles for. Even of *coloured* shreds they make brown papers, so that for those they will give you something. Your old Shoes too, the gun makers will purchase, as they cannot polish their work without them. Woollen shreds if not of use to gardeners to nail up fruit trees, will make iron or kettle holders, or clean your tins, &c. with the addition of tallow that cannot be used up in your candlestick. In short *nothing* should be *wasted ; nothing* should be *burnt.* There is no necessity to make your house untidy by preserving all these things, for every thing may be laid by in *its proper place.* Paper may be filed on a needle and thread, and preserved till wanted, pack-thread wound up, and every thing else in the same order. With regard to eatables, when you are fortunate enough to keep a pig, you will find that everything must be made the most of, even to the very skimmings of your pans, which you are too apt to throw into that general consumer, the fire. Apple-peelings and cores, the kernels of plums, which are in such abundance here, and which may so easily be collected, acorns when they can be procured, as well as many productions, such as sow thistles, &c. in short almost anything that is green are all great helps in fattening a pig. But recollect that regular feeding, and a clean bed, will go a great way in this affair. You should always give it something three times a day, and where you can contrive it you should give it food as dry as possible in one trough, and what it drinks in another. It will fatten quicker, and be much firmer by this management. Never give it your potatoe peelings raw, (if you have pared them first,) but let them be boiled and well skimmed, and if you did the same to your cabbage stalks and leaves, your turnip and carrot peelings and tops, and all other vegetables, you would find how much better your pig would get on, and particularly if you added a handful of coarse-ground meal flour, refuse corn, which I should think you might easily procure. Grains too from the brewers or from any one that did not use them. The farmers would thank you for collecting the weeds from their fields, and when they saw you so industrious, they might possibly help you with a peck or two of beans, or dross corn. I need not remind you of your washings, which must be used up to the uttermost. I have no doubt by this management that almost any poor family might feed a pig to the size they usually kill them here ; and think what comfort and plenty you would enjoy when you came to reap the fruits of this attention. I should not be so sanguine in my hopes of your making this answer, if I had not seen an instance of it in the North of England, where their pigs are nearly double the size of these, and where, incredible as it may appear, the farmers give them 30 or more bushels, before they have them as fat as they wish them. A poor woman, whose husband seldom earned more than 10s. a week, with a family of six children, contrived to feed a pig, and that a good large one, in the manner I speak of, getting perhaps a bushel of refuse corn at the last, which she probably paid for when she killed the pig. She left not a place around unsought for any weeds or greens she could pick up ; and she was continually boiling something or other for her pig ; Christmas was therefore plentiful, and a happy season to her, when she killed it.   *To be continued.*

THE VILLAGE CHURCH.

FEW persons of religious feeling can visit the Village Church-yard without deep and serious emotions. The reflections that naturally arise, bear with such solemn import upon our present and future condition, that it seems impossible to resist their influence. To contemplate those walls which have resounded with the voice of penitence and prayer from age to age;—to tread upon those sods which conceal the remains of generation after generation from the eye;—to read the brief lines of friendship and affection on the moss-covered stone;—to trace the course of death from the infant of a day old, to one whose years, perchance, had been extended beyond the usual span of man's existence,—and then to think that we shall meet them all hereafter, when every one will receive " according to that he hath done, whether it be good or bad;"—such reflections as these, we say, will naturally arise in the mind of every reflecting person, in such a spot, and be turned, with solemn application and inquiry upon himself.

There was a time when the blind fury of unsanctified zeal would have destroyed these sacred monuments of our faith throughout the land;—when under the pretence of propagating a purer creed, the leaders of rebellion, with the bible in one hand and the sword in the other, could exult in the misery and death of multitudes of their fellow-countrymen, and the murder of their king. Let us take heed that the rancour of party spirit do not again break loose with such a frightful devastation. To our shame

be it spoken,—the hate that has arisen from religious feuds has exceeded, in intensity, all other hate; and if men, for the sake of advancing themselves, are continually reviling each other, charity and peace will take wing for a holier sphere, and leave us to brood over our common ruin for ever.

The recent diffusion of information upon the subject of ecclesiastical architecture, has tended very much to increase the interest afforded by our Parish Churches. It is highly satisfactory to be enabled to affix, with much accuracy, the dates, to the various proportions of them, — beginning with the Norman period, with its semicircular arches, and zigzag ornaments, which style was in use from A.D. 1066, to the end of the 12th century, gradually merging into the Early English, which continued to the commencement of the 14th century. The arches of the latter style are usually pointed, long, and narrow; the mouldings and foliage generally well executed, and bold in design and relief. The next style is the decorated English, used until about the end of the reign of Edward 3rd, A.D. 1377. Most of our country churches are very much in this style, of which a ball, placed in the centre of three leaves, forming a cup round it, is a frequent indication. The fourth style is the perpendicular English which existed down to A.D. 1649. The tracery of the windows runs in perpendicular lines up to the head.—We have no space for the enlargement of this sketch, but recommend the study to our readers, as rational, amusing, and instructive.

THE LOVE OF NOVELTY.

There is scarcely any description of mind, less capable of substantiating a claim to be considered respectable, than that which is easily moved out of its settled convictions, (if indeed such a mind can be supposed to have any settled convictions,) by a plausible representation of some new-fangled notion. It matters not much what the notion is, or whence it originated, provided, only, it has the sound and aspect of novelty. This quality, whatever else it may, or may not, have, to recommend it, is sure to find for it an easy access, and an eager reception. It matters not how whimsical, or absurd, the new opinion may be; the superlative quality of novelty, posesses an irresistible charm, under whose influence, common sense is abjured, and the unenviable condition of second childhood, prematurely attained. It is needless to remark, that these observations do not apply to any really original conception, or useful discovery. Such a mind has nothing to do with originality, and nothing with usefulness. Indeed, it is one of its characteristics, that it exists doggedly, and servilely, amidst common place trivialities, until some wil-o-the-whisp-like Chimera, attracts it into the labyrinth, or the bog, where it sinks in the mire, or is lost in the maze.

There always have been (whatever may be said or hoped with regard to the future,) sundry small geniuses, hovering about, as the apostles of chimerical novelty. Their sole business, like that of the Athenians, seems to be, "either to hear, or to tell some new thing." This tribe, display an amazing diligence and activity in searching after novelties; and when they happen to alight on the angle of something new, (if, what appears so to them, for a thing may have been contemporaneous with all the ages from the flood, and yet be quite new *to them,)* they exhibit a somewhat ludicrous resemblance to the Fairies, a fabulous race, reputed as having a wonderful capacity of dancing on the point of a needle. It is more than a little amusing to observe the exultation displayed by one of this fraternity, on being successful in hunting up a morsel of the delicious commodity. Like a child with a new toy, or a squirrel with the first nut of the season, he is pleased, delighted, to ecstacy. And then the air of triumph with which the self-complacent feeling within, lights up every feature, and imparts vivacity and a sort of conscious dignity and superiority to the whole person, admits of but one interpretation; "Hide your diminished heads, ye minor stars! Ye dogged and grovelling plodders, concentrate your admiring gaze upon the man who has discovered *this!*"

It is farther characteristic of this tribe, to wonder beyond the capacity of language to express, that the earth-worms they consider the rest of mankind to be, grovel on, utterly unobservant of what has the power to concentrate the energies of their whole being, such a being as it is; and to convert into food for their vanity, what would be a source of mortification and chagrin, to minds differently constituted. The very fact that their fellow mortals are not at once astounded by their discoveries, and charmed, as if by magic, into implicit discipleship, is construed into a proof of their own immeasurable superiority, and serves to swell them out into a ludicrous excess of inflation and self importance; like the frog in the fable, barring that they imitate no ox, neither do they burst

It is a mischief, however, and a calamity, that men of this stamp, are generally successful in entangling *some* minds, in the web of their flimsy sophistries. This is the description of mind glanced at, in the opening sentence. It may not be without its use, especially to young persons, to specify some of the leading features of this cast of mind. Should the attempt to do so, have the effect of inducing in them a determined hostility to a similar mental formation, in their own case, it would be a happiness indeed!

The description of mind, under consideration, is marked by its habit of skimming, like the swallow, over the surface of everything. It never dives into the mass and essence of a subject, with a view to analyze and examine it; to turn it inside out, so to speak, and to know what it is composed of. It is never guided in reference to a proposition, by the apposite and useful questions, *What* is it? *How* and why is it? and *what then*? This incapacity, indisposition, ineptitude, or whatever else it may be, to go below the surface of things, is not, it is conceived, the consequence of any defect in the original, mental constitution, so much as of sheer, habitual, idleness.

Unaddictedness to active exercise, by and by, begets an aversion, if not, an utter incapacity for it. So a mind, unaccustomed to examine, becomes. in time, entirely indisposed, if not, unable to investigate any subject presenting the least difficulty. It will force the exquisite enjoyment arising in the process of investigation, and from the discovery of truth; and allow itself to be gulled by the merest sophism, or caught by the most puerile whimsicality, rather than stir a single faculty, or relinquish its ignoble repose. Whatever may have been its original calibre; or to whatever degree of capacity, vigour, and elevation, it might have attained, had it not been so unfortunate as to be idle, it *has* acquired a character which assimilates it to the consistency of cork; it never relinquishes the surface nor dreams of a thing, so preposterous, as attempting it.

Another characteristic of a mind of this cast, is its *volatility*: not, indeed, that it is ever guilty of soaring, except it be, in the sense in which *feathers* may be said to soar. It combines the lightness of a feather, with the insubstantiality and frothiness of a bubble. It ever and anon magnifies trifles into a character of importance, and diminishes what is really important into mere triviality. Volatility, changefulness, whim, indicate the character of all its movements, and mark out the entire circle of its evolutions. It never remains long, at one point; not long enough to know what should be the reasons for retaining or abandoning it, as it was unconscious of any, definite, reason for attaching itself to it. Like chaff, it is, passively, at the mercy of every breeze, and the sport of every gust It yields, without resistance, to every new impulse, and is handed over, a helpless and a hapless thing, from impulse to impulse, in an indeffinite series.

It is unnecessary to add, that, a mind in this condition, is a pitiful and despicable thing; but it is also guilty! It cannot be affirmed of any mind that this is its character, but it must, also, be allowed that it is its own fault, that it is so. When a young person, unhappily, comes within the influence of an association of circumstances, calculated to induce this most deplorable mental formation, he does not then, and therefore, lose his character of a moral, an accountable *agent*, as by a stroke of magic; or like certain insects, which, in their passage from one condition of being to another, cast off their external covering. *That* is and must be still his character, at every stage and in every mode of life, so long as he retains that property which forms the basis of the character,—his capacity of intelligence and reason. If he yield to the influence of circumstances, hostile to a respectable and useful mental formation, his doing so will be criminal, and render him guilty: his virtue would consist in surmounting, and turning them to a good account

The disposition animadverted upon, must present a fatal hinderance to the formation of a solid, useful, social character. It is the necessary consequence of the constitution of things, that it should be so! How long would be required to build a house, if the builder should fritter away the time in comparing plans, counting bricks, tempering mortar, or in changing sites? And, on what ground can it be expected that a solid and useful character will be formed by a person, who, impelled by a feverish restlessness, which forbids his settling down into any prescribed course of action, in pursuit of a defined, useful, purpose, dissipates the time allotted for that object, in grasping at novelties, each of which is doomed, in its turn, to be laid aside in favour of something else which shall present the stimulant quality? Surprise that such a being should be useless in the world, would be no more reasonable, than to wonder, that, in an intolerably flat and monotonous country, there are to be seen, no rapid streams, dashing and foaming cascades, variegated and charming landscapes, or indeed anything at all approaching the beautiful or the sublime.

But it is easy to see, farther, that a person of this unhappy cast of mind will be something worse than a cipher on the great stage. Such a person *will* be useless, indeed, except, in so far as he may serve as a warning to others, to avoid a similar formation; but he will be, also, a hinderance, a stumbling-block and a pest. Dissatisfied with himself and with every thing and every body around him, such a person will be envious of the success and happiness of better formed and better cultivated minds. Conscious of his own inutility and of his utter disinclination for usefulness, he will misinterpret and censure, deride, and sometimes oppose the plans and efforts of others to do good. He will conceive nothing, devise nothing, himself; nor will he concur in the conceptions and schemes of others, for good. Such a being is, not only, a sort of embodied negation of practical benevolence; he is also a positive obstacle to its operation.

What can be more obvious, than, that such a mind must be miserably destitute of all internal elements of personal happiness? Unaccustomed to retire within for the purpose of self-communion and observation; a stranger to itself; having neglected all self-culture, discipline, training, it must also be destitute of the solidity, confidence and repose, necessary to the right action and well-being of every inhabitant of this world. Accustomed to live without and to derive its sole means of subsistency from external incidents and impulses, its happiness will be entirely at their mercy; like the supplies of that pitiable class of persons, who, dependent for support upon the bounty of others, are three parts of their time without suitable food and clothing; or, like a vitiated, sickly, appetite, always craving after something fresh, it will be fretful, peevish and restless, except during the rare intervals of gratification.

It is a melancholy thought, that multitudes of human beings are guilty of the enormous folly of habitually expending time and wasting the thinking principle, the mental energy, upon trifles; to the entire neglect of the momentous task allotted to all men, of aiming at personal excellence, and social usefulness. And then to think of the disastrous consequences, perpetually arising to the individuals and the successive generations of men! Some in one way, and some in another, they throw away, piecemeal, the whole term of life, in doing nothing, except mischief for themselves and their contemporaries; and, by acting as a sort of drag upon the wheel of social improvement, they retard the progress of their own and succeeding generations. Sometimes, indeed, the eye rests upon a cheering contrast in both the fact and the results. It is a happy circumstance, indeed, that there are those who constantly aim to subordinate every thing to a useful purpose, and thus serve their own generation according to the will of God; and contribute, in their measure, to the improvement of those that shall follow them. The contrast is solemnly affecting in the circumstances of the exit into another world, and in the respective destinations there. The final scene in the one case is serenely calm and delightful; in the other it is characterized by an awful gloom. What can exceed in beauty the close of a fine day in the season of the year's decline? The autumnal tinge upon the luxuriant foliage of the trees, the somewhat pensive music of the birds, the soft ripple of the clear stream, the peculiar freshness and salubrity of the air, the mild effulgence of the setting sun, smiling with promise, as he retires and commissions his faithful substitute, the moon, to shed her soft enchantment upon those regions, from which he is, for a while, retiring, to impart life and light to other regions equally dependent upon his bounty,—all conspire to invest it with a delightful charm. Similar to this is the close of a life, spent in the service of God; but a life wasted in the pursuit of trifles, or consumed in the haunts of vice, must end, like a dark winter's day, whose exit, the peculiarity of the season and its attendant inclemencies, have combined to render stormy and dismal.

How imperatively it behoves every young person to guard against a mental conformation which will subject him to the influence of every new impulse, and allow him to be borne away by chimeras, dreams, and fancies. The case with him should be such, that he will not be drawn into any course, about which there are not visibly exhibited the land marks of, at least, probable truth, nor yield assent to any proposition, which does not present, on a careful investigation, the evidence suitable to justify practical belief. Let him think of the degradation and disgrace inseparable from a being endowed with reason and intelligence in the predicament against which he is cautioned, and of the consequences which must, of necessity, arise to himself and others. Let him think of the honour and happiness which will as certainly accrue to him, who has acquired an assimilating familiarity with truth, and the habit of a cheerful conformity to it, in the entire course of life; who owns no rule of conduct but truth, and no ultimate object short of the greatest possible good; and who with an ardour which nothing shall repress, and a vigour and determination which nothing shall conquer, moves on, steadily in a career of integrity and usefulness.

If the young reader, would, for himself, avoid the former and attain the latter, let him take the following suggestions into serious consideration. First, let him addict himself to a careful, impartial, vigorous, self observation. Let him diligently examine his own mind until he shall have succeeded in making something like a complete analysis, enabling him to form a just estimate of its capabilities and its defects of its good and evil tendencies. Next, let him subject his mind to a process of vigorous self-discipline with a view to strengthen what is weak and to add vigour and muscularity to what is strong; to supply deficiencies and to repress and correct all wrong tendencies: nor let him shrink at the thought of self-dicipline; he will not have occasion to use the whip if he is docile at first. Next, let him, with humility and ardour suited to one who is conscious of his liability to err and determined to acquire a practical acquaintance with truth, seek the guidance and tuition of that Being, who is the fountain of truth, and who condescends to be the Teacher of men. Then let him go cautiously, but vigorously to work, economizing time, carefully examining the structure, proportions and evidence of every proposition which promises to be worth examination, mastering everything that is useful, and arranging it, with due regard to its relative value, in the mental repository. But let him not forget that the Divine Oracle is the centre whence all the rays of truth radiate and that this alone is the universal test. And should difficulties at first and afterwards oppose his progress, let him nevertheless, be assured, that the course of the earnest enquirer after truth resembles that of a tourist, through a beautiful and picturesque country, who having carefully examined the different scenes through which he has passed and transferred the image of them into the chambers of his mind, at length attains the summit of some lofty eminence, which commands the full dome of the sky, whence, with astonishment and rapture, he beholds them all melting and blending into the whole grand landscape.

Soham. OBSERVATOR.

OUR LETTER BOX.

The Editors do not wish to be considered responsible for all the sentiments of their Correspondents.

To the Editor of the Soham Magazine.

Sir,—A friend has communicated to me, that the following resolution has been unaniously adopted by the Guardians of the Mildenhall Union ; and I have considered that its insertion in your valuable magazine, together with a few remarks on the general administration of the Poor Laws, will not be unacceptable to your readers, and that by inviting discussion, it may lead to the dissemination of correct views on this important subject, and may tend to promote the professed object of your publication, viz :—that of "improving the condition of the Neighbourhood."

" Resolved—That in the opinion of the Board, it is desirable to endeavour to create " a greater feeling of independence on the part of the Labouring population, and to " discourage as far as possible the present craving after parish assistance, which in- " duces many of them to apply for relief on every trifling emergency ; and therefore " that out-door relief *sufficient to meet the circumstances of each case, be given " in future only to those who have shown themselves to be provident, by having sub- " scribed to the funds of Benefit Societies or otherwise, and that admissions to the " Workhouse (where practicable) be the only relief afforded to those who have made no " provision against sickness, or any other calamity which may have caused their des- " titution."*

No doubt can be entertained that the objects which the promoters of the Poor Law Amendment Act had in view, were to put an end to fraud and imposture in the reception of parish relief ; to prevent the Labourers from placing too great a reliance on the poor's rates ; to check improvidence and intemperance; to improve their moral condition ; and by stimulating them to industry and frugality, to add to the comforts of themselves and their families, and if the whole of the results contemplated by this wise act of Legislation, have not been attained, the cause must be attributed to the senseless clamour raised by inexperienced, although well meaning persons, which has deterred the parties charged with the administration of the Act, from pursuing that prudent and progressive course, which their own sound sense and correct judgment would otherwise have induced them to adopt.

It is a fact which cannot be controverted, that the test of the Workhouse has operated in a great measure to prevent able-bodied men in full health from advancing their claims to relief from the parish funds, and that it has induced them to seek more diligently for employment to gain subsistence for their families ; but beyond this result, what great change has been effected? We daily see Labourers in the receipt of high wages, spending their money at the public house with the same prodigality as heretofore ; we see the same improvident marriages effected ; we experience no increase in the number of Members of Benefit Clubs ; we witness the same disposition to crave parish relief, where the rules of the Commissioners will permit its distribution, and generally we find no decided improvement in the moral habits of the poor.

I think therefore that the Guardians of Mildenhall, have exercised a wise discretion in the execution of the powers with which they are entrusted, by adopting the resolution above quoted, which their experience has taught them to deem both practicable, and conducive to the best interests of the Labouring Classes, but that such a result would be hopeless if they had waited for orders of the Poor Law Commissioners to the same effect, or for a new interposition by Act of Parliament.

If the Poor Law Commissioners had issued such an order as this, there would have been no end to the thunderbolts of the Times, and the denunciations of Mr. Ferrand, which would have been launched against them for their cruelty, harshness, &c, "Mott's case" would have sunk into comparative insignificance, and the Andover Union Committee have been forgotten, and few Members of Parliament could vote for an Act of Legislation to the same effect, with any chance of regaining their seats when a new election sholud take place. The plain fact is, that the public are unprepared to go so far, they look to individual cases of fancied hardship, and their mistaken feelings of humanity induce them to offer all the opposition in their power, and it is only practised and experienced men who have the firmness and foresight to advocate a sound principle, which they know will eventually tend to the well being and happiness of their poorer fellow countrymen.

Now let us examine in detail, the effect of this resolution.—

It first provides that ample relief "shall be given to those who have shown themselves to be provident, by having subscribed to the funds of Benefit Societies, or otherwise," this is sound policy, as it is right to offer as much encouragement as possible to habits of prudence and foresight.

It then provides that a maintenance in the Workhouse, shall be the only relief (where practicable) afforded to those who have made no exertion to provide against sickness or other calamity.

The Poor Law Commissioners, by their orders have directed, that out-door relief shall be refused to able-bodied men in full health, but the Mildenhall Guardians go further than this, they conceive it to be the duty of Labourers to make provision to the extent of their means, against sickness, and they have determined to extend the operation of the Workhouse system, with the view of discouraging pauperism, and of endeavouring to create a more independent feeling amongst the Labouring Classes, and I congratulate them on their firmness and determination.

It is true that it may appear harsh, that a pauper brought up under the old system, and who is now beyond the age to be admitted as a Member of a Club, should be obliged in ill health to submit to the classification and dicipline of a Workhouse ; but what real hardship is there in affording, as a refuge in distress, more wholesome food, better clothing, cleaner and better ventilated rooms, and more constant medical attendance, than a Labourer could provide in his own cottage, there is no real hardship, that the Workhouse is distasteful to them is true, but long established diseases require strong remedies, and surely a remedy like this cannot be condemned, if it should have the contemplated effect of creating more independent and prudent habits amongst the rising generation.

The West Suffolk Friendly Society offers to young men and women under the age of 15, the opportunity, by the payment of 1s. 6¾d. monthly, of securing to themselves during sickness, till the age of 65, 10s. per week full pay, and 5s. per week half pay, and a weekly allowance of 5s. in sickness and in health during life, after the age of 65, and of £5. on death, and yet how few there are in comparison, who embrace the opportunity of preventing their being stigmatised as paupers, by joining this excellent Institution, and such will not be their disposition, nor will their Parents advise them to this course, as long as the present system of encouraging pauperism exists, aud therefore I again congratulate the Mildenhall Guardians on the excellent example they have set to other Boards, and to the country generally.

I am afraid of trespassing too much on your columns, and I therefore conclude by expressing a hope that the Guardians, whilst carrying into effect their resolution for the discouragment of pauperism, will unite their influence to aid the exertions of those who try to earn an honest and independent livelihood, by promoting an extension of the Allottment System, by increasing wages in proportion to the price of provisions, by facilitating the enrollment of Members of Benefit Societies, by a liberal expenditure in employment of the sums which they may save in the decreased payment of poor's rates, and by inculcating on every occasion which may offer, lessons of morality and economy, and if these necessary accompaniments of their resolution be faithfully adhered too, I do not yet despair of living to see a sturdy, honest, temperate, and independent race of Labourers, in the place of the intemperate, unthrifty, lazy, and pauperized set of men, whom we too often meet with at the present day.

I am,
Your obedient Servant,
AGRICOLA.

June, 1847.

POETRY.

In Original Poetry, the Name, real or assumed, of the Author, is printed in small Capitals under the title ; in Selections it is printed in Italics at the end.]

THE BROKEN RING

Oh ! take back the treacherous token,
The heart that confided—is broken,
The word of thy destiny's spoken,
    And sorrow must ever be thine.

The seal of thy fate is upon thee,
The arts thou hast used have undone thee,,
Thou shalt love,—and the lov'd one shall shun thee,
    The pangs that I feel shall be thine.

The thoughts of the past shall oppress thee,
Thou shalt wed, but no children shall bless thee,
Nor the hand that is thine shall caress thee,
    Thy hearth shall be desolate there.

The rack of suspicion shall wring thee,
Thou shalt trust—and the trusted shall sting thee,
Till grief to the cold grave bring thee,
    Thy refuge alone from despair.

Then take back the treacherous token,
The heart that confided is broken,
The word of thy destiny's spoken,
    And sorrow must ever be mine.

Soham.

MISCELLANY AND EXTRACTS.

THE Pagoda of Sumnaut was one of the most splendid objects of Indian superstition. Two thousand Brahmins, and numerous bands of music were devoted to its service. The lofty roof of this temple was supported by fifty-six pillars, overlaid with plates of gold, and incrusted at intervals with rubies, emeralds and other precious stones. One pendent lamp alone illumined the spacious fabric, whose light, reflected from innumerable jewels, spread a strong and refulgent lustre throughout the temple. In the midst stood Sumnaut himself, an idol composed of one entire stone, fifty cubits in height, forty-seven of which were buried in the ground, and on that spot, according to Brahminical tradition, he had been adored between four and five thousand years. His image was washed every morning and evening with fresh water brought from the Ganges, at a distance of twelve hundred miles.

THE rays of light are small particles of matter emitted from the sun, or any luminous body, with a velocity so immense, as to enable them to move at the inconceivable rate of eleven millions of miles in a minute. Eight of these particles following each other in a second of time, or at the rate of 480 in a minute, render any point visible to the eye; yet such is the velocity of light, that those particles, notwithstanding the rapidity of their succession, will be 24,000 miles asunder.

THE atmosphere of the earth is thought to extend to about 45 miles from the surface, and its gravity is such, that a man of middling stature is computed to sustain, when the air is heaviest, a weight, pressing equally over his body, of about 14 tons, without, in the slightest degree, perceiving it.

An inhabitant of London, or the same longitude, is continually being whirled in a huge circle, equal to the circumference of the earth, at the rate of about eleven miles every minute, and in another vastly larger circle, equal to the orbit of the earth, round the sun, at the rate of about a thousand miles, in the same period of time.

"MOCKERY and ridicule," says Paley, "when exercised upon the scriptures, or even upon the places, persons and forms set apart for the ministration of religion, are inconsistent with a religious frame of mind ; for as no one ever feels himself disposed to pleasantry, or capable of being diverted with the pleasantry of others, upon matters in which he is deeply interested, so a mind, intent on the acquisition of heaven, rejects with indignation every attempt to entertain it with jests, calculated to degrade or deride subjects which it never recollects but with seriousness and anxiety. Nothing but stupidity, or the most frivolous dissipation of thought, can make even the inconsiderate forget the supreme importance of everything which relates to the expectation of a future existence.

MONTHLY NOTICES.

JULY.

Middle Fen Tax payable (see advertisements in newspapers).

5th.—Dividends on several species of Stock become due.

8th.—Insurances, due at Midsummer, must be paid on or before this day.

14th.—Meeting of the County Court, at the Crown Inn, Soham.

20th.—Last day for sending in claims for voting in Counties.

31st.—Overseers to make out Lists of County and Borough Electors.

PLAYFORD'S

SOHAM MAGAZINE,

AND

Friendly Monitor.

AUGUST, 1847.

INCE there is, at the present time, a strong and increasing hostility manifested in many quarters towards the Church of England, we wish to lay before our readers one or two facts in her favour which ought to be universally known. No one of her adversaries who possesses a spark of honourable or christian feeling would desire to oppose her on any other than equitable grounds, nor to raise an outcry to her disadvantage that was not founded on truth. Without, therefore, attempting to discuss the question of the lawfulness of ecclesiastical establishments, or the divine origin and apostolic order of that branch of the catholic church existing in this realm, let us simply adduce a few arguments in support of the *utility* of such establishments for the purposes of affording the means of grace to a nation at large. We are ready to allow, that, without an established Church, particular spots might enjoy the advantages of Christian cultivation. But, at the same time, we believe that instead of that uniform and equally diffused ministration of the word and ordinances which is now amongst the greatest blessings of this favoured land, we should, under such circumstances, behold long and dreary tracts, where the sound of a Sabbath-bell had never been heard; and where not only no religious instruction had ever penetrated, but where the occasional Missionary would not find so much as even the desire for it, on the part of an uninformed and half-heathen population. The opponents of an established Church

frequently refer to America as a country where the knowledge of
Christianity is preserved without one. But the point of fact which
is the whole subject in question is,—what is the actual state of
religion in America under the system which she has adopted? No
one pretends that Christianity cannot exist, except where there is
an established Church : the doubt is as to the state in which it
will be actually found among the people at large, under a different arrangement.

Let us hear, then, the language in which their own writers express
themselves on this subject; as they may be supposed to reason
with better knowledge of the facts, than those of our own country
are likely to possess.

Mr. Bristed, the author of the work called "America and her
Resources."—a writer of unimpeachable credit, and warmly attached
to the country of his birth, says,—" Full three millions of our
people (that is, more than one-third of the then population of the
United States) are altogether destitute of Christian ordinances;
and as the population of this country increases with a rapidity
hitherto unexampled in the history of nations, unless some effectual means be adopted to spread the light of the Gospel over those
sections of the Union which now lie prostrate in all the darkness of
unregenerated depravity, before half a century shall have elapsed,
our federative republic will number within its bosom more than
twenty millions of unbaptized infidels."

The other American writer from whose work we will make a
brief extract is Dr. Mason, who, in speaking of the western portion
of the Union observes ;—" Sanctuary they have none ; they lose
by degrees their anxiety for the institutions of Christ ; their feeble
substitutes, the small social meetings, without the minister of grace,
soon die away ; their Sabbaths are Pagan ; their children grow up
in ignorance, vice, and unbelief; their land, which smiles around
them like a garden of Eden, presents one unbroken scene of
spiritual desolation. In the course of one or two generations the
knowledge of God is almost obliterated. We have already a population of some millions of our own colour, flesh and blood, nearly
as destitute of evangelical mercies, as the savage who yells on the
banks of the Missouri !"

It is a notorious fact that, with the exception of that large and
rapidly increasing body in America who have retained the doctrines

and the liturgy of the English Episcopal Church, the number of orthodox Christians is becoming every day less. But speaking of the established Church simply as that, without which the knowledge of religion, if preserved at all, can only be diffused partially among the people, the extracts given above are sufficient, we think, to show that the actual condition of America affords an irresestible argument in its favour.

But it may perhaps be said that the opinion of those who desire to suppress the existence of an established Church altogether, is confined to a few persons; but that which is the subject of general complaint is the unnecessary wealth of the clergy, and the enormous expenses of the present establishment. A modern writer, whose language is as intemperate as untrue, asserts that "the revenues of the Church amount to more than eight millions a year; and that the average salaries of those of the clergy who do nearly all the ministerial work of the Church, is considerably under 150*l.*" Now according to public documents, which may be readily examined and the laborious investigations of men, who have devoted their time to the inquiry, it appears that the revenues of the Church do not reach one third of the above sum, that the average amount of income enjoyed by the parochial clergy of England and Wales is about 181*l.*; and that the average annual income received by the five thousand Curates,—those of the clergy alluded to as "doing nearly all the ministerial work of the Church,"—is not more than 81*l.* per annum. In the year 1823 there were 3,067 benefices in England not exceeding 98*l.* per annum, of which 422 were from 10*l.* to 30*l.*; 1207 from 30*l.* to 60*l.*; 645 from 60*l.* to 75*l.*; and 793 from 75*l.* to 98*l.*

But even supposing that the expenses of the present establishment were as great as its enemies desire to represent it,—on whom do these expenses fall? "Not on the poor;—that can hardly be pretended. Not on the householders in our large towns; for they contribute nothing towards the support of the clergy, except in the shape of fees for services actually performed. Not on the farmer; for he is quite aware that what he pays to the Church is subtracted from his rent, and would be added to it were there no Church to be maintained. Not on the landowner; for if the rent charge were done away tomorrow, he cannot be so ignorant as to suppose that it would be made a present of to him. Not on the state; for the tithes never belonged to the state. The documents are innumerable which still exist, with the very names of the individuals by whom they were allotted to the Church, many hundred years before the land from which they accrue came into the possession of the ancestors of any person now alive. The property of the Church, whatever its amount may be, is as sacredly her own as the property of any individual in the world, and if the time should ever come when it shall fall a prey to rapacity, all other property beside ecclesiastical will have to look around for protection." All we ask, then, is that our opponents would meet us upon fair and honourable terms :—that they would read before they write,. and think before they speak. We are tired of continual contest with misrepresentation, but fear no assaults that will bear the broad light of day.

NOTES UPON BOOKS.—No. 1.

The Chinese have an aphorism importing that something is learned every time a book is opened. We hope our readers will, with some degree of pleasure, admit the truth of this aphorism, though the good people of Mentmore, in Buckinghamshire appear to have held a different opinion, for so recently as within the present century—yea, but a few years since, having a small antient library of intrinsically good and pecuniarily valuable works, they suffered the Lord of the Manor to claim and take possession of it, "because it had been disregarded for years!" Can it then be a matter of surprise that Buckinghamshire should so long have borne the unenvied distinction of being the most ignorant county in England? It is to be hoped that this fact is without parallel in the country—certainly in a county which has for so many centuries borne the high honour of possessing one of the chief seminaries of learning in the Kingdom.

But the neglect of knowledge is not a subject upon which we are inclined, at present, to dilate; our object is merely to interest our readers by a few facts in connection with the history of books themselves. The *contents* of books will furnish we hope many subsequent papers from various pens. We invite the favours of correspondents, by the cheerful offer of our pages to their criticisms.

The earliest mentioned library in history is that founded in Egypt by King Osymandyas 2000 years before the Christian era, and which was appropriately inscribed "The office or Treasury of remedies for the diseases of the Soul."

The most antient library in this kingdom is at Merton College, Oxford, founded by Rede, Bishop of Chichester, in 1376; and the most extensive is that belonging to the Nation—accessible to all—the British Museum.

A recent American author, comparing the literature of his own country with that of the kingdoms of the old world, says: "It is uncertain what is the number of books now extant in all languages. I have used a library of 250,000 volumes which contained no duplicate, and it was so perfect that it was difficult to ask for an author not to be found in it. The largest library in Europe contains near 400,000 volumes, duplicates not included; and perhaps it may be about right to estimate the whole number of printed books in the world at 500,000. This being the case, America furnishes about one-seventeenth of the means necessary for extending learning to the utmost, and about one-thirteenth of what the city of Paris alone affords. Another comparison will shew her poverty in a manner equally striking. Germany contains 30,000,000 of people, who have 2,000,000 of books in public libraries for their instruction, exclusive of those of the sovereign princes which are always accessible to scholars. America contains 10,000,000 of people, who have 150,000 for the same purpose; but the 2,000,000 in Germany are not more read than the 150,000 in America."

The collective number of volumes in the five great libraries of Paris is 1,000,978, and those for public use in the eighty-six departments approach to four millions. The Vatican, the Imperial of Vienna, and the Royal Libraries of Munich, succeed to that of the Royal Library at Paris in relative value; while that of the British Museum holds a comparatively subordinate place in the great collections of Europe.

The library of the late Earl Spencer, at Althorp, in Northamptonshire, contained nearly 35,000 volumes. The books are the choicest copies of the choicest editions of the choicest authors, in the choicest bindings, and "as the acquirement of an individual the collection far exceeds any other ever formed."

The library of Sir Walter Scott, contained near 30,000 volumes, most of which were "presentation copies" from authors desirous of gaining his good opinion, or from friends anxious to testify their respect and admiration.

The Harleian library, it is said, cost its collector, the Earl of Oxford, more than 18,000l. to bind; but the library itself was sold to Osborne, the bookseller, for only 13,000l.

The first library ever sold by auction, was that of the Reverend Lazarus Seaman, nonconforming minister, at Leicester, who died in 1675. It produced the sum of 700l.

In 1810 the Duke of Devonshire offered 25,000l. for the library of Count M'Carthy, of Toulouse, if landed in England. Napoleon prohibited the deportation of the collection, and it was sold by auction in Paris, and realised only 16,600l. It was particularly rich in vellum copies of printed books, which exceeded that of any other private collection. They amounted to 601; while those in the Royal Parisian Library, by far the richest in the world, did not exceed 1500.

The sale of the library of the late Mr. Heber, in 1834-6, occupied nearly 200 days, and realised between 50,000l. and 60,000l. They were all collected by himself and were for the most part the choicest editions. He appropriated a large house in Westminster entirely to their reception. To this depot they were taken immediately on being purchased, and there he used to spend the principal part of his time in arranging them. They were then sent to his residence in Pimlico, or taken under his own personal care to his seat at Hodnet, in Shropshire. The latter library was distinguished for its extraordinary assemblage of early English Poetry.

Previous to the fifteenth century, books were all in Manuscript, and were so scarce and expensive that none but the wealthy could become possessed of them. At Bologna and Milan the copying of books was a regular occupation, at fixed prices. The price for copying a bible about the year 1300, was 80 Bolognese livres; three of which were equal to two gold florins. In this country at an earlier date, 1274, the price of a small bible was 30l., a sum equal to at least 300l. of our money.

The Bible supposed to have been written by the learned Alchuine, a native of York, and Abbot of Tours, for the Emperor Charlemagne, to whom it was presented at his Coronation, in 800, is now in the British Museum, by the trustees of which establishment it was purchased for 750*l.* of M. de Speyr Passavant, whose first demand, it is understood, was 12,000*l*! It was originally bound in gold and silver; but re-bound in the tenth century in wood and ornamented with six copper bosses representing the Lamb, the Crucifixion, and the four Evangelists. At the close of the 16th Century it was again bound in wood and ten other bosses added. It is now in a modern binding covered with black velvet, which is ornamented at the corners and middle with bosses of brass or copper of a modern date. It is enclosed in a box cased with iron, and lined with crimson velvet, the lid of which is embroidered with fleur-de-lis in gold, with a crucifix in silver foil in the middle, resting on an imperial crown in gold.

A beautiful vellum copy of "the Complutensian Polyglott," or Ximene's Polyglott, which exhibited the first printed text of the Greek Septuagint and new Testament, "the most precious of existing volumes," formed part of a library bequeathed with a valuable collection of paintings, a short time since, to the King of the French, by the late Mr. Frank Hull Standish, It was the only one, of three originally struck off, that ever was exposed to sale, and is known to have formed part of the Pinelli library, and to have been purchased by the late Count McCarthy of Toulouse. It cost the Count 483*l.* the largest sum ever paid, up to that period, for any printed work, and at his sale in 1817 was purchased by Mr. Hibbert for about 650*l.*, when the late royal librarian of France, M. Van Praet, in vain solicited Louis XVIII. to add it at any price to the royal collection. When Mr. Hibbert's library was dispersed by auction, it passed, through the medium of Messrs. Payne and Foss, into the hands of Mr. Standish, whose bequest of his collection to France is in every way a reproach to this country.

An imperfect copy of Mathews' translation of the Bible, folio, printed in 1537 was sold by auction, in 1845, for 105 guineas.

A copy of the New Testament (the vulgate) written before the year 700, is in the library of Durham Cathedral, where is also another copy in the hand writing of the Venerable Bede. The price of one of Wickliffe's New Testaments, in 1429, was four marks and forty pence, as much as would now purchase nearly 150 copies of the New Testament.

In 1174, the Homilies of Bede with St. Augustine's Psalter, were bought by a prior in Winchester for twelve measures (five quarters) of barley and a pall richly embroided in silver. And it is recorded that Grecia, wife of Geoffroi Martel, sovereign Count of Anjou, who was a great book collector in the middle ages, gave for a copy of the Homilies of Haimon, Bishop of Halberdstadt, "200 sheep, twelve measures of wheat, a similar quantity of rye, and as much millet; several marten skins, and eight marcs of silver." Great as this may appear, it is trifling in comparison with the Missal of the Monks of St. Florent, the price of which it is said was large enough to build a Monastery with!

The purchase of a book was an affair of the highest importance; and was usually transacted in the presence of witnesses of high rank and character, who made a formal record of their being present on the occasion. The borrowing of a book, too, was a very different kind of thing in those days. The Bishop of Winchester, who borrowed a Bible in two volumes folio, in the year 1299, gave to the Convent to which it belonged, a solemnly indited bond for its safe return.

AN ADDRESS TO THE TEACHERS IN A NATIONAL OR SUNDAY SCHOOL.

BY DAVID GUNTON.

Continued from page 103.

Pedagogical demeanour and attire had their value in olden times, and the measured step, stately gait, and pompous voice, bespoke the great man, whose words were oracular, and whose dogmas disclaimed controversy. But so altered is general opinion now, that men gain little by wise looks or distinctive habiliments, being rather valued for what they really are, than what they seem to be, hence, the schoolmaster is no longer

> Like to heaven's glorious sun,
> That may not be gazed on with saucy looks.

and instead of throwing into his childrens' mind, from a remote and studied distance, a few thwarted rays of intelligence, he courts them to his influence, and rules and commands his pupils, more by the respect they bear him, than by any towering authority he was wont to establish. Waving, however, any reflection on this point, we may say, that like the priestly office to which yours is only second, if you only keep in lively remembrance the dignity of your business, there will never be lacking an earnest mien, and a rightful conservatism of character, for, let the teacher only lose his *self-respect*, and no gifts, however exalted, and no voice, however stentorian, will give him authority over his scholars. I will hold no combat with the notions of some men, but I will fearlessly propound my own, by saying, that to be thoroughly efficient for your position, you ought to be seriously and savingly acquainted with the verities of our holy religion. Let it not be enough for you to be charmed with the ethics and morals of sacred truth ; to hear the deep-toned voice of heaven in its prophecies ; to see the fire of inspiration in its poetry, and infinite wisdom in all its pages, but seek to possess and live out its amiable and practical spirit.

Most of you, we believe, have had the advantage of christian parentage, were early inducted into the visible church by baptism, have heard impressive sermons, and have vocally breathed out, at least, the beautiful and godly formularies of the sanctuary. We have good hopes on your account, yet, to-day, on your advancing to a post of momentous trust, we wish to impress you with a double responsibility. Aforetime you lived more to yourself than you can now.—Here you will begin, more or less, to make these little ones, unconsciously what you yourselves are, for children are never in a disposition to be taught, until they can believe their Educator next to infallible, and since the Almighty has wisely given them this trusting confidence, in those who are placed over them as instructors, I beseech you to tremble for your situation, and to see to it, that you are not only able thoroughly to instruct the head, but soundly to impress the mind, with the importance of youthful religion.

And here, if it were granted me, I would ask what sight under heaven is so lovely as educated and pious youth ? What adornment so becoming their years as " the ornament of a meek and gentle spirit," which is, in the sight of God, of great price.

Then there is a peculiar interest in educating the children of the poor, since they are left implicitly to you, and because the poor, shall not only never cease from among us, but will always have a numerical preponderance in the nation.

Parents who possess some imperfect smattering of education, and who have gathered their notions of it, from peripatetic lectures and penny publications, are great annoyers to the teacher, constantly expressing their vulgar wonder, that as during their time, locomotion has at once gone from the pack horse to the steam-engine, there should be no royal road to learning, no vapoury mental vehicle, to carry the rude dullard from the slough of ignorance, to the apex of science, in a few months. Many of the poor feel their want of learning, and in proportion to this are they anxious for their children to be educated. They hold no pecuniary restraint over you, and they not only very readily defer the whole task of instruction to your hands by necessity, but we believe also, in most instances, with feelings of gratitude,

My young friends, Archimedes might boast of his ability to raise the world, if he could only have a resting place for his mechanical power, and a modern statesman might exclaim, "Let me write the national songs, I care not who makes the laws." But you are the humble directors of a force more stupendous than lever, fulcrum, pulley, or screw, and possess an enchantment that, better than Orpheus, and more brilliant than the Muses, will lead through the paths of conscious enlightenment to the very summits of happiness. Yes, we shall have to mourn over degeneracy of manners, instability of character, overspreading wickedness, and calendars of youthful depravity, until those who hold the young world, the next generation in their hands, mould them, by God's grace, into the form of virtuous promise. He helping us then, "let us set our mark on the rising generation." Let not our boys grow up, and receive their very initial of instruction, in the arena of a Mechanics' Institution, and matured men, thumb out the lessons of puerility.—This is the season of labour, that, of culture, and succeeding years, of satisfaction and delight, whereas adult instruction is like sowing in July. The whole process is inverted, unnatural, and productive of nothing, but a few stray ears, forced into hasty life, with the form and figure, but not the durability or use of spring corn.

Besides, we would spare the lungs and labour of the dictator at the Athenæum, who begins at the second floor, to raise a solid superstructure, when the foundation of the building itself, rests on a shifting sand.

And to you, in whose interests I have intense sympathy, and for whose welfare, I would rather work than talk, to you, who are to be thus educated, I leave a few lines of affectionate advice.

Be regular in your attendance at school.

Attend with great care to the instruction given.

Perform every duty imposed by your teacher with cheerfulness.

Remember what Quintilian says "He who loves not his Schoolmaster, must be suspected of a lack of Parental affection, for the teacher, is a sort of second father,"

Speak the truth—Avoid impure language—Observe general good conduct —Love the Bible—Fear God, and make frequent prayer to Him.—

> To Thee Almighty God ,to Thee
>   Our childhood we resign;
> 'Twill please us to look back and see,
>   That our whole lives were Thine.

And now my young friends, I beg you to respect these observations, because they arise out of long experience and observation. They are not difficult of practice, nor ephemeral in result, for they challenge your attention on their own open reasonableness, and the assurance that they inculcate, and will as certainly convey, blessing to yourselves, and those upon whom, whatever be your future position, you must undoubtedly exercise influence. I look for the regeneration of the whole world on the promise of Holy Writ, and I gather confidence in asserting, that whenever the blessed time shall arrive, and come it must, when "Righteousness shall cover the earth," the Schoolmaster, under God, will be rendered one of the mightiest instruments, in the universal mental and moral re-creation. The Latin writer said, *nullus spiritus, nulla vita;* we exclaim, more oracularly, and moved by livelier inspiration, NO EDUCATION, NO LIFE.

Soham Classical School, August 1847.

ECONOMICAL HINTS TO COTTAGERS.

Continued from Page 104.

———

Another proof of her good management was in regard to eggs; she had but half-a-dozen hens, yet she contrived, by good feeding, to have a supply of new-laid eggs whenever I wanted them, and, I may safely say, I have laid out some pounds with her for that article alone.—I tell you all this that you may see what *can* be *done* by *good management.* Where this poor woman lived, beer was a greater luxury than the generality of the poor could accomplish, so she substituted treacle-beer, and made it not only palatable, but brisk, I believe she only boiled the treacle and water together, and when cool, set it to ferment with a little yeast, and in a day or two bottled it, when it was very soon fit for use. Whilst speaking of this, let me remind you what an agreeable beverage you can always secure yourself by filling up your teapot, when done with, with boiling water, and letting it stand to cool. Balm, mint, and other herbs that have a pleasant flavour, make very agreeable tea, to use occasionally, and are very cooling. If you have a small piece of ground in the front or at the back of your house, you may make it very serviceable to you, not only in planting thyme, marjoram, parsley, chives, a few shallots, or anything else that is necessary to you in cooking; but you may have a hop-plant against the walls, a bush of senna,, rue, sage, and also a small bed of camomile, which would all be of use to you in case of illness. By a proper knowledge of these simples, and taking complaints *in time,* you may often spare yourself a doctor's bill, which in general is a serious consideration. As it may be of service to you to remind you of a few of these simple remedies, I shall insert them here. In the first place, *never neglect a cold.* A number of complaints are brought on by such neglect that might very easily be avoided.—If you find yourself the least chilly, go immediately and put on a warm shawl, or some other addition to your dress. and *keep it on till you go to bed.* You need not be afraid you will miss the warmth in the morning, for if you have taken it in time, you will feel no more of your chills, and will probably have prevented a heavy cold.—If this additional clothing does not remove the chills before the evening, take a good handful of bran, and let it boil in two quarts of water, down to a pint, then strain it and sweeten it with coarse sugar, honey, or treacle, and drink it quite hot when in bed. A treacle posset is also very good for a cold, taken in the same manner. If your cold turns to a cough, recollect the ever-ready remedy of sugar and vinegar; but what you sometimes fail in, is, the not stirring it sufficiently in the cup by the fire, which makes it candy, and stick to the bottom, when it ought to be all smooth and clear as honey fresh from the comb. You know it takes three large spoonsful of coarse sugar to two of vinegar.—Do not take more than a tea-spoon-full at a time, but repeat it frequently,—You will seldom know what a cough is, if you apply this remedy *very early.*

Liquorice-root (which you might easily have in your garden) sliced and bruised and boiled in a quart of water down to half-a-pint, is a very good remedy for a settled cough; as is also horehound tea.—When you require a little medicine, you have only to procure two or three ounces of salts, which you can purchase very cheap,—dissolve them in a quart of boiling water, covered close till cold, and then put the mixture into a quart bottle, and take a wine-glass-full every morning while you require it,—you will find this plan better than taking an ounce at one time.— If you mix it with hot camomile tea instead of water, it will be still better, as it will strengthen your stomach if a weak one.   Hop tea too, taken the first thing in the morning, is also very good for the latter purpose.   When stronger medicine than salts is required, procure half-a-pound of French plums, and an ounce or two of senna ; stew them together in an earthen pipkin on a very slow fire, for an hour or two ; then strain it and take a tea-cup-full of the juice.   You can put the remainder by in a bottle well corked up till required :—it will not keep long.   This medicine is often given to children, and formerly people never omitted giving them in the spring, a spoonfull every morning of the following mixture : a pound of treacle, two ounces of cream of tartar, two ounces of flower of sulphur, and one ounce of worm-seed :   children, in general, are very fond of this as they only taste the treacle. Rhubarb and magnesia of nearly equal quantities, with rather less of the latter, and the deficiency made up with ginger is a very good powder for a child, or even a grown person, and a skillful druggist, who is in the habit of selling it, will readily tell you the quantities according to the age of the person ; it is so innocent you need not be afraid of it.   The very first symptom you find of a sore throat, gargle it with cold water, and repeat it frequently ; this often prevents an attack of this complaint.   A piece of flannel with some hartshorn and oil should directly be applied to the neck, and if that is not at hand, goose-grease, although it smells very dis-agreeably is equally serviceable.   Even your stocking, put round your neck at night, will sometimes remove it.   When the throat is relaxed, get an ounce of tan-ners' bark, and boil it in three pints of water down to one pint, and add a spoonful of powdered allum : this is a very good gargle till the throat is ulcerated, and then you must have something acid.   Sage leaves boiled well in water make a very good gargle ; also a table-spoonful of port wine, one of vinegar, and one of water, with a little loaf sugar is often a good preventive.—Sometimes a little saltpetre kept in the mouth will take off the attack, if but slight ; or a piece of allum.

Soham.   *To be continued.*

FORESTS OF JAVA : PET SNAKES AND LEOPARDS.

THE forests of Java are inhabited by the rhinoceras, tiger, black tiger, leopard, tiger-cat, boa-constrictor, and a variety of animals of milder natures.   The elephant is not found in its wild state in these woods, though numerous in those of the neigh-bouring island.   I am not aware of any other animal that may be called dangerous to man in these unrivalled forests, nor is there much to be apprehended from occa-sionally coming in contact with either of those above named, though accidents happen now and then.   I have known a carriage and four attacked on the main road, between Batavia and Samarang, by a tiger and one of the ponies killed by the fierce onset.   This, however, is a rare occurrence, and can happen only when the tiger is hard pressed for food, which is seldom the case in the woods of Java, overrun as they are with deer, wild hog, and other royal game.   The boa is harmless to man, unless his path is crossed, when a speedy retreat is advisable.   A friend of mine, in Samarang, once kept one of these monsters as *a pet*, and used to let him crawl all over the garden : it measured exactly nineteen feet.   It was regularly fed twice a month—viz., on the 1st and on the 15th.   On the 1st day of the month, a moderate-sized goat was put into his house.   The poor animal would scream, and exhibit every symptom of extreme terror, but was not long kept in suspense, for the snake, after eyeing his victim keenly,, would spring on it with the rapidity of thought, coil three turns round its body, and, in an instant, every bone in the goat's skin was broken.   The next process was, to stretch the carcase to as great a length as he could before uncoiling himself ; then to lick it all over ; and he commenced his feast by succeeding, after some severe exertion, in getting the goat's head within his mouth.   In the course of twenty minutes, the whole animal was swallowed : the snake would then lie down, and remain perfectly dormant for three or four days. His lunch, (as I may call it) on the 15th of the month, used to consist of a duck. This snake was given, in 1815, to Lord Amherst on his return from China, and reached the Cape in safety; there it was over-fed to gratify the curious visitors, and died in consequence, before the ship reached St. Helena.

While on the subject of wild animals, I may mention a leopard that was kept by an English officer in Samarang, during our occupation of the Dutch colonies. This animal had its liberty, and used to run all over the house after his master. One morning, after breakfast, the officer was sitting smoking his hookah, with a book in his right hand, and the hookah-snake in his left, when he felt a slight pain in his left hand, and, on attempting to raise it, was checked by a low, angry growl from his pet leopard, On looking down, he saw the animal had been licking the back of his hand, and had, by degrees drawn a little blood. The leopard would not suffer the removal of the hand, but continued licking with great apparent relish, which did not much please his master, who, with great presence of mind, without attempting again to disturb the pet in his proceeding, called to his servant to bring him a pistol, with which he shot the animal dead on the spot. Such pets as snakes, nineteen feet long, and full-grown leopards are not to be trifled with. The largest snake I ever saw was twenty-five feet long, and eight inches in diameter. I have heard of sixty feet snakes, but cannot vouch for the truth of the tale.

In my enumeration of animals dangerous to man, I omitted the alligator, which infests every river and muddy creak in Java, and grows to a very large size. At the mouth of the Batavia river, they are very numerous and dangerous, particularly to Europeans. It strikes one as extraordinary to see the copper-coloured natives bathing in the river, within view of a large alligator. *They* never seem to give the animal a thought, or to anticipate injury from his proximity; yet, were a European to enter the water, by the side of the natives, his minutes in this world would be few. I recollect an instance that occurred on the occasion of a party of troops embarking at Batavia for the eastward, during the Java war. The men had all gone off, with the exception of three sergeants, who were to follow in the ship's jolly-boat, which was waiting for them at the wharf. Two of them stepped into the boat, but the third, in following missed his footing, and fell with his leg in the water, and his body over the gunwhale of the boat. In less than an instant, an alligator darted from under the wharf, and seized the unfortunate man by the leg, while his companions in the boat laid hold of his shoulders. The poor fellow called out to his friends, "Pull!—hold on!—don't let go!" but their utmost efforts were unavailing. The alligator proved the strongest, and carried off his prize. The scene was described to me by a by-stander, who said he could trace the monster's course all the way down the river, with his victim in his immense mouth.

Davidson's " Trade and Travel in the Far East."

THERE are thousands so extravagant in their ideas of contentment, as to imagine that it must consist in having every thing in this world turn out the way they wish—that they are to sit down in happiness, and feel themselves so at ease on all points, as to desire nothing better and nothing more. I own there are instances of some, who seem to pass through the world as if all their paths had been strewed with rose-buds of delight,—but a little experience will convince us, 'tis a fatal expectation to go upon. We are born to trouble: and we may depend upon it whilst we live in this world we shall have it, though with intermissions;—that is, in whatever state we are, we shall find a mixture of good and evil; and therefore the true way to contentment is to know how to receive these certain vicissitudes of life,—the returns of good and evil, so as neither to be exalted by the one, nor overthrown by the other, but to bear ourselves towards every thing which happens with such ease and indifference of mind, as to hazard as little as may be. This is the true temperate climate fitted for us by nature, and in which every wise man would wish to live,

Sterne.

ENGLISH HOUSES.

THE study of domestic architecture affords a curious insight into the manners and habits of a nation. In some instances we find immense tribes, whose sole protection from the inclemency of the weather consists of a few yards of canvass, stretched upon slender and elastic poles; while, in others, the solid rocks have been perforated in every direction, with astonishing ingenuity and art, to afford a more secure, and more durable retreat. In the wilds of America, the log hut of the native supplies him with every luxury and accommodation that he requires; while his fellow mortal, in a different quarter of the globe, reposes upon his gilded couch, beneath domes and turrets of stupendous altitude, upon which have been expended the labours of many years.

But in this way, moreover, may be traced the history of a nation from its first rude and obscure formation, through all its various changes, from age to age till it attains the highest eminence of civilization and refinement. If we go back. for instance, no further than the Norman conquest, and compare the massive walls and narrow loop-holes of the baronial residences, with the mansions of the present day, how strongly do we see depicted the contrast between times of insecurity, oppression, and wrong; and the tranquility and peace which so happily distinguish the present times!

Even the ordinary manor house of the 12th century was constructed on protective principles,—no communication between the lower and upper floors but by means of a staircase outside, which, on emergency, might be easily defended;—while, in comparatively recent years, few houses of any size were destitute of the moat, and draw-bridge,—an example of which we have given above, and a fine instance of which was to be seen in our neighbourhood, at Lanwade; the remains of which are now being removed to make way for edifices more adapted to the habits of the 19th century.

In the construction of cottages for the poor there is much and urgent need of improvement, and the subject should long ago have occupied the attention of the community at large. The health, not only of body, but of the mind, of the great mass of our population is greviously injured by the miserable condition of the hovels in which vast numbers of them are compelled to reside.

If the poor are allowed to live without a sufficient regard for decency, comfort, or convenience, they will remain in a condition which the best principles of general education will not materially affect, and a few years hence they will become an overwhelming burden to society, from which no political expedients will afford a permanent relief.

POETRY.

In Original Poetry, the Name, real or assumed, of the Author, is printed in small Capitals under the title; in Selections it is printed in Italics at the end.]

THE BARD'S LAMENT.

H

I ne'er again may wake a strain in which my heart may share,
When pleasure brought no bitter thought, nor folly cost a tear;
My Harp upon the willow hangs, and leaves me to repine,
It never more will yield to me the music of " Lang Syne!"

There let it murmur to the breeze as Heaven may chance to blow,
All warm and sweet the summer greet, like winter stormy grow,
Warble to spring as wild birds sing, with autum's notes decline—
So fitful would my feelings be to sing thee of " Lang Syne!"

Yoxford.

FAREWELL.

Who hath not shed the silent tear!
Who hath not felt his bosom swell
With grief that could not be suppress'd,
When came the parting word—farewell!

Who ever left his native shore,
In far and stranger land to dwell;
But treasur'd in his memory still,
The look that spoke the long—farewell!

Joyful, the Captive drops his chain,
But ere he quits his gloomy cell,
The only voice that cheer'd him there,
Shall pain him with its sad—farewell!

'Tis sorrow's note wherever heard,
Its power, the dark magician's spell,
It checks the smile that fain would play,
But withers in the deep—farewell!

Yet 'tis a word we all must breathe
Like a departed spirit's knell,
It strikes with anguish on the heart,
'Tis broken with the last—farewell!

Soham.

SONG.

H

" I am always sad when I hear sweet Music."
SHAKSPEARE.

Do not marvel, dear maids, when ye leave
me, to see
The tear of despondency starting,

Since friendship, thro' life when it visited
me,
Seemed to bring less of pleasure than
parting:

Your voices this eve filled my ear with
delight,
And ere long may be charming another's;
Bright eyes, I have bask'd in your lustre
to night,
And to-morrow ye'll shine upon others.

As the butterfly gossips with every flower
So from circle to circle ye flutter,
Unhinging young hearts with your fairy-
like power,
And the soft, siren notes that ye utter:
Oh, is it a pleasure, or is it a pain,
When, (tho' true as the needle to duty)
The heart for an hour is whirl'd round
like the vane
To each point in the compass of beauty.

Dear friendships of youth, shrin'd in
memory's urn,
Oh! sweet beyond Poet's expressing!
Ere from me ye are passing no more to
return,
With a sigh, I bequeathed you my
blessing!
Go—charm younger bosoms,—on mine
but reflect
The calm sunset of visions gone o'er me
Though I may not renew let me still re-
collect
The delight ye can never restore me!
Yoxford.

THE HOME OF MY CHILDHOOD.

CHARLES HASSEL.

The home of my childhood is dear to me
    still,
  Though now it is far from my sight;
Let me stray through the wide world
    wherever I will,
  I think of it still with delight.

To many an eye it may have but few
    charms;—
  They may call it but barren and wild;
But a sight of those scenes my fond
    heart ever warms,
  Where I roam'd, when a free happy
    child.

My fancy still pictures the happy young
    throng,
  Who met me so joyously there;
When we danc'd to the sound of the lin-
    net's gay song,
  And our bosoms were strangers to care.

But ah! the bright vision recedes from
    my sight,—
  I may taste those pure pleasures no
    more,—
Those bright sunny days, when my
    young heart was light,
  Alas! they for ever are o'er.

But the uplands and meads, where in
    childhood I roved,
  Are still looking blooming and green,
And the tall rugged trees, whose cool
    shade I then lov'd,
  Still wave in their pride o'er the scene.

The chill blast of winter each rude limb
    may shake,
  And scatter their leaves o'er the plain,
Yet spring shall once more from her
    slumbers awake,
  And sun them to verdure again.

So I, when life's tempests around me,
    shall low'r,
  And I feel keen adversity's blast,
Would patiently bow, in the terrible hour
  On the firm ground of hope, rooted
    fast;

Till the drear course of time, like the
    winter, is o'er,
  And my spirit shall wing its last flight,
Beyond the earth's bounds, and shall joy-
    ously soar
  To the realms of unceasing delight.
    Richmond.

A cloud lay cradled near the setting sun,
A gleam of crimson tinged its braided
    snow,
Long had I watch'd its glory moving on,
O'er the still radiance of the lake below;
Tranquil its spirit seem'd and floated slow,
E'en in its very motion there was rest,
While every breath of eve that chanced
    to blow,
Wafted the traveller to the beauteous
    west;
Emblem methought of the departed soul,
To whose bright robe the gleam of bliss
    is given,
And by the breath of mercy made to roll,
Right onward to the gates of Heaven;
Where to the eye of faith it peaceful lies,
And tells to man his glorious destinies.
    Professor Wilson.

OUR CHILDREN'S PAGE.

FACTS WORTH REMEMBERING

Leap year is the year which divides evenly by 4.

Epiphany, or Twelfth Day, celebrates the arrival of the Wise Men
    from the East.

Plough Monday, was the feast of the Plough, in honor of Agriculture.

The Purification, or Candlemas, celebrates the Jewish ceremony of
    the presentation of the Mother of Jesus.

Quadragesima Sunday is the first Sunday in Lent. On Ash Wednes-
    day commences the 40 days of Lent.

MISCELLANY AND EXTRACTS.

WIND moving 3 miles an hour is scarcely felt; 6 miles is a pleasant breeze ; 20 or 30 is a brisk gale ; 60 is a storm ; and beyond 80 a hurricane.

SOME idea of the velocity of a cannon ball may be formed from the consideration, that, if shot horizontally upon a plane, it would reach the ground at the same moment as it would have done if let fall from the cannon's mouth, although it would go about 800 feet in that time.

WHEN a ship founders near the shore, the wreck generally floats, and is cast upon the beach ; but when she sinks in deep water, the great pressure forces water into the pores of the wood, and renders it so heavy that no portion ever rises to reveal her fate.

IN the reign of Elizabeth, the Laws of England were denied to the Irish, although eagerly requested; and the wretched natives, neither secure in property nor life, fled to the woods and bogs for shelter: and looking on mankind in general, and the English in particular, as their enemies, made reprisals on any stranger who fell into their hands. *Henry's History.*

MAJOR RENNELL estimates that the river Ganges imports daily into the bay of Bengal, in the flood season, a quantity of mud, which is nearly equal in weight to 74 times the great Pyramid of Egypt.

LIGHT, from whatever source it proceeds, is composed of the various coloured rays that paint the grass, the flowers, and every coloured object in nature. Take away the light, and these beautiful tints disappear, and every object becomes colourless, or black. Their colours are caused by their absorbing rays of light of a certain colour, and reflecting others. Thus, for example, the leaves of plants and trees reflect both blue and yellow rays, and therefore their appearance is green, which is a combination of these colours.

THE great coral reef, on the last coast of New Holland, extended unbroken for 350 miles, forming with others, more or less connected with it, a reef of upwards of 1,000 miles in length, and varying from 20 to 50 in breadth.

SOUND, strictly speaking, is a perception excited in the mind by the motion of the air on the nerves of the ear. There is no sound in a drum or a trumpet, or a bell,—these are merely instruments by which that peculiar species of motion is communicated to the air, which, falling upon the nerves of the ear, causes the sensation of sound. The vibration of the air, which we call sound, extends in all directions around the body by which it is excited, in waves of condensation and rarefaction, which move at the rate of about 1142 feet in a second. The uniform velocity enables us to determine the distance of the object from whence it proceeds, as that of a cannon, or a thunder cloud. If we do not hear the thunder till half a minute after we see the lightning, we conclude the cloud to be at the distance of six miles and a half.

THE pains we take in books or arts, which treat of things remote from the use of life, is a busy idleness. If I study, it is for no other science than what treats of the knowledge of myself, and instructs me how to live and die well.

Montaigne.

THE world is like a vast sea: mankind like a vessel sailing on its tempestuous bosom. Our prudence is its sails : the sciences serve us for oars : good or bad fortune are the favourable or contrary winds, and judgement is the rudder. In a word, obscurity and indigence are sometimes the parents of vigilance and economy ; vigilance and economy, of riches and honour ; riches and honour, of pride and luxury ; pride and luxury, of impurity and idleness ; and impurity and idleness may again produce indigence and obscurity. Such are the revolutions of life !

Goldsmith.

THE best resolution we can take is to suffer with patience what we cannot alter; and to pursue, without repining, the road which Providence has marked out to us; for it is not enough to follow; and he is but a bad soldier who sighs and marches on with reluctancy. We must receive the orders with spirit and cheerfulness, and not endeavour to slink out of the post which is assigned us in this beautiful disposition of things, whereof even our sufferings make a necessary part.

Bolingbroke.

FALSE hopes and false terrors are equally to be avoided. Every man who proposes to grow eminent by learning, should carry in his mind at once the difficulty of excellence, and the force of industry; and remember that fame is not conferred, but as the recompense of labour, and that labour, vigorously continued, has not often failed of its reward.

Johnson.

VIRTUE is to be considered, not in the light of mere innocence, or abstaining from harm; but as the exertion of our faculties in doing good.

WHEN Aristotle was once asked what a man could gain by uttering falsehoods, he replied, " not to be credited when he shall tell the truth."

MY young readers must excuse me for calling upon them to acquire, while their minds may be impressed with new images, a love of innocent pleasures, and an ardour for useful knowledge; to remember that a blighted spring makes a barren year; and that the vernal flowers, however beautiful and gay, are only intended as preparatives for autumnal fruits.

Johnson.

WISDOM and knowledge do not always go together. There may be wisdom without knowledge, and knowledge, without wisdom. A man without knowledge, if he walk humbly with his God, and live in charity with his neighbours, may be wise unto salvation. A man without wisdom may not find his knowledge avail him quite so well. But it is he who possesses both that is the true philosopher. The more he knows, the more he is desirous of knowing; and yet the farther he advances in knowledge, the better he understands how little he can attain, and the more deeply he feels that God alone can satisfy the infinite desires of an immortal soul. To understand this is the height and perfection of philosophy.

NATURE has perfections, in order to show that she is the image of God; and defects, in order to show that she is *only* his image. *Pascal.*

MONTHLY NOTICES.
AUGUST.

On the first of this month, and until two Sundays have elapsed, County Lists to be fixed on Church and Dissenting Chapel doors.

11. County Court, at Crown Inn, Soham.

20. Last day for leaving with the Overseers objections to County Electers.

25. Last day for service of objections to Electors on their Tenants.

29. Overseers of Parishes or Townships to send list of Electors and number of objections to the High Constable of the Hundreds.

Churchwardens and Overseers are to make out before the first day of September, a list of all persons qualified ro serve on juries, and affix a copy of such list on the three first Sundays in September on the Church or Chapel door.

PLAYFORD'S

SOHAM MAGAZINE,

AND

Friendly Monitor.

SEPTEMBER, 1847.

NE of the greatest evidences of individual and national apostacy from God is, the desecration of the Sabbath Day. For, as this day was a sign by which the Israelites might know that God was their sanctifier, and their deliverer from Egyptian slavery, so it is a sign by which every christian may discover his personal interest in the promises and privileges of the gospel. Considered in this light, it must be a matter of deep concern to all who are imbued with right sentiments upon the subject, to observe the growing indifference towards the sanctity of this day, which has become so apparent among us. And we shall esteem ourselves happy, if, from a brief view of its nature and obligations, we should be instrumental, in any degree, towards its more religious regard. Every one acquainted with the recent history of a neighbouring country will remember that the abolition of the observance of the Sabbath Day was one of the chief acts of that infidel and awful power which deluged the streets of Paris with blood, and which, setting up the image of silence amid their graves, proclaimed to the world their impious hope, that death was only an eternal sleep! May our highly-favoured country be ever preserved from so frightful a desolation ;—a desolation in which all the worst propensities of human nature seemed to combine, till the cup of human misery was poured out to the very dregs, and the principal actors in the tragedy were themselves crushed beneath the engine of their own devising, amid the execrations of the civilized world.

No. 9. Vol. I.   K

In the first place then we may notice, that the first day of the week has been set apart for the uses of religion, from the earliest ages of christianity: for the history of the acts of the apostles bears the fullest testimony to this fact. The observance of the *seventh* day of the week having been closely connected with the Jewish law, it was abrogated at the commencement of the christian dispensation, when the shadows of that law were dissipated for ever, by the rising of the Sun of Righteousness. "It appears from Gen. ii., 3, (says Bishop Tomline) that God "blessed the seventh day and sanctified it;" and thus ordained, that every seventh day, or one day in seven, should be exempted from the ordinary cares and business of the world, and more immediately dedicated to religious uses, and the service of God. This ordinance which, from the nature of its origin, must necessarily be binding on all mankind, was repeated as one of the ten commandments given on mount Sinai, which our Lord expressly declared to be of perpetual obligation, (Matt. v., 17, 19.) The strict observance of the seventh day, or Sabbath, was enforced upon the Jewish nation by peculiar commands, adapted to the general tenor of institutions designed to separate them from the rest of the world, and declared to be founded in circumstances peculiar to that people (Deut. v. 18.) These positive injunctions, designed to commemorate their deliverance from Egyptian bondage, which was "a shadow of things to come," (Col. ii., 17) were of a temporary nature, and ceased to be binding on them when the Jewish law was abrogated by the coming of the Messiah; and the Saviour of the world having risen from the dead on the first day of the week, that day was then appointed to be set apart for the purpose of religious worship, *according to the original institution at the creation,* to commemorate the emancipation of all mankind from the power of sin and death. The sacred writers do not mention that the apostles received any express direction to make this change in the day, which had been so long appropriated to the service of God; but, as we know that they acted by inspiration on all occasions where religious doctrines or duties were concerned, it is impossible to doubt their authority on this point; and indeed this change seems clearly to have been sanctioned by the appearance of Christ in the midst of them, when they were assembled together, (John xx. 19,) and by the descent of the Holy Ghost, both on the first day of the week.

It is difficult to imagine circumstances more strikingly calculated to prove the universal and perpetual obligation of devoting the seventh day, or one day in seven, as "holy unto the Lord," and the abolition of the Jewish ritual by the establishment of christianity."

To these remarks we may add, that as our Lord continued forty days with his disciples after his resurrection, "speaking of the things pertaining to the kingdom of God," (Acts i. 3.) that is, directing them concerning the government of His kingdom or church on earth, we may rest assured of his full sanction, if not of his express direction for the change; and that in this, as well as in every other catholic practice, we are fulfilling the will of the divine Author of our holy religion.

The observance of the Sabbath in the Patriarchal ages, before the time of Moses, may be traced in various parts of the Old Testament. Noah, for instance, having sent forth the dove from the ark at intervals of seven days. (Gen. viii. 10, 12.) It appears as if he expected a blessing on the seventh day rather than on any other: it being the day devoted from the beginning to religious services. It is also spoken of by Moses himself, (Exod. xvi.) as a day of rest, previous to the institution of the ceremonial law.

With regard to the observance of this day by the early christians, we find from heathen sources, that it was very strict and uniform. Pliny, for example, in his letter to the Roman Emperor Trajan, written probably only six years after the death of the evangelist St. John, says, that he found nothing to allege against the Christians, except their obstinacy in their superstition, and their custom of meeting together on a set day before it was light, and binding themselves by a sacrament to do no evil. Justin Martyr also, who wrote about forty years after the death of the same apostle, states, that on Sunday, as the day of our Lord's resurrection, all the Christians met together to read publicly the writings of the Apostles and Prophets; that, after this, the president made an oration to them, exhorting them to imitate and practise the things which they had heard, and that, after joining in prayer, they used to celebrate the sacrament and to give alms.

"It is a gross mistake says, Bishop Horsley, to consider the Sabbath as a mere festival of the Jewish Church, deriving its whole sanctity from the Levitical law. The contrary appears, as well from the evidence of the fact, which sacred history affords, as from the reason of the thing, which the same history declares. The religious observance of the seventh day has a place in the Decalogue among the very first duties of natural religion. The reason assigned for the injunction is general, and has no particular relation or regard to the Israelites. The creation of the world was an event equally interesting to the whole human race ; and the acknowledgment of God, as our Creator, is a duty in all ages and in all countries, epually incumbent on every individual of mankind. The worship of the Christian Church is properly to be considered as a restoration of the Patriarchal in its primitive simplicity and purity : and of the Patriarchal worship, the Sabbath was the noblest and perhaps the simplest rite." The obligation, therefore, upon Christians to comply with the religious odservance of Sunday arises from the authority of Apostolic practice, and the express sanction, *at least*, of the great head and ruler of the Church.

The chief uses proposed by it are :—

1. To facilitate attendance upon public worship.

2. To meliorate the condition of the laborious classes of mankind, by regular and seasonable returns of rest.

3. By a general suspension of business and amusement, to invite and enable persons of every description to apply their time and thoughts to subjects appertaining to their salvation.

" The duty of the day is therefore violated, as Archdeacon Paley observes, first, by all such employments or engagements as (though differing from our ordinary occupation) hinder our attendance upon public worship, or take up so much of our time as not to leave a sufficient part of the day at leisure for religious reflection ; as the going of journeys, the paying or receiving of visits which engage the whole day, or employing our time at home writing letters, settling accounts, or in applying ourselves to studies, or the reading of books, which bear no relation to the business of religion.

Secondly, by unnecessary encroachments on the rest and liberty which Sunday ought to bring to the inferior orders of the community ; as by keeping servants on that day confined and busied in superfluous preparations for our comfort or convenience.

Thirdly, by all such recreations as are customarily forborne out of respect to that day ; as fishing, public diversions, frequenting taverns, and playing at cards or dice. "

Does the conscience, then, of one of our readers tell him that he has been guilty of any of these things ? Let him be persuaded to a wiser and happier course. Let him no longer employ the sacred hours of the Sabbath about his temporal gains, or the empty politics of the world, but remember the account he must shortly give at the bar of eternal justice, who will render to "every man according as his work shall be." Let him shun the dark retreats of the drunkard, the sensual, and the vile, where the language of blasphemy and licentiousness is continually falling upon the ear ; and apply himself diligently to the study of his Bible, "while the evil days come not, nor the years draw nigh when he shall say, I have no pleasure in them."

ECONOMICAL HINTS TO COTTAGERS.

Continued from Page 122.

When an infant is newly-born, you should never omit giving it a tea-spoonful of castor oil ; it prevents many complaints that they are subject to ; and may be often repeated with great safety when their bowels are disordered. I, by no means, recommend magnesia, which lies cold and heavy on the infant's stomach, and should never be given alone.—In case of eruption, as measels, chicken-pock, &c., if the complaint come out freely, a very small quantity of weak onion-tea often assists it ; but you must be very careful, for it is rather powerful when too strong. Never be persuaded to give an infant any sleeping medicine, for you may depend on it, if they are cross, they only want a little aperient medicine, and I know of none more efficient than castor oil. You add to their uneasiness by giving them what only lulls them for a few hours, as it confines their bowels when they ought to be relaxed, In the hooping cough, nothing relieves the patient so much as slight emetics, but of these I speak with caution, as they are dangerous to tamper with. You cannot, however do harm by rubbing the chest every night with some oily substance, and keeping it warm with flannel. I also believe that the sugar and vinegar is very serviceable in this complaint, as it relieves the chest.

As agues are so prevalent here, the most frugal and ready remedy, you will be surprised to hear, is the *snuff* of the *candle.* Strange as it may appear, it is now frequently used with great success. You may mix it with a little honey, treacle, or some other sweet that may disguise it, and you need not tell your patient what it is. Bark and snake root, mixed in beer or wine, is another remedy ; but the most certain cure is the quinine, bark, which now most druggists know how to make up in proper quantities. It is, however, a very dear medicine. Cayenne pepper, or a large quantity of ginger taken in warm beer or spirits, often stops it at first. You know I, by accident, found out the most simple and pleasant remedy for a scald or burn, that is, putting the part afflicted into the hottest water you can bear your hand in (an infant, of course, could not bear it so warm) and keeping it there for a considerable time, adding to the heat of the water as it cools, till, on your taking it out, you feel no return of the pain, if so, you return it to the water again, and add again to the heat of it.—You feel no pain in this case, but in the first plunge, which you must not mind being very severe, If the skin is broken, put on some of the following ointment, which you can easily make in summer :—to a pound of sweet hog's lard add a quarter of a pound of mutton suet melted, and poured in a little at a time, till all is well mixed, with a table-spoonful of salt.—Get all the rose leaves you can, and put some in every day, working it well with your hands, for as long as you can get rose leaves.—Then put it into a jar tied close down, and set it in a kettle of water, stirring it now and then till in a liquid state, taking care that no water gets in.— Then strain it through a fine sieve into a basin, and, when settled from the lees, pour it off into small vessels for use : you may make a quarter of the quantity, which will last a long time.   I have just heard of a recipe for weak eyes, which may be of service to you at some time or other.   It is 20 grains of sugar of lead, mixed in a pint of water, and to a small tea-cupful of this liquid. add 5 drops of laudanum, when you use it.—You must take great care of it, as the sugar of lead is a *strong poison*.   Brandy and water, in equal proportions, is very strengthening to the eyes, used every morning.   For a sudden pain in the stomach, you cannot have any thing more simple than a little ginger tea, made very hot.—Pepper mixed also, either the oil of it, or on a lump of sugar, or the plant itself made into tea, is often very efficacious.   If you are ever rich enough to possess a clock, you may save yourself the expense of a watchmaker in regulating it, by the following method :— take hold of the pendulum in your left hand, resting the weight on your thumb. If you want it to go faster, turn the nut at the bottom a little to the right; if slower, to the left.   You will easily perceive whether it rises from, or falls on your thumb, and stop as soon as you feel the motion.

To be Continued,

A PEEP INTO CANTON.

THE sail from Hong-Kong to Canton is very interesting, particularly to a stranger. The numerous islands he passes, and the entirely new scenes that everywhere attract his eye, cannot fail to delight and amuse him.   Here, the unwieldly Chinese junk ; there, the fast-sailing Chinese passage-boat ; now and then, the long snake-like opium smuggler, with his fifty oars ; innumerable fishing-boats, all in pairs, with a drag-net extended from one to the other ; country boats of all descriptions passing to and fro, their crews all bent on money-getting, yet never failing to cast a glance of mingled contempt and scorn at the " *Fanqui* ; " the duck-boats on the river banks, their numerous tenants feeding in the adjacent rice-fields ; a succession of little Chinese villages, with groups of young celestials staring at him with never-ending wonder ; here and there a tall pagoda, rearing its lofty head high above the sur- rounding scenery, as if conscious of its great antiquity and of the sacred objects for which it was built ; the Chinese husbandman, with his one-handled plough, drawn by a single wild-looking buffalo ; smiling cottages, surrounded with orange and other fruit-trees ; the immense fleet of foreign ships anchored at Whampoa ; these, and a thousand other objects equally strange and new, attract the attention of the stranger, as he sails up the " Quang Tung " river.   On nearing the city itself, he is still more astonished and pleased with the sights that literally confuse his ideas, making the whole scene to seem the creation of magic, rather than sober reality. Here, the river is absolutely crowded with junks and boats of all sorts and sizes, from the ferry-boat of six feet long to the ferry-boat of a thousand tons burden. Long rows of houses, inhabited principally by boat builders and others connected with maritime affairs, and built on the river, line its right bank.   Outside of these, are moored numerous flat-bottomed boats with high roofs ; these come from the interior with tea and other produce, and resemble what I fancy Noah's Ark must have been, more than anything I have seen elswhere. On the left bank, the shore is lined with boats unloading and loading cargoes, while the different landing-places are completely blocked up with ferry-boats seeking employment. The space in the centre of the river is continually crowded with boats, junks, &c., proceeding up and down. The scene altogether is bewildering to the stranger. Busy as the scene is which the Thames presents at London, its superior regularity and order, in my opinion, prevent its coming up to the scene I have just faintly traced, in the strange and excited feelings it calls up. Amidst all this, there is a constant clatter of tongues strongly recalling the confusion of Babel. A Chinaman never talks below his breath; and if one may judge from the loud tones in which the whole community express their sentiments, whether in a house or a shop or in the street, the only conclusion that can be come to is, that in China, the word secret is not understood, or rather, that the idea corresponding to that word has no existence in their conceptions.

Of the immense city itself, the home of a million of souls, what account can a traveller give who has seen little more than the portion inhabited by foreigners? I must say a few words, however, about that part of it which I have seen.

I begin with the foreign factories. These buildings stretch along the left bank of the river about three-quarters of a mile, (or rather, they did so, for one-half of them have recently been destroyed by fire,) and extend back about two hundred yards. They are large, substantially built, and comfortable houses; but those situated behind the front row must be (indeed, I know they are) oppressively hot residences in the summer season. The space between the factories and the river is reserved for a promenade, where foreigners may take a little recreation after their day's work. Although but a limited space, it is invaluable. Here, in the evening, may be seen Englishmen, Americans. Frenchmen, Spaniards, Dutchmen, Portuguese, Parsees, Moslem, and Hindoos; all enjoying the evening breeze, and talking over the affairs of the day, or the news brought by the last overland mail, while a crowd of Chinese coolies surround the square, gaping with noisy wonder at the strangers attired in all the costumes of Europe and Asia. The streets principally resorted to by foreigners are China Street (old and new) and Carpenters Square. In the former, a very choice collection of Chinese articles may be purchased, either in the way of curiosities or of valuable merchandize. In Carpenter's Square, the new-comer may fit himself out with everlasting trunks, dressing-cases, &c.; or if in search of furniture, he may here, in half an hour, furnish his house with well-made, substantial articles. The houses in these streets are all of two stories, with very narrow frontage, ground being valuable. A large quantity of timber is used in their construction, which renders any chance fire in this city so very destructive. The streets in Canton are all very narrow, most of those I have seen, not exceeding six or seven feet in width; the two China streets are probably twelve feet wide. The city does not cover half the space which a European one with the same population would do. Its streets, from their want of breadth, always appear, and indeed always are crowded; and the unwary passenger is very liable to get knocked down by some heavily-laden porter running out against him if he does not keep a sharp look out. Like Macao, it is infested with loathsome beggars, who are, if possible, still more clamorous in their demands for charity than those of that place. Here the stranger will be surprised to see dogs, cats, and rats hawked about, dead and alive. I do not say that these animals form the daily food of the people of Canton, but they are daily and hourly hawked about its streets and purchased by the poorer classes. The Canton market is, nevertheless, remarkably well supplied with the good things of this life; and the European who cannot live and be contented with the provisions procurable in it, must be hard to please. By nine o'clock at night, this huge city is perfectly quiet, and nine-tenths of its inhabitants are wrapped in sleep. At either end of each street is a gate, which is shut at that hour, and ingress or egress put a stop to for the night. This regulation, as may be supposed, is an excellent check upon night robbers, whose peregrinations can extend no further than the end of the street they live in. Another equally salutary regulation is that which makes the inhabitants of the street responsible for each other's good conduct. Thus, if A's servant steals anything from B, A must make good the loss. Prowling being put a stop to during the night, I have seen robberies attempted and detected during the day; and I certainly never saw a poor thief treated elswhere with such unrelenting cruelty. A Chinaman seems to have no mercy for a thief; nor is this feeling to be wondered at in an over-peopled country, where all have to work for their bread and where idlers are sure to starve. During the winter, in Canton, the lower classes suffer severely from cold ; they are poorly fed and worse clothed; and hundreds of them may be seen about the streets, shivering and looking the very picture of absolute wretchedness. Amongst these, a few old women may be seen sitting by the side of the streets earning a scanty subsistence by mending and patching the clothes of people as poor as themselves. These poor women, having all undergone the barbarous operation of cramping the feet during infancy, are consequently unable to undertake anything but sedentary employment to gain their bread. The very small size to which the feet of some of the Chinese females have been distorted by cramping them with bandages during the first six years of their lives, is almost beyond belief. I have seen a full-grown woman wearing shoes, and walking in them too, not more than three and a half inches long. Their walk resembles that of a timid boy upon ice; it is necessarily slow; and, indeed, some of them require the aid of a staff in one hand while they lean with the other on the shoulder of a female attendant. The smaller the eyes and feet of a Chinese beauty the more she is admired. I once asked a respectable Chinaman what he thought of this custom of cramping their daughters' feet? His reply was, "Very bad custom." On my inquiry further, whether he had any daughters, and whether their feet were treated in the same way, he answered in the affirmative, but asserted, that they had been subjected to the cruel ordeal by their mother against his will. He added, that in a Chinaman's house, where there were young girls, no peace could be had, night or day, for their cries, which lasted till they were six years old. He gave us a reason for the mother's insisting on her daughters' submitting to this long course of pain and suffering. "Suppose *he* no small foot, no man wantjee make *he* number one wife." A respectable Chinaman, it appears, chooses a small-footed woman for his principal wife, while for number two, three, and four, he contents himself with ladies whose feet are as nature made them, and who are, consequently, more able to make themselves useful in household matters. *Davidson's " Trade and Travel in the Far East.*

‑‑•‑‑

OUR TOWN.

IT would really be a just punishment of those who are continually prating about antiquity, and who condemn every thing that is modern because it *is* such, to put them, if possible, down to the savagery of a thousand years ago. The world has been travelling onward as regularly as day-light, and our forefathers were only gropers in the darkness, whilst we are moving in open and conscious noontide. This statement gains especial force when applied to our own country, and the most emphatic illustration when referred to " Our Town."

One may imagine its condition, when perched on a tiny hillock elevation, it looked like an unsubmerged relic of the Adamic world. There was its large religious house, its residence of monks, nodding dutiful respect to its superior of Ely. Miles around presented a waste of waters, and truth, like Noah's dove found no other resting place for the sole of its foot. Let me send away to this age the misanthrope and grumbler, and try whether his sentimentality could find food for entertainment, in an isolation more dread and horrible than that of Napoleon at Helena, and not less frightful than the maddest fiction ever depicted.—Fancy, may draw upon winds whistling through endless osier beds, the flapping wing and discordant note of water fowl, and the dull tone of monastic bell, but let me prefer the honest facts and circumstances of the year of our Lord, 1847. At such a period, " Our Town" was made up only of a sombre brotherhood and their retainers, for few, save the seekers of hospitality, ever put foot, within the precincts of the monastery. Here, was a clustering spot of the charity, learning, and piety of the times, and hence issued all the tones of music and devotion, that arose toward heaven for miles. One can hardly decide the reason, why these good brethren clung to this wild spot, whether they were really, the conservators of morals and letters, waiting the times of their favourable extension ; or, whether they were carnal enough to love loneliness, for laziness sake, and a ghostly life, for good living.—Modern historians have made their own comments, and broached their own opinions on the subject, but the better and undoubted authority of Bede, makes their religion, a system of gross error, tyranny, and superstition, and shows that the public mind, from peasant to prince, felt its grovelling subjugation. Thank God for these better times, when, if men fall into moral error, they at least do it wittingly, and in the blaze of day. If indeed these men were learned, and such they were, they had the craft to use their learning illegitimately, and became only the more expert, in chaining down the minds, binding the consciences, and putting out the mental eyes of the nation, and therefore we cannot but rejoice for the period, when Providence permitted the barbarous Vikingr, or Sea Kings, to break up these cells,—to take the bushel off the candlestick,—to scatter this Alphabet to the common use.

Who can really think of the broils of the heptarchy without a shudder ; or, contemplate the bead roll, of the potentates of East Anglia, without dismay. Where *might* took the place of *right*, and the throne was oftener wrested, by violence and murder, than by less harmful means, and whilst occupied, only held by an ignorant and imbruted potentate,—who can think that personal safety could be ensured, much less, that any of those arts should be discovered, and appliances resorted to, that mould and fashion a people, and put them into a disposition, for the almost spontaneous growth of virtue. So many independent states, would naturally enough, soon blend into one kingdom. Streams adjacent, are prone to seek a common course, and, although their junction may be cut out by the sword, yet, we are wont to justify the means, by the results which ensue.

It gratifies us to trace the onward struggles of liberty and enlightenment, now chained, then under a cloud, now receiving new impulses, again being retarded, until the last and bravest prince of the Saxon Line, found defeat and death, under the power and arms of the Norman William, who, making important modifications of the English Constitution, and material additions, laid the ample platform of our laws, and opened out the way to that national glory and honour, which make us now, the envy and admiration of the world. " Our Town," then, has put on more phases than autumn presents, and shown as many hues as the chameleon, yet, slow as have been its transitions, it has been moving onward. It has been pumped and drained into territorial existence, and dragged itself out of the bog, like an Alligator from the slime of the Nile. This Soham, of Saxon Times, begotten in ignorance, nurtured at the very teats of barbarity, and dandled in the arms of superstition, made its bow to the rigorous court of William, and, taking up the complexion and usages, common to the reigns of nearly eight hundred years, stands out, in all the immunities of the blessed times of Victoria. It would be a wasteful and fruitless research, to enquire into our early social circumstances, for so tiny an affair as ourselves, is lost in the dust and distance of ages, to look for a needle in the bed of the Thames, would be as wise a pursuit, as to search for any particular record of Soham, in the tomes and folios of the historical writer of very remote times, but, what truth cannot entirely accomplish, imagination may help along, and those who do not like the peacock's feather, may pull it out if they please.

We shall not then stand on tip-toe, to fetch down the musty and clasped volume, but prefer the "Life and Times" of Soham, some two hundred years since, just as she seems to rise into a clear horizon, and cognizable form. Let us date from the stirring times of the Commonwealth, and see how our little microcosm has been affected, civilly, domestically, and morally.   G.

To be Continued,

THE RELATION OF ATHEISM TO A FUTURE STATE OF BEING.

BY JAMES STEELE.

MORAL writers, in describing the appalling consequences of atheism, enumerate, among others, a total oblivion of all the fears and hopes of a world beyond the grave. They tell us that the fool who says in his heart "there is no God," in the same spirit of absurd impiety says also there is no hereafter,—nought after death but "the dark, unbroken sleep of nothingness " But let us, in dealing with the atheist, ever bear in mind that the two points admit of being argued on different grounds. Independently altogether of the existence of a Supreme Being, we might argue for a future state on on the principle of a mere continued existence.

Discarding the idea of an infinite series of men, let us suppose a point in remote antiquity, in which one man was created. This being, whether the creation of chance, fate, or a fortuituous concussion of atoms, or whatever the atheist substitutes for a Supreme intelligent mind, might have started into existence with the intellect of a Newton. In this there is nothing incredible, even if the hypothesis of the atheist be admittted ; for surely the power, whatever it be, which created a mind capable of producing the Principia, might have conferred at once that vigour of intellect which was the growth of years. This man, on surveying but his solitary self, but the one unpeopled planet on which he stood, would, by a rapid act of thought, land in the inference that that which created him could create other beings, that that which had given existence to one planet could have given existence to others. He would not infer that creative energy had exhausted itself in him, and the place of his abode. Nor might this be all. On contemplating life, and if made aware, by any means, of its cessation at death, he would not fail to perceive that if there at first existed any energy sufficient to have called him into existence from nothing, that same energy could raise him from the dust, and make him to be again all that he was before.

All this the atheist could not deny. He may speak of the improbability of future being, but its possibility he must admit. His own existence does away with all difficulty in the case. His own reason must suggest that there is in *this*, ground for tormenting anxiety. The very uncertainty of the case generates doubts of the most harrassing description. The very fact that he may live for ever is sufficient to give a sting to every pleasure. The hand-writing upon the wall is that dread word—Eternity. He must, if he thinks at all, come to this awful conclusion,—the same power, however blind and unintelligent, which placed me here, may transpose me elsewhere ; it may perpetuate all the pains I feel, increase their number, and augment their intensity, and all this where no wisdom rules, where no mercy pities, where " chaos umpire sits," where all is hopeless woe and irremediable confusion. It may be that my future destination may be a happy one, but who can assure me that it will not equal in misery all the felicity which is fabled of the heaven of the New Testament ?

And such is Atheism. The man who, insensible to the multitudinous proofs of the divine existence and attributes which meet him on every hand, which press upon all his senses, which occupy in their succession every moment of his existence, can yet afford to deny his Creator, must, if he thinks at all upon his future destiny, contemplate but a chaos of disorder. Under the influence of that moral disease which he has suffered to obtain the mastery in his spirit, he can see no truth in religion, no God, no mercy, no life and immortality. Without believing in a place of punishment, he realizes, in his moments of most sober reflection, the essential evils of that place which, separated from the divine presence, contains the fire which never shall be quenched,—" the worm that will not sleep and cannot die."

NATURAL HISTORY.

THE HORSE.

VARIOUS and essential are the services performed by the animals of this tribe, to mankind. In many countries they are almost the only beasts of draught and burden that are empl6yed. They are gregarious, and in a wild state inhabit the most retired deserts. In the southern parts of Siberia large herds of them are occasionally seen. They are extremely swift, active, and vigilant; and have always a sentinel who gives notice to the herd of the approach of danger, by a loud neigh, on which they gallop off with astonishing rapidity. In Ukraine they are used as food. The Cossacks catch the wild horses on each side of the Don in the winter, by driving them into the vallies filled with snow, into which they plunge and are captured. Their excessive swiftness is such as entirely to exclude any other mode of taking them.

The horses of South America live in herds, some of which are said to consist of ten thousand. As soon as they perceive domestic horses in the field, they gallop up to them, caress, and by a grave and prolonged neighing, invite them to run off.

In Arabia they are found in their highest perfection, and are as dear to the Arabs as their own children. They are the fleetest animals of the desert, and are so well trained as to stop in their most rapid course by the slightest check of the rider.

The French consul at *Said* once offered to purchase the whole stock of a poor Arabian, which consisted of a mare, with an intention to send her to Louis XIV, the poor man having arrived with his magnificent courser, dismounted, and looking first at the gold, and then steadfastly at his mare, heaved a deep sigh:—"To whom is it (he exclaimed) that I am going to yield thee up? To Europerans! who will tie thee close, who will beat thee, who will render thee miserable! Return with me, my beauty, my jewel! and rejoice the hearts of my children!" As he pronounced the last words he sprang upon her back, and was out of sight almost in a moment.

The horses of the Bedouin Arabs, whose lives are spent in traversing the scorching sands, are able, notwithstanding the fervency of the sun, and the suffocating heat of the soil over which they pass, to travel three days without drinking, and are contented with a few handsful of dried beans given once in twenty-four hours.

But there are few countries that can boast a breed of Horses so excellent as our own. The English hunter, a portrait of which we have given above, is allowed to be among the noblest, most elegant, and useful animals in the world.

The celebrated race Horse "Childers" was capable of passing over eighty-two feet and a half, in a second of time : while, as it regards strength, a horse has been known to draw, for a short space, the weight of three tons, and to carry at one load the weight of more than nine hundred pounds.

OUR CHILDREN'S PAGE.

FACTS WORTH REMEMBERING.

A span was 11 inches nearly.   Ezekiel's reed was 10 ft. $11\frac{1}{8}$ ins.

Behold a wall on the outside of the house round about, and in the man's hand a measuring reed of six cubits long.—EZEKIEL, 40 c., 5 v.

A Sabbath Day's journey was 1155 yards; or about two-thirds of a mile.

Then returned they unto Jerusalem from the mount called Olivet, which is from Jerusalem, a Sabbath Day's journey.—ACTS, 1 c., 12 v.

Jerusalem is distant from London about 2000 miles.

Lady Day celebrates the Virgin's miraculous conception.

Palm Sunday celebrates Christ's entrance into Jerusalem.

Easter is the first Sunday after the first full moon that occurs after the 21st of March.

Ascension Day is forty days after Easter Sunday.

Whitsunday is 49 days after Easter Sunday.

Trinity Sunday is the next after Whitsunday.

Michaelmas is a festival in honour of Michael and the Angels, recorded in the Revelations.

Advent Sunday is that which is nearest to St. Andrew's Day.

St. Stephen and the Holy Innocents' celebrates the massacre of the first martyr; and the children by Herod.

All Saints' is a day of prayer for saints who have no special days.

POETRY.

[In Original Poetry, the Name, real or assumed, of the Author, is printed in small Capitals under the title; in Selections it is printed in Italics at the end.]

THE PANGS OF MEMORY.

She leaned upon her harp and sighed,—
  Deep thought had shadow'd o'er her
    brow;
In vain some lovely air she tried,
  Each chord, alas! was sorrow now.
There was a time when ev'ry string
  Would vibrate with her touch of joy:
Then Hope was young and blossoming,
  Then pleasure's dream had no alloy.
But Hope and Pleasure quickly fled,
  And left her but the wreck you see,
Those early blossoms withered,
  And what remains is misery.
The trembling strings too truly tell,
  That memory is busy there.
And each soft note's melodious swell
  Seems but the breathing of despair.
Soham.

HARVEST,

BY ONE OF THE THANKFUL.

"Praise God from whom all blessings flow."

Thank God for harvest! many a sigh
  Has travell'd onward for to day;
Thank God for harvest! many an eye
  Will wipe its sorrow all away,
For soaring lark, and glowing sun.
Tell happy harvest is begun.

How many days has it been said,
  Sometimes in hope, yet oft in fear,
" Give us this day our daily bread,"
  " Lord, let Thy goodness crown the
    year,
And whilst Thy priests and people pray,
  These threatened judgments turn away."

What is it makes the world so fair,
  And earth and heaven with music
    ring,
What gives this freshness to each air,
  That moves on Zephyr's noiseless
    wing;
And why with such spontaneous voice,
Does all the universe rejoice?

Each beast and bird no longer mute,
  In varied tones attune His praise;
Is man the most insensate brute,
  Shall he no song of triumph raise?
Shout Britain shout, with loud acclaim,
The honours of God's blessed name.

A thousand glittering blades are lift,
  With rustling music in their sound,
And nature's wooed and bounteous gift
  Falls a rich harvest on the ground.
Dejection, grief, and fear are fled,
And peace and plenty reign instead.

Soham Town's End.

THE THREE MANSIONS.

" O homeless and unsheltered head!"
  Desponding pilgrim, weep not so:
Three mansions are before you spread—
  To one you *must*, to all *may* go!

Each offers freely, and has room
  For all earth's travellers, rich and
    poor—
The House of God, His Heaven, the Tomb,
  Have each, for all, an open door.

Go lowly to the House of Prayer,
  With steadfast faith and contrite
    breast;
Then shall the Narrow House prepare
  For weary limbs, a welcome rest.

Cherish the three in daily thought—
  The House of God, the Grave, and
    Heaven,
And all by sin and sorrow wrought
  Shall pass away and be forgiven.

       Mrs. C. E. Richardson.

CONSCIENCE.

Conscience distasteful truths may tell,
But mark her sacred lessons well;
With her whoever lives at strife
Loses his better friend for life.

Dr. Lettsom's Moral Thermometer.

....

TEMPERANCE.

70—	WATER	Health Wealth, Serenity of mind,
60—	Milk and water	Reputation, long life and
50—	Small beer	Happiness,
40—	Cider and Perry . . . . . :	Cheerfulness,
30—	Wine	Strength and nourish-
20—	Porter . . :	ment—when taken only at meals, and in moder-
10—	Strong Beer	ate quantities.
0—		

INTEMPERANCE.

		Vices.	Disease.	Punishments.
10—	Punch . .	Idleness; . Peevishness	Sickness ;	Debt.
20—	Toddy . .	Quarreling . Fighting .	Tremours of the hands in the morning ;	
			Bloatedness ;	Black eyes.
30—	Grog, and	Lying ;	Inflamed eyes ;	Rags.
	Brandy and Water .	Swearing ; .	Red nose and face; Sore & swelled legs;	Hunger.
			Jaundice ;	Hospital.
40—	Flip & Shrub	Obscenity ; Swindling ;	Pains in the limbs, and burning in the palms of the	Poor House.
50—	Bitters infused in spirits Usquebaugh		hands, and soles of the feet ;	Jail.
	Hysteric Wa- ter	Perjury ;	Dropsy ;	Whipping.
			Epilepsy ;	
60—	Gin, Anniseed Brandy, Rum, and Wiskey in	Burglary ;	Melancholy ; Madness ;	The Hulks.
	the *morning*	Murder ;	Palsy ;	Botany Bay.
70—	Ditto, during the *Day* and *Night* . .	SUICIDE ;	Apoplexy ; DEATH ;	GALLOWS.

"After this the Judgment."

MISCELLANY AND EXTRACTS.

TIMOUR the Tartar exclaimed to the prostrate citizans of Damascus; "You behold me here, a poor, lame decrepid mortal. I am not a man of blood, and in all my wars I have never been the aggressor," Notwithstandnig this boast, millions of miserable victims were sacrificed at his command, and every great city of the east felt for years the loss of population. Human bodies, curiously piled to an immense height, marked the progress of his conquests; and two several pyramids on the road to Delhi, of one hundred thousand, and on the ruins of the venerable city of Bagdad, of ninety thousand heads, gratified his unnatural ferocity. The indignation of the Persians against the invaders, occasioned the murder of a few Moguls in the streets of Ispahan. But the conquered people repented their imperfect submission, and the skulls of seventy thousand Persians were piled in the forms of towers in the principal squares of the city.

THE rainbow is formed by the refraction of the sun's rays in their passage through a shower of rain, every drop of which acts as a prism, in separating the coloured rays as they pass through it. The union of these coloured rays produce white. This may be proved by painting a card in compartments with the seven prismatic colours, and whirling it rapidly on a pin. The card will appear white.

WATER is composed of minute particles which are not in contact, for spirits of wine may be poured into a glass quite full of water without increasing its bulk or making it overflow. A considerable quantity of salt may likewise be dissolved in water, with the same result, because the particles of salt will lodge themselves in the pores of the liquid, so that the salt and water together will not occupy more space than the water did alone.

SENSUALITY contaminates the body, depresses the understanding, deadens the moral feelings of the heart, and degrades man from his rank in the creation.

IT is pleasant to be virtuous and good, because that is to excel many others: it pleasant to grow better; because that is to excel ourselves: it is pleasant even to mortify and subdue our lusts; because that is victory: it is pleasant to command our appetites and passions, and to keep them in due order, within the bounds of reason and religion; because this is empire.

Modern discoveries have taught us that the sea, the earth, the air the clouds, are replete with a subtile and penetrating matter, which, while at rest, gives us no disturbance; but when excited to action, turns into a consuming fire, which no substance can exclude, no force can resist: so that the "elements," which are to "melt with fervent heat," want no accidental matter to inflame them: Since all things may be burnt up by that matter which now resides within them, and is only waiting for the word from its Creator.

HE that witholdeth corn, the people shall curse him: but blessing shall be upon the head of him that selleth it.
Proverbs xi, 26.

WHAT an anchor is to a ship in a dark night, on an unknown coast, and amidst a boisterous ocean, that is the hope of future happiness to the soul, when distracted by the confusions of the world. In danger it gives security; amidst general fluctuation, it affords one fixed point of rest.

CAN the stream continue to flow when cut off from the fountain? Can the branch flourish when torn away from the stock which gave it nourishment? No more can dependent spirits be happy when deprived of all union with the Father of spirits, and the fountain of happiness.

IF we delay till tomorrow what ought to be done to day, we overcharge the morrow with a burden which belongs not to it.

THE Outa Snake is about twenty-five inches long, and entirely white, except the top of the head, which is a deep shining black. These creatures always go in pairs, and it is remarkable that if one is killed, either by man or beast, the survivor will follow until it is either destroyed or obtains its revenge by biting the author of its bereavement. It has been known, under such circumstances to keep up the pursuit with the most patient perseverance, for upwards of three hundred miles.

INSCRIPTION FOR A WATCH PAPER.

Onward,
perpetually moving,
these faithful hands are ever proving,
how swift the hours steal by;
This monitory, pulse-like beating
Is constantly, methinks, repeating
Reader, be ready!
For perchance before these hands
have made one revolution more
life's spring is snap't,—
YOU DIE.

YOUNG minds cannot be too strongly impressed with the simple wonders of creation by which they are surrounded. In the race of life they may be passed by, the occupation of existence may not admit attention to them, or the unceasing cares of the world may smother early attainments, but they can never be injurious: they will give a bias to a reasoning mind, and tend, in some after thoughtful sobered hour, to comfort and to soothe.

MONTHLY NOTICES.

SEPTEMBER.

Churchwardens and Overseers are to make out before the first day of September, a list of all persons qualified to serve on juries, and affix a copy of such list on the three first Sundays in September on the Church and Chapel doors.

1. On this day, until two Sundays have elapsed, Lists of objections to County Electors to be affixed to Church and Chapel doors.

Between Fifteenth of September and the last day of October, Revising Barristers to hold their Courts.

15. County Court held at Soham. All Plaints for this Court must entered by the 4th.

PLAYFORD'S

SOHAM MAGAZINE,

AND

Friendly Monitor.

OCTOBER, 1847.

A MONG the many irresistible proofs of the truth of the Christian Religion, the literal fulfilment of prophecy, has ever claimed peculiar regard. To the pretended philosopher who affects to treat Revelation as a fable, it offers a species of evidence which cannot be met by a sneer, for it is a plain matter of fact, open to the observation of the world. It has been said by Mr. Hume, "that the Christian Religion, even at this day, cannot be believed by any reasonable person, without a miracle." Every prophecy is a miracle, and is even admitted to be such by this inconsistant writer; and yet, so great was his hatred towards the truth, that he steeled his heart against its reception to the last. Let it be remembered by all those who may be disposed to admire the vain reasonings of this unhappy man, that he was the apologist, if not the advocate for one of the grossest crimes that can be committed against society. Such is almost universally the history of unbelief: "professing themselves to be wise, they become fools:" "not liking to retain God in their knowledge, he gives them over to a reprobate mind:" they abhor the *purity* of the gospel, and therefore pour forth all the venom of their malignity against it.

The *doctrine of chances* (says Dr. Keith) or calculation of probabilities, has been reduced into a science, and is now in various ways of great practical use, and securely acted upon in the affairs of life. But it is altogether impossible that short sighted man could select, from the infinite multitude of the possible contingencies of distant ages, any one of such particular facts as abound in the prophecies; and it is manifest that, upon the principle of

No. 10.   Vol. I.   L

probabilities, the chance would be incalculable against the success
of the attempt, even in a single instance. But without enumerating
all the particulars included in the volume of prophecy respecting
the life, and character, and death of Christ,—the nature and extent
of Christianity,—the destruction of Jerusalem,—the fate of the
Jews in every age and nation,—the existing state of Judea, of
Ammon, Moab, Edom, Philistia, Babylon, Tyre, Egypt, the Arabs,
&c.—the Church of Rome, and the prophetic history which extends
throughout two thousand three hundred years; may it not be
assumed (though fewer would suffice, and though incontestible
evidence has been adduced to prove more than double the number)
that a *hundred* different particulars have been foretold and fulfilled?
What, then, even upon *these* data, is the chance that *all of them
would have proved true?* Such is the desparate hazard'to which the
unbeliever would trust, that it is *mathematically demonstrable*
that the number of chances against him is far greater than the
drops in the ocean, even if the whole world were one globe of
water. Such is the stake on which unbelievers put to certain peril
the interests of eternity.

By way of brief example, let us notice the prophecies respecting
the seven Churches of Asia, recorded in the 2nd. and 3rd. chapters
of the Revelation of St. John.

The CHURCH OF EPHESUS, after the commendation of their first
works, were accused of apostacy, and threatened with destruction,
except they should repent. The city was chiefly famous for the
temple of Diana, "whom all Asia worshiped," which was adorned
with one hundred and twenty-seven columns of Parian marble, each
of a single shaft, and sixty feet high, and which formed one of the
seven wonders of the world. It is said that twenty thousand people could easily have been seated in its theatre. But what is its
present condition? A few heaps of stone, and some miserable
mud cottages, occasionally tenanted by Turks, *without one Christian
residing there,* are all the remains of ancient Ephesus. It is described by different travellers, as a solemn and most forlorn spot.
The Epistle to the Ephesians is read throughout the world; but
there is none in Ephesus to read it now. They returned not to
their "first works," and the great city of Ephesus is no more.

The CHURCH SMYRNA was approved of as "rich," and no

judgment was denounced against it. They were warned of a tribulation of ten days (the ten years persecution of Dioclesian) and and were enjoined to be faithful unto death, and they would receive a crown of life. Unlike Ephesus, Smyrna is still a large city, containing nearly one hundred thousand inhabitants, with several Greek churches; and an English and other Christian ministers have resided in it: the light has indeed become dim, but the candlestick has not been wholly removed out of its place.

The CHURCH OF PERGAMOS is commended for not denying the faith in a time of persecution, and in the midst of a wicked city. But there were some in it who held doctrines which the Lord hated. Against them He was to fight with the sword of His mouth; and all were called to repent. But it is not said, as of Ephesus, that their candlestick would be removed out of its place. It still contains at least fifteen thousand inhabitants, of whom fifteen hundred are Greeks, and two hundred Armenians; each of whom has a church.

In the CHURCH OF THYATIRA, some tares were soon mingled with the wheat. He who hath eyes like unto a flame of fire discerned both. Against those to whom was given space to repent, and who repented not, great tribulation was denounced. These, then warned while on earth in vain, have long since passed, whither all are daily hastening, to the place where no repentance can be found, and no work be done. But there were those in Thyatira, who could save a city. It still exists, while greater cities have fallen, Mr. Hartly, who visited it in 1826, describes it as "embosomed in cypresses and poplars." The Greeks are said to occupy three hundred houses, and the Armenians thirty. Each of them have a church.

Tha CHURCH OF SARDIS differed from the churches of Pergamos and Thyatira, *they* had not denied the faith, but there were some evil doers among them, on whom, if they repented not, judgment was to descend. But in Sardis, though the church had been founded by an Apostle, there were only a few who had not apostatized from their faith. The state of Sardis now is a token that the warning given to her was in vain. The city was the capital of Lydia: the wealth of Crœsus its king was accumulated within its walls. But now, a few wretched mud huts, scattered among the ruins, are the only dwellings in Sardis. Turkish herdsmen are its only inhabitants. As the seat of a Christian Church, it has lost all it had to lose—*the name.* No Christians reside on the spot.

"And to the Angel of the CHURCH IN PHILADELPHIA write, these things saith, He that is holy, He that is true, He that hath the key of David, He that openeth, and no man shutteth, and shutteth, and no man openeth; I know thy works ; behold 1 have set before thee an open door, and no man can shut it ; for thou hast a little strength, and hast kept my word, and hast not denied my name.— Because thou hast kept the word of my patience, I also will keep thee from the hour of temptation, which shall come upon all the world," Rev. iii. 7, 8, 10. "Among the Greek Colonies and Churches of Asia (says Gibbon, the infidel,) Philadelphia is still erect ; a column in a scene of ruins." Divine service is performed every Sunday in five Churches. "Him that overcometh will I make a pillar in the temple of my God," even as Philadelphia, when all else fell around it, "stood erect," our enemies themselves being judges, "a column in a scene of ruins."

"Unto the Angel of the CHURCH OF THE LAODICEANS write,— I know thy works, that thou art neither cold nor hot : I would thou wert cold or hot. So then because thou art lukewarm, and neither cold nor hot, I will spue thee out of my mouth." *The character and the fate of lukewarm Christians is the same in every age.* Laodicea was the metropolis of the greater Phrygia. It was the mother Church of sixteen Bishoprics. Its three theatres, and the immense circus, which was capable of containing upwards of thirty thousand spectators, the remains of which are yet to be seen, give proof of the greatness of its ancient wealth and population, and indicate too strongly, that in the city where Christians were rebuked for their lukewarmness, there were multitudes who were "lovers of pleasure more than lovers of God." But there are no sights of grandeur, nor scenes of temptation around it now. Its own tragedy may be briefly told. lt was lukewarm, and neither cold nor hot, and therefore it was loathsome in the sight of God. It was loved, and rebuked, and chastened in vain. It has been blotted from the world. As described by Dr. Smith in his travels, it is "utterly desolated, aud without any inhabitant, except wolves, and jackals, and foxes."

Does then the Sceptic demand a miracle before he will believe the truths of the gospel? Here are seven, out of the multitude, which he may *see with his own eyes!* The fate of these seven Churches of Asia was predicted eighteen hundred years ago; and infidels themselves, without knowing it, have borne witness to its literal fulfilment. How contemptible do all the vain reasonings of man appear beside this naked fact! He then "that hath ears to hear, let him hear what the spirit saith unto the Churches."

—◆—

OUR TOWN.

Continued from Page 138.

The reign of the Martyr Charles was favourable to the increasing importance of "Our Town," he having granted certain assistance to the Duke of Bedford, in draining his large possessions in the fens.—One of the most violent opposers of these improvements, was a Mr. Oliver Cromwell, who, from this very act of stupidity, was recommended as an able man to be sent to parliament, as the *defender of the public rights!* Such a better state of drainage however ensued, as to cause an increase of population through all the low district, and Soham, although then a long and straggling place, was of some note from the number of its inhabitants. The plough had now been driven through many an acre of new and rich soil; the green slopes were dotted with sheep and herds; and many a sunny nook embosomed the cot of the bluff peasant of the fens.

The times were however far from tranquil, and, whatever either malignity or prejudice may say of Charles the First, it is certain that his enemies were base and merciless, and that his murder is a stain on our national escutcheon, and a sin, for which our country must ever bewail itself. The *defender of the public rights*, was the fell spirit that tracked upon the heels of this unhappy monarch, and, having dyed his ruffian hand in kingly blood, with sanctified hypocrisy, pleaded himself as God's agent, and held up the sacred volume as the text book of Revolution.—To gaze from the summit of our own age, on the revolting scenes of the Commonwealth, is enough to make us love "our glorious constitution" with renewed affection, as well as to teach us the value of just subordination and loyalty. The whole framework of society was now so disjointed, and the nation thrown into such a paroxysm of embroilment, as no other person but a *Protector* could have accomplished, Episcopacy being abolished, a host of erratic preachers scoured the country, and expounders of the gospel were started from every class of society, the military not excepted. Without entering upon all the profanities which were uttered by this herd, we may present a single instance of their extravagance from Walker's History of Independency.—"About this time, there came six soldiers into the parish church of Walton-upon-Thames, near twilight; Mr. Fawcet, the preacher there, not having till then ended his sermon. One of the soldiers had a lanthorn in his hand, and a candle burning in it, and, in the other hand, four candles not lighted. He desired the parishioners to stay awhile, saying he had a message from God unto them, and thereupon offered to go into the pulpit. But the people refusing to give him leave, he went into the church-yard, and there told them that he had a vision, wherein he had received a command from God to deliver his will to them on pain of damnation; consisting of five lights. (1,) That the Sabbath was abolished as unnecessary. And here, (quoth he) I should put out my first light, but the wind is so high I cannot kindle it. (2,) That tithes are abolished as Jewish and ceremonial, and here I should put out my second light, &c, (3,),That ministers are abolished as antichristian and of no longer use, now Christ himself descends into the hearts of his saints, and enlightens them with revelations and inspiration. And here I should, &c. (4,) Magistrates are abolished as useless, now that Christ himself is in purity amongst us, and hath erected the kingdom of the saints upon earth. And here, &c. (5,) Then, putting his hand into his pocket, and pulling out a little bible, he shewed it open to the people, saying, Here is a book you have in great veneration, I must tell you it is abolished; it containeth beggarly elements, milk for babes; I am commanded to burn it before your eyes. Then putting out the candle, he said, And here my fifth light is extinguished."

Remember too, that yon venerable and beautiful church of our own, could tell of polluted ruffians pacing its sacred precints, of soldier parsons spouting blasphemy and treason from its pulpits, and of an infatuated mob joining in their declamation. If the quiet rest of the grave could be broken into, and human dust become vocal, he who was consecrated to the offices of the sanctuary, and who Sabbath after Sabbath fed the people with the word of truth, and with uplifted hands prayed that "we, being defended from the fear of our enemies, may pass our time in rest and quietness,"—if the broken-hearted parish priest could revisit the glimpses of the moon, he could tell us how he prayed betwixt the porch and the altar, wept away the watches of the night, supplicated Heaven to defend the right, and then died, just as the troubled waters rolled back their last surge, the dark cloud faded from the east, and the blessed star of the RESTORATION rose upon us.

> Who in the dust for years have slept,
> Are still in holy memory kept,
> And deathless Truth in glowing page,
> Transmits their fame from age to age.

If one may credit an oral tradition, which has travelled down from Job Standfast, the rotund landlord of the Royal Arms, that occupied the spot now known as the "Fountain Inn," we had enough Roundheadism in Soham, to poison the country, and as stentorian an advocate of the puritanic creed, in Nehemiah Gracelip, as the times could boast of. Our modern Church-gate Street has been paraded by men with cropped poll and shorn chin, bedizened in buff jerkin and sugar-loaf hat, and anon by others of elongated visage, and a head of long lank hair, cut all round, and confined in a black cap with white edge; a frightful ugliness which they explained as an avoidance of "the vanity of dress." The Scriptures too, were quoted with chilling profanity, whilst weak wives and fuddling men, discoursed with daring tongue on sacred mysteries, which the schoolman and priest drew back from as holy ground.

It is marvellous, if we did not know the gross state of mind into which our townsmen had sunk, that, notwithstanding a Barebone's parliament, a military government, a tyrant Protector, and a whole nation thrown off the pivot of order, they still retained their prejudices against the late king, and their wild and fanatical liking of Cromwell. Indeed, with the exception of Cambridge, the whole county supported his cause, but, no where had he more ardent spirits in his lists, than at Soham.

It is not so very wonderful then, that, by some direction, his son Henry and his daughter Frances should have fallen upon this neighbourhood, for their abode. By the way too, we may mention that a direct descendant of Cromwell resides in "Our Town," who, while avowing all the liberal political attachments of his ancestors, exhibits them through the Christian feeling, and enlightened mind, of these better times.

From careful research, we find that the religious tendencies of this place, toned and directed as they were by the peculiar notions of those protestants who, in Mary's reign fled to Geneva rendered them very likely to be betrayed into Cromwell's interests; and it is pretty certain, that Nonconformity dates its full establishment amongst us, from the Protectorate.   G.

To be Continued,

ECONOMICAL HINTS TO COTTAGERS.

Concluded from Page 134.

As my wish, in all this, is to keep you as much as possible dependent only on your own labour and exertions for your support.   I have endeavoured to recollect the most minute particular, which may be of service to you,—most truly and sincerely should I rejoice to see the same spirit of independence revive again amongst the Cottagers of England, which, when I left the north, was so predominant a feature in that class of people.   I shall conclude these long remarks with an event which happened to a worthy old man 'who often worked for me, and which I think deserves to be recorded.

He was a stone mason, which, in that part of the country, is a very good business. He had brought up a family very respectably, but they, having families of their own, could not contribute much to the support of their aged parents, who made use of all their feeble efforts to support themselves, he by his toiling as long as he was able at his employment, and she labouring at her wheel.—Sickness, at length, overtook him; and after suffering a great deal, he was most reluctantly compelled to apply to the parish for relief, an act which his high spirit could not brook the idea of, but which was most readily promised him from his known character. He was however obliged to go about two miles in a cart to attend the meeting; he bore the journey very well, and stood to receive his money, when just as it was put into his hand, his feelings overpowered him, and he dropped down dead ! ! ! Poor honest Joseph Nixon, long may you be remembered ! and may a tear arise in every independent eye at your most sensitive end. *His was spirit becoming every English Peasant, and till this revives, this otherwise favour'd country will never flourish as it has once done.* Cherish it therefore, as much as in you lies; labour night and day rather than submit to apply to your parish while you have health and strength, keep your independence of its bounty,—so will you be happy here and eternally blessed hereafter!

THE BISHOP AND HIS BIRDS.

A worthy Bishop, who died lately at Ratisbon, had for his arms two fieldfares, with the motto—"Are not two sparrows sold for a farthing?" This strange coat of arms had often excited attention, and many persons had wished to know its origin, as it was generally reported that the bishop had chosen it for himself, and that it bore reference to some event in his early life. One day an intimate friend, with whom he was taking his morning's walk, asked him its meaning, and the bishop replied by relating the following story :—

Fifty or sixty years ago, a little boy resided at a village near Dillengen, on the banks of the Danube. His parents were very poor, and, almost as soon as the boy could walk, he was sent into the woods to pick up sticks for fuel. When he grew older, his father taught him to pick juniper berries, and carry them to a neighbouring distiller, who wanted them for making hollands. Day by day the poor boy went to his task, and on his road he passed by the open windows of the village school, where he saw the schoolmaster teaching a number of boys of about the same age as himself. He looked at these boys with feelings of almost envy, so earnestly did he long to be among them. He thought it was in vain to ask his father to send him to school, for he knew his parents had no money to pay the schoolmaster ; and he often passed the whole day thinking, while he was gathering his juniper berries, what he could possibly do to please the schoolmaster, in the hope of getting some lessons. One day, when he was walking sadly along, he saw two of the boys belonging to the school trying to set a bird-trap, and he asked them what it was for? The boy told him that the schoolmaster was very fond of fieldfares, and that they were setting the trap to catch some. This delighted the poor boy, for he recollected that he had often seen a great number of these birds in the juniper wood, where they came to eat the berries, and he had no doubt but he could catch some.

The next day the little boy borrowed an old basket of his mother, and when he went to the wood he had the great delight to catch two fieldfares. He put them in the basket, and, tying an old handkerchief over it, he took them to the schoolmaster's house. Just as he arrived at the door, he saw the two little boys who had been setting the trap, and with some alarm he asked them if they had caught any birds. They answered in the negative ; and the boy, his heart beating with joy, gained admittance into the schoolmaster's presence. In a few words he told how he had seen the boys setting the trap, and how he had caught the birds, to bring them as a present to the master.

"A present, my good boy !" cried the schoolmaster ; "you do not look as if you could afford to make presents. Tell me your price, and I will pay you, and thank you besides."

"I would rather give them to you, sir, if you please," said the boy.

The schoolmaster looked at the boy as he stood before him, with bare head and feet, and ragged trowsers that reached only half-way down his naked legs. "You are a very singular boy!" said he; "but if you will not take money, you must tell me what I can do for you : as I cannot accept your present without doing something for it in return. Is there anything I can do for you?"

"Oh, yes!" said the boy, trembling with delight; "you can do for me what I should like better than anything else."

"What is that?" asked the schoolmaster, smiling.

"Teach me to read," cried the boy, falling on his knees; "oh dear, kind sir, teach me to read."

The schoolmaster complied. The boy came to him all his leisure hours, and learnt so rapidly, that the schoolmaster recommended him to a Nobleman who resided in the neighbourhood. This gentlemen, who was as noble in his mind as in his birth, patronised the poor boy, and sent him to school at Ratisbon. The boy profited by his opportunities, and when he rose, as he soon did, to wealth and honours, he adopted two fieldfares as his arms."

"What do you mean?" cried the bishop's friend.

"I mean," returned the bishop, with a smile, "that the poor boy was MYSELF."

EARLY RISING.

"Redeeming the Time." Eph. v. 16.

" See then that ye walk circumspectly," says the Apostle St. Paul, " not as fools but as wise, Redeeming the Time," saving and obtaining all the time you can for the best purposes, for the health of the soul, and also, the health of the body, rescuing every fleeting moment from the hands of sin and sloth, ease and pleasure ; and that the more diligently, because we read " the days are evil."

Redeeming the time from sleep, is, we fear, little considered even by those amongst us who are most eminent for piety and virtue. Numbers have been very conscientious in other respects, in attending diligently upon the duties and ordinances of religion, both in public and private, but have not been so in this, they do not look upon it as forming an important branch of Christian *self-denial*, and seem to think it a matter of total indifference whether they sleep more or less, whether they rise at six o'clock in the morning, or at nine.

But let us consider, *what it is to redeem the time from sleep.*

It is briefly and simply this,—to take just that measure of sleep which nature requires, and no more ; that measure which is most conducive to the health and vigour both of body and mind.

Now, we affirm, that one measure will not suit all, neither will the same measure suffice even the same persons at one time as at another. Whoever therefore, they are, that attempt to find one measure of sleep for all persons, do not understand the nature of the human body, so widely different in different persons, as neither do they, who imagine, that the same measure will suit even the same person at all times.

If a person be ill, or weakened by preceding sickness, he wants more sleep and rest than he does when in perfect health, and so he will when his strength has been exhausted by long continued labour.

I knew a young man, a Student at one of the Universities, who was absolutely persuaded, and who would listen to no argument in favour of a contrary opinion, that no one living need to sleep more than four hours and a half out of twenty-four.

I know another young man, about the same age as the former, who in a letter to me, writes thus : " I cannot, under any circumstances, do with less than seven hours sleep, after being behind the counter all day, and nine hours if I have to undergo any extra fatigue.

Now I think that the joint testimony of these two persons, tends very much to favour the point we contend for, viz : that one measure will not suit all, neither will the same measure suffice the person at one time as at another. We have one affirming, and absolutely contending that four hours and a half rest are quite sufficient for any one, and the other stating that he cannot do without seven hours sleep under ordinary circumstances, and nine when he has laboured longer in the day. For my own part, I am fully convinced from personal observation, and experience, that whatever may be done by extraordinary persons, or in some extraordinary cases in which persons have gone on with little sleep for some months, the human body can scarcely continue in health and vigour with a less amount of sleep than six hours in the twenty-four.

If any one would desire to know the exact amount of sleep his constitution requires, he may easily do so by means of an alarum, which is now so cheap as to be within the grasp of every person, and so contriving it that it may wake him half an hour sooner every morning, beginning we will say from seven o'clock, (for not a moment later ought a healthy person to be in bed) let him spring up and begin to dress himself immediately, and, I had almost said *not look back at his bed*, for the temptation to lie down again is so great, especially in the dark and cold winter mornings, that it requires a fixed and determined resolution, replete with every good argument in favour of early rising, to combat with false and foolish reasoning on the comfort of enjoying " a little more sleep and a little more slumber."

But why should we be so exact? What harm is there in doing as our neighbours do? What occasion have we for being so very particular, so nice about an hour or two in the morning? Suppose we lie in bed from ten until eight or nine o'clock in the winter, and six or seven in summer, what harm is there in that?

" Do you really desire to know what harm there is in not redeeming all the time you can from sleep? Suppose in spending therein an hour a day more than nature requires? Why, first, it hurts your substance, it is throwing away six hours a week, which might turn to some temporal account. If you can do any work, you might earn something in that time, were it ever so small; and you have no need to throw even this away. If you do not want it yourself, give it to them that do; you know some of them that are not far off. If you are of no trade, still you may so employ your time that it will bring money, or money's worth to yourself or others."

+

To be Continued,

—●—

THE CHANNEL ISLANDS.

THE wonder of the public is so frequently excited by some new invention, deemed hitherto supernatural, at home, and is so entirely engrossed with the mightier affairs and interests of our own country, that but a very small degree of its attention is possessed by those little fertile spots, which deck the Channel, and which, though separated from the maternal island by an arm of the mighty Atlantic, still hold allegiance to her sovereign. Thinking, however, that a short description of Guernsey, the principal and characteristic of the whole, will not be without interest to those unacquainted with the history, mode of government, &c., of these interesting portions of our dominions, we submit the following :—

Guernsey is supposed to have been discovered by the Romans (B.C. 17); it was then an uninhabited island, overrun with briers and brushwood; but through the instrumentality of a settlement formed by them, it gradually began to assume the appearance of a cultivated island. But little more is heard of it until the sixth century, when the introduction of Christianity by Sampson, Bishop of Doll, undoubtedly tended greatly to the enhancement of the social condition of the people, and to a great improvement in the appearance of the island. This man erected a chapel for Christian worship somewhere near that bay, which now, in commemoration of him, is called Sampson's Bay. In the tenth century the Danes, aware of the advantageous situation of the island, made several attempts to possess themselves of it, and in order to ward off their attacks, a castle was built at a place called the End of the Vale, which was used as a Monastery for the lay brotherhood, the hospitality and kindness of whom, Robert, Duke of Normandy, experienced, when adverse winds, and contending elements, shattered his fleet and drove it on the shore. He sojourned three months with the Abbot, and, as an acknowledgement of their benevolence, left engineers, and other artisans, who instructed the natives in the art of war, built mounds (some of which now remain) in order to enable them the more easily to detect the approach of a warlike incursion, and in time to take means of defence, and constructed many fortifications which added materially to the safety of the island.

Philip, King of France, in the time of King John, sent out a fleet against Guernsey, and though he had the advantage of coming upon them unexpectedly, he still found that his project was not so easily achieved, for, after a short engagement, he was obliged to put to sea again. But though this island was so successful against the invasion of a foreign power, it was doomed to fall a prey to the civil war between the parliamentarians and royalists; for, having embraced the side of the King, Oliver Cromwell, exasperated at its temerity, soon hove in front of Cornet Castle, with a fleet of armed men. But they had a little mistaken the nature of its defenders; for, added to the impregnable position of the castle (being built on a rock) it was well fortified with a garrison, who obstinately withstood his assault for fourteen days, but, at last, overcome by hunger, they capitulated on honourable terms.

Guernsey resembles a triangle in shape; on its north side it is almost a plane, but descends with a gentle slope towards the south, which, by reason of narrow vales, and deep, romantic glens, presents a very charming prospect to the eye. It is intersected by streams, and rivulets; and its supply of wood, though not equal to that of Jersey, is still sufficient to add to the beauty of the scenery. Travelling is rendered rather inconvenient through the badness of the roads, there being but few good ones in the island : the best are those which lead from some of the parishes to St. Peter's Port.

Its climate is mild and healthy, and combines the more genial air of France, with the somewhat more fickle climate of England. Frosts are very seldom severe, or of long duration, and, on the whole, it is much warmer than many other lands in the same latitude. Although the soil is very productive, the cultivation of grain is not rendered so serviceable as it otherwise might be, on account of the minute division of the land. A man who holds twenty or thirty acres is considered a large farmer, while from six to twelve is the ordinary quantity attached to a farm. Peas and beans are the most plentiful, and though corn is grown, it is thought by some that it can be imported cheaper. Its productions comprise most of the useful vegetables and herbs of England, to which it unites the more delicious fruits of France. The fig-tree abounds and arrives at great perfection. [Aloes are not uncommon; and many of those delicate plants which all the skill of the horticulturist in England will sometimes fail to rear, grow here in out-door luxuriance, without the aid of artificial means, and may very often be met with in a wild state. Although nature in the distribution of her favours has not furnished Guernsey with that useful substance coal, she has, in order to supply the deficiency, covered those rocks which surround the island with a sea-weed, called by the natives *vraic*, which, when dried, not only supplies the place of coal, but is useful for many other domestic purposes; and in the culture of the land is the principal manure used by them. There are two seasons set apart for the gathering or harvest of this weed, viz., March and July, and as the value of it is fully understood by the inhabitants, the days of gathering are ushered in by a general rejoicing, and both women and children assist the men in procuring it. As soon as morning dawns numbers of small vehicles, occupied by the workers, each equiped with a small instrument resembling a scythe, may be seen hastening towards the scene of action ; and such is their anxiety to make the best of their time, that their impatience will scarcely await the preparing of the boats to carry them to the rocks, so that it is not an unfrequent sight to see cars floating, and horses swimming from all directions to the long-wished-for goal. After the day's labour is over, they turn to feasting and merriment, and their repast consists principally of vraicing cakes, made for the occasion, and at this important time the best cask of cider is tapped. The vraic, when cut, is spread on the coast to dry, and is then either stored for fuel, and other purposes, or sold.

The islanders have a very singular, and no less economical method of spending their winter evenings, which originated probably in their poverty. Each house has its *lit de ville*, a square frame similar to that of a bed, which, covered with dry fur, or hay, forms a very comfortable seat, and is generally stowed in one corner of the room. Each in its turn is patronized by the youths and maidens of the neighbouring houses. Sitting close together around the frame, with a lamp in the centre, suspended from the ceiling, a very comfortable degree of warmth is thus imparted, which supersedes the necessity of a fire. They pass the evening in singing, reading, &c. The language spoken by the poorer classes is purely Norman; whilst in the upper circles of life, both the English language and manners are rapidly gaining the ascendancy. The chief occupation of the men is fishing, at which they are very adept; and as the coast is supplied with various sorts of fish, they obtain a very comfortable livelihood. A very curious custom relating to their fishing was in vogue in the olden times, which was that of presenting a tythe of all the fish caught by them to their clergy. As cider forms the principal beverage of the islanders, the growth of the apple is an object of great attention, and large orchards of them are very common.

The principal town is St. Peter's Port, the view of which, from the sea, is extremely picturesque. It is romantically situated on a gentle slope, running towards the sea, and is studded with villas, shaded with trees and tasty gardens, denoting the residences of the more opulent, while the institutions of religion and benevolence add not a little to its appearance. On a nearer approach, however, the streets are discovered to be narrow and irregular. One of the principal buildings is the Public Seminary, founded by Elizabeth, (A.D. 1563) which holds out, by its privileges and variety of literature, an incitement to the youth of Guernsey to dig deep into the mines of knowledge, and even places them on an equal footing with students at our own universities. Benevolence also extends the arm of encouragement to the poor and needy, in a building, called (rather improperly) the Hospital. It answers for the several purposes of,—an Asylum for the unfortunate,—a Workhouse for the destitute,—and a School for young children, or, indeed, for any other good purpose in which charity can exert her benign influence. The fish markets are very spacious, and well fitted up with marble slabs, &c., and, as may be easily supposed, there is generally a good supply of fish. In their vicinage are the Public Library and Assembly Rooms. There are several large and showy shops, and clever artisans and mechanics, contribute to the social comfort of the Town. The Harbour is formed by two piers, and affords both safe and convenient anchorage. It is screened from the south-western gales, and its entrance is guarded by Castle Cornet, situated about half-a-mile from the shore.

Both Guernsey and Jersey have a political constitution of their own, called "The States of Deliberation," at the head of which is the Bailiff or Governor of the island, elected by the Crown of Great Britain, and the other members, comprising Rectors, Constables, and Jurats, are chosen by the islanders. Our space will not permit a description of their respective duties. The Revenue is gained by taxation upon various articles, as publicans' licenses, harbour dues, &c. But in no case, except that of great emergency, have the States the power of imposing a new tax, without sovereign permission.

These Islands are six in number, and were first joined to the Crown of England, when William the Conqueror ascended the throne, (A.D. 1066) and though various events have served to detach the remaining part of the Duchy of Normandy, these still remain. They are surrounded by huge rocks, which, with the rapidity of the currents about them, render an approach very hazardous, except under the guidance of a pilot, well acquainted with their coasts.   S. R.

APPLICATION.

If young persons enter into their various pursuits with becoming ardour, and steadily persevere in a course of diligent application, it is impossible to foresee the eminence to which they may attain. Difficulties, which timidity and indolence would deem insurmountable, are overcome; and knowledge in all its variety, and with all its honours, advantages, and pleasures, is rapidly and effectually gained. Among the students who obtained classical honours and distinction in the late examinations at the University of Oxford, was Mr. Seymer, of St. Alban Hall, who, notwithstanding the disadvantage of blindness from his infancy, was placed in the highest class but one. When this circumstance came to the knowledge of Lord Grenville, the Chancellor, he addressed a most kind letter to the learned Principal of St. Alban Hall, enclosing a draft for twenty pounds to be laid out by Mr. Seymer in the purchase of books. Let no youth despair.—*The Youth's Instructor.*

BAYHAM ABBEY, SUSSEX.

WE have been so accustomed, from early youth, to associate ideas of indolence and superstition with monastic establishments, that, notwithstanding the advocacy they may have received in recent times, we are slow to admit their advantages. Advantages, however, they certainly did possess, which, in the days of their grandeur, could scarcely be obtained from any other system. Books were then both rare and ponderous, and the means of communication between the learned and studious, were difficult and uncertain. Under such circumstances, therefore, the monasteries afforded a nucleus, here and there, round which was gathered most of the erudition of the land; while we cannot deny that some of the most exalted instances of self-denial and piety, have found a refuge within their walls. Their dissolution was determined on, not so much from any faults or vices inseparable from the system, or actually existing in them in the aggregate, but from the grasping avarice of Henry and his court.

What would England be without her ten thousand parochial churches and magnificent cathedrals? Her hills and dales would appear as wearisome to the eye of the painter, as, perchance, the moral condition of her people would be painful to the contemplation of the philanthropist. And yet we owe the greater part of the natural and moral gratification in these particulars which we now enjoy, to monkery,—with all its real or supposed evils and barbarisms.

We must, at least, give our ancestors of the cowl, great credit for taste and judgment in the selection of the sites for their turreted abodes. Rich pastures, umbrageous woods, and silver streams, —as in the case of Bayham Abbey above, —form the invariable accompaniments. Secluded in some romantic glade, the student and the saint could each enjoy that quiet and retirement which they loved; and while indulging in the highest gratification which can be afforded to an intellectual being on this side the tomb, could prepare with intense and entire devotion for the life beyond.

POETRY.

[In Original Poetry, the Name, real or assumed, of the Author, is printed in small Capitals under the title; in Selections it is printed in Italics at the end.]

THE YOUNG MARINER'S ADIEU.

Avast, while I swab off the spray from my cheek,
　Trim the Skysail of Hope and Sheet home;
Freedom's bark's in the offing,—her anchor's apeak,
　And the ocean invites me to roam.
　　Yes, now for ever, my home must be,
　　The trackless, boundless, fathomless sea.

Farewell to the land, that has cradled my birth,
　To the friends who have had me in tow,
On Memory's log is recorded their worth,
　And gratitude's tide's at the flow.
　　Yes, now for ever, my home must be,
　　The trackless, boundless, fathomless sea.

Heaven's arch is above me,—the horizon clear,
　And tho' storms, it is true, may o'erwhelm,
Yet He, who commands them, the vessel can steer
　Tho' the tempest should shiver the helm.
　　Yes, now for ever, my home must be,
　　The trackless, boundless, fathomless sea.

Soham.

The golden palace of my God,
　Towering above the clouds I see;
Beyond the cherub's bright abode,
　Higher than angels' thoughts can be!
How shall I in those courts appear
　Without a wedding garment on?
Conduct me Thou life-giver there,
　Conduct me to Thy glorious throne!
And clothe me with Thy robes of light,
　And lead me through sin's darksome
　　night.

Dr. Bowring.

THE BOW IN THE CLOUD.

BEAUTIFUL bow! in mercy given.
A token of love to earth from heaven;
When thou art beaming bright and fair,
May I ever behold the promise there!

Beautiful bow! when the rain-drops fall,
And the cloud is dark like a funeral pall,
When the sun hath hidden his shining
　ray,
And the birds seek shelter beneath the
　spray:

Beautiful bow! I will look on high,
For thou wilt appear to paint the sky,
And bid earth's mourning children see
The sign of a covenant God in thee.

Beautiful bow! a brighter one
Is shining round th' eternal throne;
And when life's little storm is o'er,
May I gaze on that bow for evermore!
　　　　　Charlotte Elizabeth.

FAITH, HOPE, LOVE.

Faith is the Christian's shield in fight,
　And Hope his anchor in the storm;
Love makes his heaviest burden light,
　And gives to every grace a charm.

Where foes and storms for ever cease,
　Shall faith and hope their charge resign
While love in heaven, her native place,
　Shall sweetly sing and brightly shine.
　　　　　J. Churches.

THE STRANGER AND HIS FRIEND

'Ye have done it unto me.''—MATT. XXV. 40,

A poor wayfaring man of grief
Hath often crossed me on my way,
Who sued so humbly for relief,
That I could never answer, " Nay":
I had not power to ask his name,
Whither he went, or whence he came,
Yet was there something in his eye,
That won my love, I knew not why.
Once when my scanty meal was spread ;
He entered ;—not a word he spake ;—
Just perishing for want of bread :
I gave him all : he bless'd it, brake,
And ate,—but gave me part again ;
'Mine was an angel's portion then,
For while I fed with eager haste,
That crust was manna to my taste.
I spied him, where a fountain burst
Clear from the rock; his strength was
    gone :
The heedless water mocked his thirst,
He heard it, saw it hurrying on :
I ran to raise the sufferer up ;
Thrice from the stream he drained my
    cup,
Dipt, and return'd it running o'er ;
I drank and never thirsted more.
'Twas night: the floods were out; it blew
A winter hurricane aloof ;
I heard his voice abroad, and flew
To bid him welcome to my roof ;

I warm'd, I cloth'd, I cheer'd my guest,
Laid him on my own couch to rest ;
Then made the hearth my bed, and
    seem'd
In Eden's garden while I dreamed.
Stript, wounded, beaten, nigh to death,
I found him by the highway-side ;
I roused his pulse, brought back his
    breath,
Reviv'd his spirit, and supplied
Wine, oil, refreshment ! he was heal'd
I had myself a wound conceal'd ;
But from that hour forgot the smart,
And peace bound up my broken heart,
In prison I saw him next, condemn'd
To meet a traitor's doom at morn ;
The tide of lying tongues I stemm'd,
And honour'd him, 'midst shame and
    scorn ;
My friendship's utmost zeal to try,
He ask'd, if I for him would die ;
The flesh was weak, my blood ran chill,
But the free spirit cried, " I will."
Then in a moment to my view,
The stranger darted from disguise :
The tokens in his hands, I knew,
My Saviour stood before mine eyes :
He spake ; and my poor name He named;
" Of me thou hast not been asham'd ;
These deeds shall thy memorial be ;
Fear not, thou didst them unto me."

James Montgomery.

—◆—

OUR CHILDREN'S PAGE.

FACTS WORTH REMEMBERING.

The Quarter Days are,—March the 25th, June the 24th, September
    the 29th, and December the 25th.
London is in latitude 51 degrees, 32 minutes north; Dublin, 53 deg.
    20 min. ; Edinburgh, 55 deg. 58 min., and 395 miles from
    London.
Mercury is said to be about 37 millions of miles from the sun ;
    Venus, 69 millions; the Earth, 95 millions ; Mars, 144 mil-
    lions; Jupiter. 490 millions : Saturn, 900 millions ; Georgium
    Sidus, 1,800 millions.
The hourly motion of Mercury, in its orbit, is about 105,000 miles ;
    of Venus, 76,000; the Earth, 68,000; Mars, 55,000; Jupiter,
    25,000; and of Saturn. 22,000 miles.

MISCELLANY AND EXTRACTS.

THE circumference of the visible horizon, on the top of Etna, cannot be less than 2000 miles· Malta, which is nearly 200 miles distant, is often discovered from about one half of the elevation of the mountain; so that, at the whole elevation, the horizon must extend to near double that distance, or 400 miles, which makes 800 for the diameter of the circle, and above 2,400 for the circumference.

PERHAPS every man may date the predominance of those desires that disturb his life, and contaminate his conscience, from some unhappy hour, when too much leisure exposed him to their incursions: for *he* has lived with little observation, either on himself or others, who does not know that "to be idle, is to be vicious."

NEVER delay till to-morrow, what reason and conscience tell you ought to be performed to-day. To-morrow is not yours; and, though you should live to enjoy it, you must not overload it with a burden not its own.

IT is the custom of the Mahometans, if they see upon the ground any printed or written paper, to take it up and lay it carefully aside, as not knowing but it may contain some pieces of their Alcoran. Might not many professing Christians take a lesson from them?

THE LAKE OF COJUTEPEKE.—It is about twelve miles long, of an irregular shape, on an average about five miles broad, and surrounded on all sides (except a small opening at which a stream of water runs out) by majestic and precipitous mountains. Some small rivulets flow into the lake, and the surrounding scenery is most romantic and beautiful. The lake is, in some parts, of great depth, though no attempts have been made to ascertain it with exactness. In smooth weather the water has no peculiar appearance or difference from that of other lakes, nor can parties then walking on the banks observe any fish; but after a brisk wind it assumes a dark green colour, and the fish flock to the shores in such numbers that the natives not only catch them in large quantities with nets, but in buckets, and even with the hand. This singular phenomenon is called by the natives *la cosecha de pescadoes*, (" the fish harvest"); and the Indians suppose that a demon, who lives in the middle of the lake, then troubles the water, the fish escaping from his presence to the border of the lake. The most likely explanation would appear to be, that the middle of the lake contains a number of thermal springs, charged with carbonic acid gas and some minerals, which colour the water. This water, being heavier than that which enters from the mountain streams, remains at the bottom of the lake, and the pure water covers the upper surface, so that in smooth weather the fish find no difficulty in maintaining themselves in the uncontaminated water, readily avoiding that at the bottom of lake, in which they cannot exist; but, when the lake is agitated by strong winds the mineral water becomes mixed with that which is superincumbent, and the whole body of the lake then becomes destructive to the fish, which are compelled to repair to its borders, where it is shallow, and consequently composed entirely of pure water, without any understrata of that charged with the gas or other noxious principles. *Travels in Cen. America.*

MONTHLY NOTICES.

OCTOBER.

10th.—Dividends on several species of Stock become due.

13th.—Insurances, due at Michaelmas, must be paid on or before this day.

13th.—County Court, at the new Court House, Soham.

20th.—Isle of Ely Quarter Sessions, at ELY.

PLAYFORD'S

SOHAM MAGAZINE,

AND

𝔉riendly 𝔐onitor.

NOVEMBER, 1847.

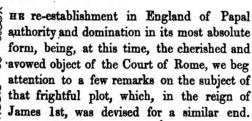

Hᴇ re-establishment in England of Papal authority and domination in its most absolute form, being, at this time, the cherished and avowed object of the Court of Rome, we beg attention to a few remarks on the subject of that frightful plot, which, in the reign of James 1st, was devised for a similar end. Popery has always shown itself regardless of the means it uses in its machinations against the freedom of mankind, and few of us seem to be aware of the formidable and ceaseless efforts that are now being made to bow this nation again beneath its crushing and blood-stained yoke. The ties of the tenderest affection, the sanction of the most solemn oaths, the strongest obligations of honour and of duty, and the plainest injunctions of the word of God, have all been thrown to the winds before the onward stride of that most awful power that is now uncoiling its monstrous folds in every region of the globe. If light be more desirable than darkness, liberty more sweet than the galling chain,—if we would preserve our hearths from the pollution of the confessional, and our altars from blasphemy and idols, we must sternly repel this "woman drunken with the blood of saints, and with the blood of the martyrs of Jesus."

Mild as James the 1st was in toleration, there was a project contrived in the very beginning of his reign (says Dr. Goldsmith) for

No. 11. Vol. I.   K

the re-establishment of Popery, which, were it not a fact known to all the world, could scarcely be credited by posterity. This was the gunpowder plot, than which a more horrid or terrible one was never conceived by the human heart.

The Papists had expected great favour and indulgence on the accession of James, because he was a decendant of the rigid Papist Mary, and had shown much partiality to their corrupted form of christianity in his youth. They soon, however, discovered their mistake, and were at once surprised and enraged to find him expressing, on all occasions, his resolution of strictly executing the laws enacted against them, and of persevering in the conduct of his predecessor. This declaration determined them upon more desperate measures; and they at length formed a resolution of *destroying the King and both Houses of Parliament at one blow.* The scheme was first projected by a gentleman of good abilities and an ancient family named Catesby, who conceived that a train of gunpower might be so placed under the parliament house, as to blow up the king and all the members at once.

How horrid soever this contrivance might appear, yet every one of the conspirators seemed faithful and secret in the league; and about two months before the sitting of parliament, they hired a house in the name of ' Percy' adjoining the scene of their intended operations.

Their first intention was to bore a passage under the parliament-house from that which they occupied, and they set themselves laboriously to the task. But when they had pierced the wall, which was three yards in thickness, they were surprised to find that the parliament-house was vaulted underneath, and that a magazine of coals was usually deposited there. From their disappointment on this account they were soon relieved by the information that the coals were then selling off, and that the vaults would be let to the highest bidder. They seized the opportunity of hiring the place, and bought the remaining quantity of coals, as if for their own use. They next conveyed there *thirty-six barrels of gunpowder* which had been purchased in Holland; and covered them over with the coals, and with some fagots bought for that purpose. The doors of the vaults were then boldly thrown open, and every body admitted, as if they contained nothing dangerous.

Confident of success, they now began to plan the remaining part of their project. The king, the queen, the prince Henry, the king's eldest son were all expected to be present at the opening of parliament. The king's second son, by reason of his tender age, would be absent, and it was resolved that Percy should seize or assassinate him. The princess Elizabeth, who was also a child, was kept at Lord Harrington's house, in Warwickshire; and Sir Everard Digby was to seize her, and immediately proclaim her queen.

The day for the sitting of parliament now approached, and never was treason more secret, or ruin more apparently inevitable. The hour was expected with impatience, and the conspirators gloried in their meditated guilt. The dreadful secret, although communicated to above twenty persons, had been religiously kept during the space of near a year and a half. But when all the motives of piety, justice, and safety were too weak, a remorse of private friendship saved the kingdom.

Sir Henry Percy, one of the conspirators conceived a design of saving the life of Lord Monteagle, his intimate friend and companion, and an anonymous letter which he wrote for this end, although at first but little regarded, even by the secretary of state, led the King himself to suspect the real cause of the danger. The Earl of Suffolk was directed to search the vaults, which he intentionally delayed to do till the day before the meeting of parliament, when he siezed a man preparing for the terrible enterprize, dressed in a cloak and boots, with a dark lantern in his hand. This was no other than Guy Fawkes, who had just disposed of every part of the train for taking fire the next morning, the matches and other combustibles being found in his pocket. The whole plot was soon divulged. The conspirators who were in London, fled into Warwickshire, where Sir Everard Digby was already in arms. Beset on all sides, about eighty of them determined to sell their lives as dearly as possible. But many of them were mangled by the accidental explosion of some gunpowder, while others were cut to pieces by the indignant populace. Several fell by the hands of the executioner, and others experienced the King's mercy. Garnet and Oldcom, who were *Jesuits*, and privy to the plot, suffered with the rest; and notwithstanding the attrociousness of their guilt, Garnet is to this day considered a *martyr* by the popish party, *and miracles were said to be wrought by his blood.*

We have thought it right to publish this extract from Dr. Goldsmith's history of England at the present time because, in the first place, many efforts are being made to efface the remembrance of this infamous conspiracy from the public mind; and secondly, because we wish to show, that such a dreadful crime was not the mere effect of a treasonable design, existing in the minds of a few, but was in entire consistency with the avowed policy of the Pope of · Rome, in his official character, and with the decrees of his *infallible* and *immutable* church.

Now, Emanuel Sà, in his aphorisms, affirms it lawful to kill a King, if the Pope has sentenced him to death. Not the obligations of the oath of allegiance, nor the sanction of God himself, must reverse the sentence of the Pope against the King, but any one of his own sworn subjects may kill him.

This iniquitous position of Sà was not made public till forty years after his death, and is *now* the ordinary received manual for the *Fathers confessors of the Jesuits' order*. Mariana goes further than this, for he descends to the very manner of doing it with the most convenience. He thinks poison to be the best way, and that, for greater secrecy, it should be cast upon the chairs, and clothes of his Prince. He also gives examples of this method of King-slaughter, telling us that it was by poisoned boots that Henry of Castile was destroyed. Neither was *this* the opinion of an individual, for there was an apology printed in Italy, in the year 1610, *by permission of the superiors of the popish church*, that says, "they were all enemies of that holy name of Jesus that condemned Mariana for any such doctrine."

But to come nearer to the case in hand,—Garnet, the superior of the English Jesuits, who was executed for his share in the gunpowder plot, was defended in his act of high treason, by writers of no less eminence than Bellarmine, Gretser, and Eudæmon!

Let us now briefly enquire whether there existed, at that particular period, any recent decisions of the Pope, which could have instigated men who thus moved in the highest circles, to become traitors and murderers.

Queen Elizabeth preceded James upon the throne, and, in consequence of her hostility to Rome, the Pope issued a Bull or letter against her in which he declared her a heretic, deprived her of her kingdom, absolved her subjects from their oaths of allegiance, ex-communicated her, and gave power to any one to rebel against her. This was his first step. He then procured a gentleman of Florence to incite her subjects to a rebellion against her for her destruction. Further yet,—he thought this would be such a real benefit to christendom, that he was ready to aid in person, to spend the whole revenue of the See Apostolic, all the chalices and crosses of the church, and even his very clothes to promote so pious a business.

Antonius Gabutius also tells us that the Pope's design was to take away her life, in case she would not turn papist.

The rebellion was to be under the conduct of the Duke of Norfolk, a papist, and the Pope intended to use "*the utmost and most extreme remedies to cure her heresy, and all means to strengthen the rebellion.*"

"I durst not have thought so much of his Holiness (says Bishop Taylor,) if his own had not said it."

Such proceedings of the court of Rome we think are quite sufficient to account for the deadly project which we have narrated above. But there is another slight incident worth recording, which doubtless, would tend to quicken the traitor in his hateful plot. Pope Sixtus the 5th compared the assassination of Henry 3rd, by Clement, to the exploits of Eleazer and Judith, mentioned in the scriptures; and after having aggravated the faults of the murdered King, concludes him to have died impenitent, and prays that "*God would finish what in this manner had been begun!*"

"Let us remember, then, (as Bishop Jewel urges) that the Pope hath conference with traitors, that he raiseth subjects against their Princes, that he causeth Princes to plague their subjects, that he hath no regard of the stranger and the fatherless, that he suffereth those who trade in vice to live in wealth and peace with him at Rome; and yet will not suffer a lawful Princess to live in the peace of her own country at home; that he is the procurer of theft and murder, of rebellion and dissention in the land, and that he sent in a Bull against Queen Elizabeth to work our disquiet, *fraught with blasphemy and untruth.* Let these things never be forgotten! Let your children remember them for ever!"

OUR TOWN.

Continued from Page 151.

We stay to make little observation on the character of Charles 2nd., nor is it our intention to act the critic on the various occurrences of his reign, and the doings of his government. His personal excesses, and general public acts, were the fair issues of such a state of things as we have lately looked at. Hating the sour hypocrisy of the Commonwealth, he launched himself into the very vortex of gaiety, and in his political movements, while he could not obliterate from the deeply-graven tablets of memory, the murder of his father, or his own disasters, he used every effort to conciliate and gain the good services of his enemies, and anon, as other, and less forgiving feelings gave momentum to his will, he tried to secure peace by more inflexible appliances. Nor can we wonder, with all our ardour after true liberty, that in such times, a corporation and test act, and an act against conventicles should have received the royal assent, since whatever clamour may assert, and those who stand at a distance may state, this *seemed* the safest way of gagging a power whose early efforts were notorious for much misdirection, and to the commonest judgments, lacked most of the gentle and commendable attributes of truth. It is no libel to say of yon sun that he arose out of the dark cloud, and grey mists, with broken and refracted ray ; that when we first saw his distant glances, he darted through a creviced and sombre curtain work ; nor can it be unfair to Nonconformity to assert, that whatever it had of the *angel* in this age, these portions were hidden under thick folds of drapery, which rendered it both undefinable and frightful.

The word *liberty* has been a stalking-horse for the most frightful enormities : it throws upon crime a sort of fascination that makes it popular, and transforms sin itself into an angel of light. Who would believe it, that many of the quaint beings of " Our Town," who, a few days agone were scattering fire brands and death, and deeming it sport now that a scrutiny was made to see if any sparks were left behind, with well feigned horror spoke of conscience, freedom, religious toleration, and such stock terms of the new brotherhood. But we will pass on a few years until these virtuous uproars having partly subsided, men exercised their brains instead of their lungs. Now our townsfolk had lost half their cant vocabulary, and instead of reforming governments, hunting kings to death, and persecuting the priesthood, they might be seen and heard in snug half-dozens laughing at their late madness, and mysteriously talking of magic lanthorns, glass coaches, looms, a post office, a royal society and the like ; but the most famous invention was, that of newspapers.

Look into the parlour of the Royal Arms, ay, and such a parlour too for magnitude and good company as has no parallel in this age of No. 1 and 2, you will see a fair specimen of our forefathers, for whatever *religious* differences existed, the parlour floor formed neutral ground, and here such topics were never introduced until the oft repeated and potent draught made the tongue out-strip reason, and knock down the dam by which prudence held back their prejudices. Our friend Job loved conciliation, and although he called himself no party man, he wiled away the loose moments of the day in snatches of ballads, plainly indicating his political bias, and when pressed by his customers for a tribute to their merriment, he was wont to break out in old remembrance.

If I were a gay young Cavalier,
I'd fight till my sword was worn to the hilt.

When " Prithee cease, the times are changed," closed his loyal and lugubrious pipes. Smoking, that nerve soother and brain rocker, was here carried on to a considerable extent, and yonder, especially, might be seen the round visage of Shortell, the hosier, laughing like the sun through a cloud, Mumps, the melancholy cobbler, meanwhile perusing the " Public Intelligencer," for here, once in a while, this first periodical paper lent and sent to our landlord, by the trustworthy valet of a neighbouring Knight, might be seen, and from its columns, and the tongue of rumour, the folk of "Our Town" heard of the Plague of London, in which 90,000 persons died, and where all infected houses were shut up ; and a red cross chalked on the door, with these words over it : " Lord have mercy upon us." " Bless *me*," cried Mr. Puff, the baker, " some of the King's folk are *now* at the Newmarket Palace, and no doubt they've brought the infection down from the great city, and I trow it will be here directly," and away he hied, for bakers it seems had *then* a fearful conscience, which in times of danger, presented to them visions of light weights, pirated joints, and abcissions of tit bits.

Another year brought the great Fire, and amidst so much, likely both to move and amend, it is certain that the movements of the Sohamites, were too often in the direction of Job's ' Hostelrie,' and the great solace of sorrow sought in the lusty potations retailed there. Numerous however were the conjectures as to the origin of this Fire, and singular were the oral descriptions of its ravages. Mumps, who made the worst of everything, averred that it had burnt millions of houses, and thousands of churches, and as none of the party had ever seen London, and only knew of it from exaggerated report, this hyperbole was written down for an honest fact.

Perhaps the most remarkable social change of the year appeared in the altered character of the attire of the people, who, finding out that the cut of the cloth was no credential of sound faith, soon launched out into all the gay toggery of the time. The court rules the country, and as the attendants of a certain wry necked monarch carried their heads on one side out of compliment to the King, so blue or yellow adopted there, is found in some shape or other from Land's-end, to John O' Groat's. Alas, how many who once deprecated " the vanity of dress," and were as spare and demure as scissors and sancitimoniousness could make them, now disported themselves in long flowing wigs of *false* hair covering the shoulders, and a cravat round the throat, tied in a great bunch under the chin.

But yon knot of men hard by the church wall calls us away from these remarks, for there, one of the cleverest men in the parish, according to his own valuation, (none other than Doublesight, who saw the witch at " Hanie,") is exclaiming, " Odds fish masters " Our Town," 'ill be a a brave place for larnin, if matters go thus, for at yon big school about which our parson has been so busy, every chick in the place may get to read as 'clart' as the clargy, and know as much lingo as a Strologer.'' " Tut," cried a little crabbed looking man at the outskirt, " it be not so much for larnin, that this huge house be built, as to teach the bairns to hate the Pope and the Roundheads." " By my sabbath doublet then," shouted the only Foxite in the parish, "my Obadiah's brain shall the rather rest untilled." And so one by one they separated after doing what has been enacted again and again, scouting secular teaching, lest a spice of religion should be mixed with it, especially any grain that didn't suit 'their own individual palate. It appears that this was one of a class of schools now first instituted, and generally established in the next reign, for the conservation of the sound protestant feeling of the country, against the inroads of error and popery. Stupid prejudices wearing away, it was found of essential use to "Our Town," affording for many years the only instruction to be obtained. Here therefore the sons of farmers and cowherds, of shopkeeper and peasant were grouped together in literary emulation, and in the contest, it most likely has often occured that the first has been last, and the last first.

> "Delightful task." mid buzz, and hum, and noise,
> To train these crooked human branches—boys.

To be Continued,   G.

EXCURSION TO THE DEAD SEA AND THE JORDAN.

HAVING visited nearly all the remarkable localities in Jerusalem and its environs, we resolved to conclude our pilgrimage by an excursion to the Dead Sea and the Jordan. The governor of Jerusalem is bound once a year, to convey all the pilgrims who may desire to visit those places, with a guard sufficient to preserve them from the attacks of the Arabs; but, as this would not occur till a fortnight later, and our time would not allow us to wait, we applied for permission, and an escort for ourselves, which were readily granted. A detachment of four soldiers was appointed to conduct us to Rihhah, pronounced Yarikah, *i. e.* Jericho, with an order upon the garrison of the fort there to join us in our advance to the Jordan, which is the place considered most liable to Arab attack.

Our intentions were speedily noised abroad, and, in consequence we had numerous applications from pilgrims to be allowed to accompany us. Among the applicants were several of the fair sex; but as the Turks, to enhance their services and increase the *bucksheesh*, magnified the danger, fearful that they might prove an impediment to our movement, we were compelled to silence our gallantry, and refuse their request. One buxom Grecian dame was most pertinacious in her entreaties, returning four times to the charge, and at last fairly seating herself in our apartment, as if determined to take no denial; so we had no resource but to evacuate the place and leave her in full possession, when, I presume she gave the affair up, as we heard no more of her. There came, also, a mad Russian priest, raving and ranting in so extraordinary a manner, that forcible ejectment was found necessary. Two Muscovite grenadiers were next ushered in, craving permission — tall, stout fellows, decorated with several crosses and medals, who had belonged to the army of occupation at Paris. Thinking that such old campaigners would be no bad allies, in case of a brush with the Arabs, we gave our assent, upon condition that all should bring us a certificate from the Russian Chancellor of having procured horses, that they might be no hinderance to us. One immediately acquiesced: the other, with a doleful countenance, produced an empty purse as evidence of his inability to hire an animal. This excited our compassion, and we gave him wherewith to furnish a conveyance. His gratitude was unbounded; before we could hinder him, he, greatly to our annoyance, prostrated himself upon the ground before us, and commenced kissing our shoes.

The rendezvous was appointed next morning, half an hour before sunrise, at the convent-gate, at which time about a dozen of them appeared well mounted, and I was carried down, and set upon my horse, in very poor condition either for fighting or flying, had need required. As soon as we were joined by our escort, we issued forth through St. Stephen's Gate, our Turkish warriors (two of whom were armed with long guns, and two with spears, all having sabres and pistols,) careering before us to exhibit their horsemanship, and most beautiful it was.

As an instance, one of them galloped his horse down a very steep pitch to a level spot, which appeared scarcely large enough to receive him, and, planting his spear in the centre, like the leg of a compass, he made him describe a circle three or four times at speed, and then pulled him up short upon his haunches in a moment. The Mameluke bits are of tremendous power, having very long checks, and a strong iron ring passing through the bit, and under the horse's chin, affording a lever which no animal could resist. The mouths of the Turkish steeds are very fine; the slightest motion of the finger will turn them.

Crossing the Cedron, we skirted the Mount of Olives, above Absalom's pillar, proceeding round it to Bethany, near which, concealed behind a rock, we found a number of pilgrims waiting our approach, who, having heard our determination to admit none but equestrians into our party, had preceded us to this spot, where we had no means of preventing them from following us. They were mostly Greeks. With this addition, and the Arabs who accompanied us, to look after the horses, our numbers exceeded sixty, being generally stout, able-bodied young men; so we made a formidable show of both cavalry and infantry, and stood in no fear of the enemy.

In two miles we reached Bethany, a miserable village, where are shewn the mansion and tomb of Lazarus, and Mary Magdalen's house. Descending from hence, by a steep rocky path, we reached the Fountain of the Apostles, so called from having been their resting-place in their journeys between Jerusalem and Jericho. It is situated in the gorge of a long narrow valley, which exhibited the last signs of vegetation in a few stripes of corn: beyond it not a blade of grass is to be seen. The well is walled round, and covered with a roof: we halted a few minutes to refresh our horses, and taste of the holy element.

After leaving this valley, we wound our way among parched and barren hills of one uniform whitish-brown colour, bearing not the semblance of any green thing to relieve the eye. Never before had I formed an idea of what barrenness really was. We at last reached, on the top of a hill, an enclosure of loose stones and some ruins, which our guards rode forward to reconnoitre, as they said, it was a favourite lurking place of the Arabs; but no one was found. We had seen only two human beings upon the road, armed Arabs, perched upon a rock above us, in the valley of the Apostles' Fountain: these our guides pretended to think were scouts on the look-out: so, presenting their guns, they ordered them immediately to descend, which they did forthwith, saying, they were shepherds watching their flock. This might have been the case, as a few sheep were visible; and, in this country, where every man's hand is against his fellow, the peaceful crook of the shepherd must necessarily be exchanged for a more warlike weapon.

At the ruins we concentrated our forces, and waited for stragglers; then, with the guards in front, we began our advance through a very narrow defile, with high precipitous sides. It was here that Sir Frederick Henniker was attacked and wounded; and a better place for an attack could not be found; half a dozen rifles would have sufficed to discomfit a host: however, nothing interrupted our passage. Emerging from this gorge, we beheld the the plains of Jericho at our feet, to which we descended by a steep, rugged, and perilous path. Most of the company dismounted, and led their horses down. Being unable to walk, I was obliged to trust my safety to the surefootedness of my nag; and, being equally powerless on horseback, I gave him his head, and clung to the saddle with my hands. I was not a little relieved when this nervous descent was achieved, and I found myself once more upon level ground. About half a mile from the foot of the hills we passed some large masses of reticulated Roman brick-work. Another hour's riding brought us to Rihhah.

The plain was nearly as devoid of verdure as the hills we had left, except in the beds of some torrents that we crossed, in which were growing oleanders, tamarisks, and other shrubs, particularly the Spina Christi, supposed, and not without reason, to be the plant of whose branches the crown of thorns was plaited, with which mockery decked our Saviour's brow. It resembles a young willow in growth and flexibility, the leaves being much of the same form, but somewhat longer, and the thorns an inch in length, and very strong and sharp. Water was conducted in channels, from (I believe) the healing spring of Elisha, to supply the wants of the very scanty cultivation that was partially sprinkled over this portion of the plains. These tiny rills, edged on each side with about a foot's breadth of the most vivid green vegetation, formed a delicious contrast with the brown and arid desert around, —a feast for the weary eye. The sun was overcomingly powerful, and the wind high, raising clouds of dust, which made the latter part of our ride very distressing.

No. 11. Vol. I.   K 2

Oh! City of Palms! how are the mighty fallen! Jericho is now nothing more than an assemblage of the most miserable huts, compared with which the worst Irish cabin is a palace; so low that, at night, one might almost ride over them without being aware of the fact. In most of these, of the dimensions of a pigsty, in the midst of filth at which an English porker would disdainfully turn up his nose, an Arab, his wife and several children, are huddled together,—naked, squalid wretched-looking creatures, of a very dingy complexion; some, indeed, were nearly black. They crowded about us to indulge their curiosity.

The citadel attached to this city of human sties is quite in character, consisting of a small ruinous square tower, with a court surrounded by a wall, having a tank of chocolate-coloured water at one corner, to which rushed man and beast as soon as they were admitted, to quaff the brown element. Necessity would not allow of our being very nice; and parched, with sun and dust as we were, we found it grateful: it was thatched over with boughs to keep it cool. We found here another party, consisting of two Frenchmen and their attendants. Not a palm was to be seen; but there were two very fine fig-trees just outside this tower of strength, whose young green foliage afforded a delightful shelter,

> From off the drooping head to fend the ray
> That downward poured intolerable day.

Thither we retired from the crowd, to rest our weary limbs after the fatigues of the ride, and refresh ourselves with whatever provisions our Greek host at Jerusalem had supplied our basket with. We found nothing but four pigeons and a small quantity of bread; upon which there arose a debate whether we should finish the whole at once, as appetite impelled, and trust to chance for a fresh supply, or reserve a couple of birds for the morrow, as prudence dictated. Prudence at last carried the day; so we divided our scanty fare. But virtue was not rewarded; for, during the night, some of our worthy companions contrived to purloin the contents of the basket. Nothing was to be obtained in these inhospitable regions; consequently we were compelled to fast till our return to Jerusalem.

At sunset, the inclosure was shut, and we were desired to take our repose in the court, amidst Arabs, Russians, Greeks, horses, and donkeys, upon the bare ground. To the ground, as a couch, we had no particular objection, seeing no better bed was to be had; but too great propinquity to the human portion of this motley assembly might have entailed consequences which it would have been difficult quickly to get rid of; we therefore applied to the sheikh for admittance into his turret. At this he demurred, alleging in excuse, that he had no order from the Governor, and that it was against discipline to allow strangers to inspect the fortification! This was rightly interpreted into a hint for *bucksheesh*. We offered a dollar, which, after the usual delay and demand for more, being at length accepted, we were ushered into the interior of this superb fortification, which consisted of an upper and a lower apartment. The lower room had no window, nor any aperture whatever to admit light or air save the door, and was filled with all imaginable nastiness. Of course we declined having anything to say to that. Climbing up a steep and narrow flight of broken stone stairs, we reached the upper chamber, the roof of which had fallen in. In one corner, beneath a bower of branches plastered with mud, reposed the commander-in-chief and his garrison of six or seven men, and we were politely desired to select any of the other three corners that might hit our fancy. In spite of the hardness of our stone bed, we might have slept had it only been exempt from the annoyance of vermin; but even that couch was alive with fleas, which danced about us with untiring energies. A lamb, too, the live-stock of the garrison, resented our intrusion, practising fencing upon our persons, and bleating incessantly during the whole night. Had it not been for these discomforts, sleeping beneath the canopy of heaven would have been agreeable, as the night was warm and pleasant.

An hour before day-break we were summoned to prepare for marching. Our pigeons having flown away, and carried our bread along with them, we were compelled to defer breakfast till some future opportunity. Marshalling our forces in front of the fort now increased by the addition of the sheikh and his garrison, with the exception of one man left behind as a guard, we set out for the Dead Sea, distant about three hours, crossing the most dreary, parched and desert plain imaginable, having the appearance of land left bare by the receding waters of the lake, which seems to have shrunk considerably. *Three Weeks in Palestine and Lebanon.*

To be continued.

ON THE FOLLY OF INDULGING IN ANGER.

PERHAPS there is nothing more necessary or important to mankind, than to be in possession of that habitual self command which will enable them to guard against those bursts of anger, and ebullitions of temper, to which we are all, more or less, inclined. The man who has so studied himself, as to be able to withstand firmly such a furious assailant, has undoubtedly achieved a great work, and merits the applause and approbation of his fellow men. The only way in which this can be accomplished or possibly effected, is by seriously watching over ourselves at all times, by cultivating an acquaintance with our own dispositions, and by so learning our peculiar temperament, that we may be able, in the first rising of this Satanic passion, to oppose a firm barrier to its progress.

If man so acts, and makes it his duty to "know himself," which, as Thales the Milesian observed, was, of all knowledge, the most valuable, and consequently, the most to be desired, he will be able successfully to resist anger, with all its train of subsequent evils.

To expatiate upon the evils inevitably arising from unsubdued passion, and to point out the sin and folly of anger, seems scarcely necessary, when we have such abundant evidence of the ill consequences attending it; evidence not merely collected from the pages of history, or the verses of the poets, but also other incontestable evidence furnished by the pens of inspired writers, and from our own social intercourse in life.

If we were to attempt to heap up examples, and gather illustrations of the ruinous consequences of this dreadful passion, our pages would swell far beyond our present purpose. The poets of old sang of the direful wrath and malignant fury of degenerate man.—Homer begins his poem with discoursing of the destructive wrath of Achilles; and Euripides with the infernal spirit which led on Medea to a fatal revenge. Every historian supplies manifold instances. One informs us of the maddened rage of an Alexander, who stabbed, in a moment of exasperation, his noblest friend. Another of the ruthless Saul, who, fired at once by malice and envy, would have smote the valiant but unassuming warrior, David.

All, indeed, both ancient and modern, both sacred and profane, have united in exclaiming with a celebrated poet, that, "neither sword, nor tempest, nor shipwreck, nor even the thunderbolts of Jove himself, have been the cause of so much ruin and destruction as anger."

We see then the folly of the passion, from a glance at its effects, and thus we behold the danger of heedlessly throwing ourselves into that state of mind, which, where in the least indulged, involves us in difficulties and troubles, the extent and danger of which cannot be known, inasmuch as they cannot be confined or receive any limits.   H.

NATURAL HISTORY.

THE CROCODILE.

THE lizard division of the amphibia presents to us, as its leading class, the formidable crocodiles : a name to which dread and aversion are, by the hasty prejudices of our defective knowledge, almost inseparably attached : for, although this class of creatures is the largest of all known animals, except the elephant, the hippopotamus, and the whale, and a few enormous serpents; yet it is neither a fierce nor a cruel animal, nor ever purposely or unnecessarily injures. It seeks its appointed prey when hunger urges it; but destroys only for food, and has no passion or malignity. In its general form it is extremely similar to the other lizards ; but with distinctive characters peculiar to itself. The mouth is enormously large, opening even beyond its ears, with jaws that are sometimes several feet long. Its teeth, about thirty in each jaw, pass between each other when the mouth is shut ; and have others of a very small size, in their socket, to replace their first ones. The lower jaw is alone moveable ; and having no lateral motion, they mostly swallow what they take without mastication.

They are sometimes thirty feet long. Their whole body is covered by strong, hard scales, except the top of the head, and can be only wounded between the rows of these, which are impenetrable by a musket ball, unless it be fired very near, or the piece be very strongly charged. Having no lips, their teeth are always bare ; and from this peculiarity, though they be walking or swimming with the utmost tranquillity, the aspect seems animated with rage. Another circumstance that contributes to increase the terrific nature of its countenance, is the fiery appearance of the eyes, which being placed obliquely, and very near each other, have a malignant aspect. Over its hard and much wrinkled eyelids, is an indented rim, resembling an eyebrow drawn into a menacing frown. Its brain is extremely small. Its tail and its webbed hind toes, acting like fins, assist it swimming. Its figure being flattened laterally, with some resemblances to an oar, enables it to cut the waters with great swiftness, and with astonishing velocity when about to sieze its prey. On land, it can overtake a man in direct running ; but if he turn quickly round into a circle, he escapes with ease, as the animal cannot so rapidly wheel round its great length of body. We have reason to presume that it will live for more than a hundred years. When pressed with hunger, it devours mankind ; and the large ones even attempt to leap or scramble into boats during the night ; and in some places use their tails to overturn small skiffs, and then sieze on the men or animals within them. It has not been determined at what times, and from what causes, crocodiles acquire this voracity; for they often subsist a long time without any sustenance. In the colder climates they are torpid in the winter ; and bellow like a bull when they wake into sensitiveness from this state. They congregate together in numerous assemblies ; but not for any common purpose, like bees or beaver; nor like seals, from affection. Yet the habit shews that they have a gratification from each other's society; and their not meeting for any specific co-operation, rather implies that a pleasurable sympathy, in seeing and moving with each other, is the real motive of the association. They abound chiefly between the tropics ; but are met several degrees to the north of the one, and to the south of the other. They are smaller, however, as more distant from the equator.

In the Rio San Domingo, and on the west coast of Africa, M. Brue was astonished to find the crocodiles perfectly harmless ; insomuch that children played with them, mounted on their backs, and even beat them, without danger, or any appearance of resentment. This gentleness of disposition proceeds, probably, from the care which is taken by the natives to feed them, and treat them well. M. De la Borde saw crocodiles in Cayenne kept in ponds, where they lived without doing any harm, even to the tortoises kept in the same ponds, and fed along with them on the refuse of the kitchens. To tame these formidable animals, it is stated, nothing is necessary but to supply them abundantly with food ; the want of which is the only cause of their being dangerous.— *Turner's Sacred History of the World.*

POLSTEAD CHURCH.

AMONG the many picturesque villages which adorn the county of Suffolk, Polstead certainly claims particular regard. Viewed from the town of Stoke, it presents a very pleasing appearance, standing nearly upon the summit of a hill, embosomed in trees. To the east the eye may range over the finely-wood valley of the Stour, as it rolls its ample waters into the German Ocean; and there, in the most beautiful portion of the landscape, rises the majestic tower of Dedham Church

"lifted above the clouds
Of the dense air which town or city breeds;
To intercept the sun's glad beams."

Alas! that such a spot should have acquired so dreadful a notoriety among the blood-stained corners of our land. It was here that a wretched man, having begun his career by dishonouring his father, proceeded, step by step, along the dreadful road of crime till, at length, he forfeited his life to the offended laws of his country. It was here that the miserable partner of his vice, and victim of his murderous hand, first left the path of purity and peace, to wander onward in that course of sin, which brought her, at last to a premature and awful grave!

Let us turn from so sickening a scene with the hope that it may be made useful as a warning to all who know its fearful history. Surely we may say with the wise man, "the way of transgressors is hard,"

Polstead Church—the subject of the sketch above—stands within the Park of Polstead Hall, and is almost surrounded by trees. It contains a number of escutcheons belonging to the Brand family, one of whose monuments stands near the altar-piece, bearing the effigies of a man and his infant son, the former looking at a book, and the latter at a human skull which he holds in his hand. Here are also the monuments of Dr. Bakehouse, formerly Archdeacon of Canterbury, and of several other Clergymen who have been incumbents.

The sacred edifice, like most of those which adorn our christian country, has undergone many alterations in form and architectural detail. The decorated style, however, predominates, and it is altogether a very pleasing example of a village "house of prayer."

POETRY.

[In Original Poetry, the name, (real or assumed) of the Author, is printed in Small
Capitals, under the title; in Selections it is printed in Italics at the end.]

AN ACROSTIC.

El canta. che n'l' anima si sento.
GUARINI.

The song that's to the soul so sweet,
Oh! how it steals our thoughts away,
Misery's pulse forgets to beat,
In list'ning to the "magic lay"—
So like the healing balm of heaven,
Seems the power to music given—
Each heart attests its sway;
There is a mystic charm in song,
Religion brings it to her shrine,
And the wrapt soul then soars among
Visions,—extatic and divine:
Enchantress of the vocal train,
Remembrance can't recall a strain
So sweetly breathed as thine.

Soham.

CHRISTIAN TRIUMPHS.

THOUGH laurel crowns and victor
        wreaths
    Be for the sons of triumph twin'd:
Though song her sweetest music breathes
    For the destroyers of our kind;
O let them weep, for time shall sweep
    Their perishable pomp away;
O let them mourn, for death shall turn
    The proudest conqueror into clay.

But here's a deathless coronet,
    Wrought for the holy and the wise:
And here is music sweeter yet,
    Which never faints and never dies;
The good may see earth's glory flee,
    Heaven's ever-living glory theirs,
Their path is peace and pleasantness,
    And they are joy's immortal heirs.

John Bowring.

TO-MORROW.

How sweet to the heart, is the thought of To-morrow,
    When hope's fairy pictures bright colours display
How sweet when we can from futurity borrow,
    A balm for the griefs that afflict us to day.

When wearisome sickness hath taught me to languish,
    For health and the comforts it bears on its wing,
Let me hope, (oh! how soon it will lessen my anguish!)
    That To-morrow will ease, and serenity bring.

When travelling alone, quite forlorn, unbefriended,
    Sweet the hope, that to-morrow my wand'rings will cease:
That at home, with all care sympathetic attended,
    I shall rest unmolested, and slumber in peace.

O, when from the friends of my heart long divided,
    The fond expectation with joy how replete!
That from far-distant regions, by Providence guided,
    To-morrow will see us most happily meet.

When six days of labour each other succeeding,
    With hurry and toil have my spirits oppress'd,
What pleasure to think, as the last is receding,
    To-morrow will be a sweet sabbath of rest.

And when the vain shadows of time are retiring,
    When life is fast fleeting, and death is in sight,
The Christian believing, exulting, expiring,
    Beholds a To-morrow of endless delight.

J. Brown.

MISCELLANY AND EXTRACTS.

WONDERS OF THE OCEAN.—In one of the Tonga Isles in the Pacific ocean, there is a very curious submarine cavern. Mr. Mariner, who describes it, informs us, that being in the vicinity one day, a chief proposed to visit this cave. One after another of the young men dived into the water without rising again, and, at length the narrator followed one of them, and, guided by the light reflected from his heels, entered a large, opening in the rock, and presently emerged in a cavern. The entrance is at least a fathom beneath the surface of the sea at low water, in the side of a rock upwards of sixty feet in height; and leads into a grotto about forty feet wide, and of about the same height, branching off into two chambers. As it is apparently closed on every side, there is no light but the feeble ray transmitted through the sea; yet there was found sufficient, after the eye had been a few minutes accustomed to the obscurity, to show objects with some little distinctness Mr. Mariner, however, desirous of better light, dived out again, procured his pistol, and after carefully wrapping it up, as well as a torch, re-entered the cavern as speedily as possible. Both the pistol and torch, on being unwrapped, were found perfectly dry, and by flashing the powder of the priming, the latter was lighted, and the beautiful grotto illuminated. The roof was hung with stalactites in fantastic forms, bearing some resemblance to the grotto arches and carved ornaments of some old church.

ON LISTENING TO EVIL REPORTS.—The longer I live, the more I feel the importance of adhering to the rules which I have laid down for myself in relation to such matters. 1st. To hear as little as possible what is to the prejudice of others. 2nd. To believe nothing of the kind until I am absolutely forced to it. 3rd. Never to drink into the spirit of one who circulates an ill report. 4th. Always to moderate, as far as I can, the unkindness which is expressed towards others. 5th. Always to believe that if the other side were heard, a very different account would be given of the matter. I consider love as wealth; and

as I would resist a man who should come to rob my house, so I would a man who would weaken my regard for any human being. I consider, too, that persons are cast into different moulds; and that to ask myself, what should I do in that person's situation, is not a just mode of judging. I must not expect a man who is naturally cold and reserved to act as one that is naturally warm and affectionate; and I think it a great evil that persons do not make more allowances for each other in this particular. I think religious people are too little attentive to these considerations: * * amongst whom there is a sad propensity to listen to evil reports, and to beleive the representations they hear. The more prominent any person's character is, the more likely he is to suffer in this way; there being in the heart of every man, unless greatly subdued by grace, a pleasure in hearing anything which may sink others to his 'level, or lower them in the estimation of the world. We seem ourselves elated in proportion as others are oppressed.—*Simeon.*

A sneer is the weapon of the weak. Like other devil's weapons, it is always cunningly ready to our hand, and there is more poison in a handle than in the point. But how many noble hearts have withered with its venomous stab, and festered with its subtile malignity.

MERCHANTS' LEDGERS.—It was an ancient custom for merchants in their books of accounts, to have " Laus Deo," or, Praise to God, written on the beginning of every leaf; and it stood on the head of the page in large and fair letters, to put them always in mind, that in all their human affairs they should carry on a divine design for the glory of God.

HONEST INDUSTRY.—If there is a man who can eat his bread at peace with God and man, it is that man who has brought that bread out of the earth by his own honest industry. It is cankered by no fraud—it is wet by no tear—it is stained by no blood.

Lines by Milton, on the university carrier, who sickened in the time of his vacancy, being forbid to go to London, by reason of the plague.

Here lies old Hobson ; Death hath broke
   his girt,
And here, alas ! hath laid him in the dirt :
Or else the ways being foul, twenty to
   one,
He's here stuck in a slough, and over-
   thrown.
'Twas such a shifter, that, if truth were
   known,
Death was half glad when he had got
   him down ;
For he had, any time this ten years full,
Dodg'd with him betwixt Cambridge and
   the Bull.*
And surely Death could never have pre-
   vail'd,
Had not his weekly course of carriage
   fail'd.
But lately finding him so long at home,
And thinking now his journey's end was
   come,
And that he had ta'en up his latest inn,—
In the kind office of a chamberlain.
Show'd him his room where he must
   lodge that night,
Pull'd off his boots, and took away the
   light:
If any ask for him, it shall be said,
'Hobson has supt, and's newly gone to
   bed,'

   * The Bull Inn, Bishopsgate-street.

INCULCATE CHARITY.—Should you ever have a child to educate, teach him not merely not to condemn too rashly, lest he overwhelm the innocent with the punishment of the guilty ; but teach him also, that even the guilty may often be as deserving of his pity as his censure; tell him that misfortune is the parent of more crimes than is a wicked heart; tell him that even the fallen should retain some claim to a fallen race; and bid him, at least, leave the way to reformation open and drive not the unhappy wretch from evil to worse; and, worst of all, to the fellowship and example of those who are ever ready to seize on fresh pupils, and become tutors in crime.

DON'T GRUMBLE.—He is a fool that grumbles at every little mischance. Put the best foot forward is an old and good maxim, don't run about and tell acquaintances that you have been unfortunate. People dont like to have unfortunate men for acquaintances. Add to a vigorous determination a cheerful spirit ; if reverses come, bear them like a philosopher, and get rid of them as soon as you can. Poverty is like a panther, look it steadily in the face and it will flee from you.

A SERIOUS THOUGHT.—The following inscription is said to have been written upon a pane of glass, by Dr. Williams, of St. John's College, Cambridge :—

   "PHILIP WILLIAMS.

Frail glass, thou bear'st my name as
   well as I,
And no man knows in which it first shall
   die."

MONTHLY NOTICES.

NOVEMBER.

Middle Fen Tax Payable, (see Advertisements in Newspapers.)
20th.—Half yearly Interest on Savings' Bank deposits due, and Annual Accounts made up.
Bedford Level Corporation Tax must be paid in this month.
17th.   County Court, held at the Court House, Soham

Ilchester Church.

. PLAYFORD'S

SOHAM MAGAZINE,

AND

ꬍrienⅅlp ꭹonitor.

T was a maxim uttered by the great Lord Burleigh that, "England can never be ruined, unless it is by her own Parliament." Let us hope that the present Parliament will not stamp the Lord High Treasurer's maxim with the character of Prophecy. Certain it is that dangers of the most formidable character surround the Throne, while the great mass of the people are ignorant and unconcerned in the matter. An enemy more powerful, more subtle, and more persevering than England has ever had yet to contend with, is using every effort that the most refined policy could devise for her overthrow. Men of the highest order of intellect, with the most perfect knowledge of the secret springs of human action, and with an almost unbounded supply of pecuniary means, are urging with sleepless energy, and remorseless zeal, every engine which art and hatred can supply, for the extinction of the Protestantism of these Realms.

Alas! that any should be found who are indifferent on so momentous a subject : as if it were a matter of small concern whether the Church of England or the Church of Rome were established in this country. For the supposition that the Government can exist without any alliance with an established form of religion, is as visionary an idea as ever entered into the mind of the weakest enthusiast to conceive. But how far more deplorable is the thought that the descendants of those who shed their heart's blood at the

No. 12. Vol. I.   N

stake, under the cruel hand of Popery, should now not only not shrink with horror from that frightful power, but should open their bosoms for the reception of its deadly coil.   Popery and freedom, are as opposite as darkness and light.   Popery and truth, are as widely dissevered as two antagonistical systems can possibly be; and the moment this " Mother of Abominations," attains the ascendency she so ardently seeks, she will set her foot upon the liberties and civilization of the world.

In speaking thus of Popery, we would carefully distinguish between *individuals* and a *system*.   It is the *system of Popery* against which we feel so imperatively called to protest; for it is a system which utterly enslaves every member of its own community, and will never rest till it has trampled all the obstacles to its unlimited ambition in the dust.   The Church of Rome will never rest, we say, till she attain this object of her supreme desires. And yet, however far she may succeed, as a judgment upon apostate Christendom, the day shall surely come when an insulted Deity shall blast her with the breath of his righteous displeasure, and wo be to all those who have not joined the standard of the cross against her, for they shall be partakers in her fearful plagues.

Before the admission of Papists to seats in Parliament, every member of both Houses, previous to his admission, solemnly and sincerely, in the presence of God, and in the plain and ordinary sense of the word, without any evasion, or equivocation, or mental reservation whatever, professed, and testified, and declared that Popery was IDOLATRY.   And yet, in spite of this solemn declaration, an intimate, and perfect, and national, and legalized ingraftation of idolatry has been effected with the profession of pure and scriptural truth, and the vassals of the Pope, may now legislate for the Queen of England, whose very title to the Crown is derived from the hostility of her ancestors towards them, and from obedience to whom, every one of her subjects is declared, by the decisions of their church, to be virtually absolved.

Protestantism is the polar star of England; and if she should dare to steer her course by any of the false lights of political expediency, she will inevitably be hurled from the proud position she has so long held, among the nations of the earth,—a monument of the just retribution of heaven upon her presumptuous sins.

CHRISTMAS.

Hail! father Christmas! hail to thee,
Honour'd ever shalt thou be!
All the sweets that love bestows,
Endless pleasures wait on those,
Who, like vassals brave and true,
Give to Christmas homage due.

CHORUS TO A NORMAN CAROL.

THE feelings associated with this season, in the olden time, were of a very exuberant character; and the preparations for giving it due homage were actively commenced several weeks before. Indeed our East-Anglian housewives have been accustomed, very irreverently it is true, to consider the Collect for the last Sunday after Trinity to be the Church's admonition, "to think of mixing the ingredients of their mince-pies," and have therefore, says Forby, denominated it, from the initial words of the Collect, "Stir-up Sunday."*

Every festival had its eve; and as it was customary to devote a portion of the preceding day to the more immediate preparations for the coming feast, the spirit of the festival entered into it, and various ceremonies, observances, and marvels became a necessary adjunct. Bees were said to be heard on Christmas eve as if it were a day in June; and cattle to kneel in their stalls, their heads bowed to the east, as if in devotion.† Shakspere writes,

" Some say, that ever 'gainst that season comes
Wherein our Saviour's birth is celebrated,
The bird of dawning singeth all night long;
And then they say no spirit dares stir abroad;
The nights are wholesome; then no planets strike,
No fairy takes, nor witch hath power to charm,
So hallow'd and so gracious is the time."

The famous Glastonbury thorn, traditionally said to have grown into a tree from the stick of St. Joseph of Arimathea, which took root when stuck by him in the ground at that place, was for ages believed to put on its blossoms on the eve of Christmas,‡ and many piously disposed Christians in the times of popery, made a pilgrimage to witness this miraculous occurrence. Its fame was so great that other religious houses sought for the same attraction, and some few were favoured by the Glastonbury monks with cuttings from the original tree, which, being planted in consecrated ground, and with religious ceremonies, grew and flourished, and became trees possessing the desired peculiarity. The East-Anglian Christmas flowering thorn, at Parham in Suffolk, was doubtless a scion of the same holy stick. Among the lesser wonders of the time was the belief that bread baked on this eve never became mouldy,—probably because none of it was left unconsumed in the ensuing season of unbounded hospitality.

* That it was a very common practice, in Roman Catholic times, to denominate Sundays or Holidays from the initial words of the Collect, Anthem, &c., of the day, is seen by the Paston Letters; but this is believed to be the only, and a very sad, instance of its Protestant use.

† "An honest countryman," says Brand, in his Popular Antiquities, "living near Launceston, Cornwall, informed me in 1790, that he, with others, watched several oxen in their stalls at the above time, and at 12 o'clock at night, they observed the two oldest oxen fall upon their knees, and 'make a cruel moan, like christian creatures.'"

‡ The belief in the sudden blowing of different flowering trees, shrubs, or plants, on the eves of particular festivals, was very general. On New Year's eve, it was believed in our antient kingdom, that at 12 o'clock at night, the rosemary, the sacred emblem of faithful remembrance, burst into flower.

Ale was the accustomed beverage of our forefathers in all parts of England, and in various forms, entered into the catalogue of good things which the rustics enjoyed on great days and high seasons; but "'twas Christmas broached the mightiest ale." One of the peculiar observances, in our own district, was the offering to all comers of a jug of ale or mead, with a toast and nutmeg. In the west, the wassail* bowl, filled with Lamb's Wool, (a rural nectar, formed by roasting a number of apples on a string, till they fell hissing hot into a large bowl of spiced ale) was carried from door to door, frequently by "wenches," with much merriment and rejoicing. In Yorkshire, they were wiser than the people of the west; for, instead of parading their ale about the streets, they got a large block of wood (the most knotty being preferred) called the yule-log, and having brought it in with much ceremony, and set it upon the fire, comfortably sat themselves adown before it, and "lapped their Christmas ale, singing, with loud voices, 'Yule, yule, a pack of new cards† and a Christmas stool.'" The remnant of the yule-log was carefully put by to kindle the fire the next Christmas, not merely because it was deemed lucky thus to connect the two festivals, but because it was believed to possess the virtue of preserving the place and those belonging to it, from any spiteful intentions or devices of the devil and his emissaries.

In Rome Christmas morn is ushered in by the Pifferari (*pipers*)—shepherds from the Abruzzi mountains, who come annually to pay their homage to the Virgin mother on the birth of her Son. This they offer at each of those little shrines which are met with in niches in the various streets; playing a wind instrument like a bagpipe. They also stop at the shops of carpenters, out of respect to Joseph, the husband of Mary. In this country, carols‡ were sung, in reference to the song of the angels on the birth of our Saviour; Bishops carolled among their clergy; and Carols were substituted for the Psalms, in the service of the day; the clerk, even in protestant times, declaring at the end his "wishes for a merry Christmas and a happy new year." The carol formed too, a part of the feast itself; at the Christmas kept by Henry VIII., at Greenwich, in the third year of his reign, the Dean and others of the Chapel Royal, we are told, "sang a carall" after the first course. The earliest known carol, that from which we have borrowed the refrain at the head of this paper, is preserved in the British Museum.

These ditties—at one time the delight of kings, princes and prelates—now exclusively enliven the Irish peasant, or the industrious servant maid and the humble labourer of our country; if we except, perhaps, the happy bluecoat boy of the great Metropolis, many of whom, perhaps, like the kind-hearted Charles Lamb, have listened to the carol of our Church, sung by the elder boys, assembled in the portico beneath the hall—

> "Hark! the herald angels sing,
> Glory to the new-born King;
> Peace on earth. and mercy mild,
> God and sinners reconciled!"

* According to Steevens, this name is supposed to have its origin from the words which Ronix, daughter of Hengist, used when she drank to Vortigern, "Loverd King, was hail;" he answering her, "Drinc-heile;" and then, as Robert of Gloucester says,
"Kuste hire and sitte hire adoune and glad dronk her heil,
And that was tho in this land the verst was-hail."
The expression is supposed to be a corruption of the Saxon words signifying 'wish health.' Washaile and drinc-haile afterwards became the common phrases of quaffing among the English.
† The practice of playing at cards at Christmas is noticed by Bishop Latimer.
‡ Derived from "cantare" to sing, and "rola" an interjection of joy.

till they have "been transported to the fields of Bethlehem, and the song which was sung at that season, by the angels' voices to the shepherds." The Waits, formerly looked for with so much interest, and their soft and aerial sounds listened to with a holy rapture, having become, in general, but rude inharmonious disturbers, have been mostly discontinued; but in the neighbouring town of Cambridge, parties perambulate the town, not on the eve and morn of Christmas only, but for many nights previous, and with strains of earth enliven the werdly-minded,—the sacred carol with its holy associations being disregarded.

In some places the morn was ushered in with miraculous music. In our own country, at Raleigh in Nottinghamshire, where an entire village with its church was swallowed up by an earthquake, the bells of the entombed temple were accustomed to ring on this most sacred of days; and, even now, it is usual for the villagers to go to the miraculous valley, and placing their ears to the ground, hearken to the subterranean melody!

An early sunshine on this morning was a thing to be desired; and many are the simple folk in the west who, in our own time, peer out earnestly on Christmas morning, to see the sun shine through the apple trees; and if it do, have faith in the prospect of the boughs rejoicing under a rich burden in the ensuing season.

The festival of Christmas,—the greatest feast of the Church,—by that strange corruption which turned religious festivals into days of excessive indulgence, was formerly conducted on an extensive and regular system; and, until comparatively very lately, the hospitalities lasted to the "twelfth day."

An English gentleman of the olden time, was accustomed to be surrounded by his tenants and neighbours by day-break. The strong beer was broached, and the "black jacks" went merrily about with toast, sugar, and nutmeg, and Cheshire cheese and slices of "hackin," or great Christmas sausage, which was always ready by day-break; or the cook was liable to be taken by the arms, by two young men, and compelled to run round the market or green till she was ashamed of her laziness. In the Isle of Thanet the festivities were begun by a curious musical procession, the origin of which is inexplicable. A party of young people having procured a horse's head, affix it to a pole about four feet in length; a string is then tied to the lower jaw, and a horse cloth being attached to the whole, one of the party goes under it, and by frequently pulling the string, keeps up a loud snapping noise. Accompanied by the rest of the party, grotesquely habited and singing carols and ringing bells, they proceed from house to house; asking for money beer or cake. This practice is termed a "hodening," and the horse's head a "hoden." In High Suffolk, says Forby, in many farm-houses, a large quantity of frumenty, or *fermety** as it is provincially sounded, is prepared, and the labourers with their wives and children are invited to breakfast upon it

The old English prince, nobleman, and squire, had their tables spread, from first to last of the holidays, with sirloins of beef, capons, turkeys, plum puddings and porridge, mince pies, &c., and all who came were heartily welcome.

An Earl of Gloucester used to entertain at his manor of Keynsham, two hundred knights at his table during Christmas. On Chrsitmas day, it is recorded there were thirty eel pies smoking on his table, and they were considered a great dainty, possibly being furnished by the far-famed waters of our own Isle of Ely.

* Parched wheat boiled in milk. It is considered a great treat, and is really a most nourishing and delicious food.

Yet if we believe Massinger, the country banquets were not to be compared to those in London. In his play of the *City Madam*, he says :—

> " Men may talk of *country Christmases*,
> Their thirty-pound butter'd eggs, their pies of carps' tongues,
> Their pheasants drench'd with ambergris, the carcasses
> Of three fat wethers bruis'd for gravy, to
> Make sauce for a single peacock; yet their feasts
> Were fasts, compar'd with the City's."

And then he proceeds to describe the city feast, as containing among other rare dishes, "three sucking pigs served up in a dish, a fortnight fed with dates and muscadine, that cost 20 marks apiece. The dishes, (he adds) were raised over one another, as woodmongers do billets, and most of the shops of the best confectioners in London were ransacked to furnish out a banquet." And so great was the charm of a London banquet that it became too common for country gentlemen to spend their Christmas in London; so much so as to be considered detrimental to the public weal, and to cause Queen Bess, in 1589, to command "the gentlemen of Norfolk and Suffolk to departe from London before Xtemasse, and to repaire to their counties, and there to keepe hospitalitie amongst their neighboures.*

But amongst all the marvels in the way of feasting, we must not omit to mention the Punch Bowl of Admiral Russel.† When at Cadiz, in 1695, he gave a Christmas entertainment to the officers and merchants then resident there.—"In the middle of a garden of lemons and oranges was a fountain set with Dutch tiles in the bottom and sides. Into this was poured six butts of water, half a hogshead of strong mountain Malaga wine, two hundred gallons of brandy, six cwt. of sugar, twelve thousand lemons, and nutmegs and sugar in proportion. Dinner being ended, the company marched in order to the fountain, where, on the punch was floating a little boat with a boy in it, and cups to serve it out to the company. On the company's leaving, the mob were admitted, and they went into it, shoes and stockings and all on, "and had like to have turned the boat with the boy over; and so he might have been drowned in punch; but to prevent further danger they sucked it up."

The following particulars of some of the more usual components of a Christmas dinner may prove interesting.—

PLUM PORRIDGE.—Misson, in his "Travels in England," says, "They also make a sort of soup with plums, which they call plum porridge." It is alluded to in a Christmas song in Poor Robin's Almanac for 1695, in association with mince pies. Brand says, "The first thing at the chaplain's table at St. James's Palace, in 1801, was a tureen full of rich luscious plum porridge." So that the French cook's blunder was not quite so ridiculous as it is generally thought, when he forgot the one thing—"De pudding bag, sare." A worse mistake was made by a Spanish chemist, at Gibraltar, who being requested by a cook to *make up* a plum pudding for the officers of the garrison, when they had sent home for the receipt for their Christmas dinner, innocently enquired whether it was to be *spread upon plaister!*

MINCE PIES.—This dish is of great antiquity, and is supposed to have reference, in its savoury ingredients, to the offering of the wise men! It was formerly always made oblong, in imitation of the rack or manger wherein Christ was laid! It was held to be of great importance to every individual to eat as many of these pies as

---

* Lodge's Illustrated English History.
† Described in Moore's Almanac for 1711.

possible, seeing that the quantum of happiness to be enjoyed in the subsequent year depended on the number of pies discussed during the Christmas season. In Suffolk, the individual is said to ensure as many happy months after Christmas as he or she eats mince pies, at different houses, before it.

BOAR'S HEAD.—A soused boar's head, decorated "with garlands gay and rosemary," used to be borne with great state and solemnity to the principal table in the nobleman's hall, as the first dish on Christmas-day. It is still retained at Queens' College, Oxford, where the carol sung at its entrance is also preserved; and it is seen occasionally in some great houses, but it is more generally superseded by the collar of brawn. The dish was introduced at this feast in derision of Judaism, which especially abhors that animal. In Queen Elizabeth's time we find brawn directed to be used at breakfast at Christmas.

THE TURKEY is comparatively a modern article of Christmas fare, though introduced into this country from America early in the 16th century, and absurdly called by this name in accordance with the custom of the day of so styling every highly-esteemed foreign production. It was at first considered only as a curiosity, and is said to have been first served up in France at the nuptial feast of Charles IX., in 1570. It now shares equally with the sirloin (the knighthood of which is familiar to all) in the honors of the Christmas feast. As many as 3,000 of these birds have been known to be sent from the Norwich market alone in three days, to supply the tables of the Londoners. Some are fattened to the weight of 25 lbs. or 30 lbs., and are sold at £2 or £3 a-head to gratify the gourmands of the Metropolis.

But feasting, high and jovial as it was, was not the only characteristic of this festival: its distinguishing feature, capable of being indulged in by all, was and is, we are happy to say, the decoration of the apartments and things with evergreens— beautiful ornaments and fitting emblems of a christian's joy and gladness. Holly, ivy, bay, and mistletoe it was absolutely essential to introduce,—the yew never. In East-Anglia, and perhaps elswhere, it is still believed, that if a branch of yew should be brought into the house with the other evergreens, a death would be sure to occur in it before the end of the year. The period to which the evergreens are suffered to remain is to Candlemas eve, when every particle must be removed, or some misfortune will certainly happen to the family.

The "red-gemmed holly" is traditionally said to have been unknown before it sprang up in perfection and beauty beneath the footsteps of Christ when he first trod the earth, and that the beasts all reverence it, and are never known to injure it.

The ivy is said to have a charm against care; and to ward off all pernicious influences from the cup which it encircles. In Thom's "Anecdotes and Traditions," published by the Camden Society, it is related that in several parts of Oxfordshire, and particularly at Launton, it was till lately customary for the maid-servant to ask the man for ivy to dress the house, and if he denies or neglect it, the maid steals away a pair of his nether garments, and nails them up to the gate in the yard or highway!

Boughs of bay were considered a sure protection from fire or lightning; and a leaf of it, held in the mouth, was believed to protect the wearer from misfortune or pollution.

The mistletoe, the delight of the young everywhere, has always been invested with a sacred character, probably from its then mysterious growth; since the days when it formed part of the mystic superstition of the Druids. It was not admitted with the evergeens into churches, says Brand, but it was hung up in great state in houses, and whatever female chanced to stand under it, the young men present claimed the right of saluting her, and of plucking off a berry at each kiss.   Mr. Archdeacon Nares, in his valuable glossary, adds, " there was a charm attached to it that the maid who was not kissed under it at Christmas would not be married in the year."

The Puritans, rigid religionists, naturally disgusted with the excesses which had grown up under a licentious priesthood, sought to curtail the people's festivals ; but unhappily their zeal was without knowledge ; and they could only reform by uprooting.   The Parliament began in 1642, by suppressing the plays,—relics of the mysteries of papal times, which formed a part of the amusements of the days, in which the unhappy Charles the First, following the example of his predecessors for many ages, had frequently taken part. This was followed, in 1647, by an ordinance,[*] forbidding " the feast of the nativity," (or Christide as it was then generally termed, in abhorrence of the word *mass*) with other holidays to be . any longer observed. And, five years afterwards, not content with sanctioning the non-observance of that day, they proceeded to encourage its desecration, by directing the markets to be held thereon, and charging the city authorities "to protect from wrong and violence" those who should open their shops on that day !

It may with reason be urged, that in all the feasting and mummery of the olden time, there was not much like a commemoration of the epoch of the Gospel dispensation ; but we confess we should grieve to see a return of the gloomy severity of the Puritans.   There is a happy medium which is more generally observed in our day,—a decent, if not a devout, observance of religious ordinances, combined with the exercise of kindly feelings towards connexions, neighbours, and dependents,— the meeting of families whose members are at other times divided, the invitation to the social board of the lone beings whose home affords no gladdening circle of happy faces, the " dealing of thy bread to the hungry and the bringing of the poor to thy house," which the inspired volume declares to be the feast preferred by the Giver of all good, and which brings to the heart the " light breaking forth as the morning, and the (moral) health springing forth speedily."   Far distant be the day when such exercises of the best affections shall be restrained ; but alike removed be the scenes of noisy revelling, of excess and wantonness, which put open shame on that great Gift to the world, of which Christmas is the celebration.

Beautifully has a talented American author written of this happy season :—" Of all the old festivals, that of Christmas awakens the strongest and most heartfelt associations. There is a tone of sacred and solemn feeling that blends with our conviviality, and lifts the spirit to a state of hallowed and elevated enjoyment.   The services of the Church about this season are extremely tender and inspiring.   They dwell on the beautiful story of the origin of our faith, and the pastoral scenes that accompanied its announcement. They gradually increase in fervour and pathos during the season of Advent, until they break forth in full jubilee on the morning that brought peace and good will to men. I do not know a grander effect of music on the moral feelings, than to hear the full choir and the pealing organ performing a Christmas anthem in a cathedral, and filling every part of the vast pile with triumphant harmony."

* In allusion to these ordinances, we find Butler directing his wit against those who
" Quarrel with mince-pies, and disparage
Their best and dearest friend, plum-porridge."

OUR TOWN.

Concluded from Page 168.

In resuming our paper with a glance at the fretful and disturbed reign of the second James, we are very painfully impressed by the fact, that popery, under every circumstance, is the fell foe of all civil reforms,—the vampire that exhausts the life-blood of national greatness,—the tyrant whose iron heel falls foully on personal independence and free thought,—the huge demon that usurps the place of God, and trades with heaven and conscience as marketable commodities. The historian Hume says rightly enough, that it is a very dangerous experiment to trifle with the settled protestant complexion of the English mind, and if any stronger proof were needed, we would only advert to the present reign, furnishing as it does, on one hand an imperious bigot papist driving his kingly authority to the very utmost; and on the other, a sturdy well-principled resistance, that sent back the affront with such terrible recoil, as soon, not only to abridge the monarch's power into the narrowest circle, but to make the very throne itself totter. Let the events of this reign burn into living remembrance, and stand out in so striking a relief, as not only to be recollected by protestant monarchs, but read by every religious man in the empire. Don't tell us that the devil, transformed into an angel of light, is less satanic; nor that the papacy, under the guise of modern tissues and phases, is less monstrous and destructive. To hate its principles and dogmas, is a part of virtuous, religious, and political duty. William of Orange was called to take the reins of a mis-managed government, and though in himself a cold, inflexible, and reserved man, mistrustful of his subjects, and narrowed in his religious views, yet his firmness of command resulted in the return of a healthful state of public mind, the advancement of the sciences, and the diffusion of domestic comfort. The clouds had already rolled back from the eastern firmament, and one by one arose those fixed stars of mental greatness, Locke, Boyle, and Dryden. This was the time also when the barber's business received a new impulse, for as the long beard was reduced to a small pointed lock of hair in the reign of Charles I., and mustachios only remained in the reign of James II., now the use of beards was discontinued altogether, and men looked smooth, sleek, and christianly. It would have been no small treat to listen to the lucubrations of Tim Latherem, who saw his labours extended by the length of visage over which his razor was now privileged to glide, nor a little amusing to hear him, as tradesmen are wont, depreciate the ability of a limping shoemaker who, to fill up his time and increase his gains, had trespassed upon his immunities by commencing barber, in all its important and mysterious varieties.—"Gentlemen, he can neither bleed, nor cure corns. charm away an ague fit, nor take a body respectably by the nose. Fah! He's a cobbler and his hands"—and here he broke off, to open the door for another customer, and if he forgot to renew the strain, it is likely he did less injury both to truth and conscience. And now breaks upon us, what is called, the Augustan Age of England, radiant with those constellations of litera-ture, Newton, Addison, Pope, Steele, and Swift, and adorned by the trophies of such commanders as Marlborough, Peterborough, and Shovel. "Our Town" rang with their praise and exploits, and especially as of yore, the "Royal Arms" was the arena of politics and song. Shovel, who was the son of a Norfolk peasant, might have heard his name and doings jingled in rhyme, and trilled in such nasal measures as would have made his very sword leap out of its scabbard in madness,

> "For he's a brave lord admiral,
> With a roodle doodle diddle lel the dal."

since men's heads were much more filled with narratives of engagements than ought beside, and with the exception of the clergyman, few were improved or benefitted by the learned pens that now began to distil thoughts which are too indelible to be destroyed by time, and too valuable to be contrasted.

The House of, Brunswick-Hanover, brings us to a period when oral history is full of authenticity. Those hoary heads that lately went down to the grave like a ripe shock of corn, have amused us by stirring relations of what their fathers and our great grandsires said of the first and second Georges,—of their rough, cold, and heartless manners,—of the Pretender and the *young* Pretender,—of Sir John Blunt's South Sea bubble, a scheme to buy up the national debt,—of the barbarous treatment of the Jacobites,—the alteration in the calendar, and so on. But we must let the panorama glide off, relieved as it is by curteseying and smiling dames with painfully pinched-in waists, the skirt standing out over enormous hoops, and the elbows adorned with huge ruffles. The hair too is drawn tight up over the forehead and towers above the head like Eddystone lighthouse. Look at the flounces, frills, and trimmings, the endless variety of colours exhibited on the same dress, and whilst wondering at the tom-fool fashion, we will avert our eyes and blush that dignified beings like ourselves should be led by its certain tyranny, yet uncertain laws.

The christian King and father of the people, George III., was permitted to reign long and gloriously, over a nation progressing year by year, in all that constitutes true and permanent greatness, and it would have been utterly strange, if the rising tide of general improvement had not reached " Our Town." Space compels us to be brief, so we pass by at once the stupendous events of these times, events which disruptured empires, destroyed thrones and sent their influences through the world's centre. It is ours, under the blessed sceptre of Victoria, to enjoy peace, settled peace, and an amount of prosperity and general enlightenment, unprecedented in any other period of our History. Go through the hamlet nooks, the pretty towns, the bustling cities of Great Britain, and tell us whether you would exchange your native soil for the romantic hills of Switzerland, or the balmy air of Italy, No !—

> " England with all thy faults l love thee still."

And who can deny that " Our Town " is a fair feature in the general landscape, and especially that it presents a good degree of moral, social, and mental excellence. We have within our parish a few of the best hearts, in the universe, and some heads too, whose wisdom is worth respecting, and whose precepts are worth following. We have the cunning hand to write, and the powerful press to disseminate what is written, and by these and other means we hope, not only to become a happy people ourselves, but also the humble agents of communicating happiness to others.

EXCURSION TO THE DEAD SEA AND THE JORDAN.
Concluded from Page 171.

At the first dawning, the tints of the rising sun, purple and gold, with the deep shadows concealing the nakedness of the land, gave beauty to the landscape. The mountains encircling the lake, which lay sleeping and motionless beneath them reflecting their images, supplied a noble outline which fancy might fill up at its pleasure with a thousand Edens; but as the sun ascended, the illusion was quickly dissipated: the full glare of day displayed the wilderness in its true colouring of awful desolation—a desolation that was felt, and which depressed the spirits. The mountains assumed one uniform brown livery, unrelieved by even a passing shadow, for not a cloud was visible in the blazing heavens: the sea was of a dull, heavy, leaden hue, unlike the fresh transparent purple which the living waters of a still mountain-lake usually display. The ground over which we rode, riven into chasms and ravines showed not a blade of verdure: the few stunted shrubs that had struggled into life were masses of thorns with scarcely a leaf upon them, and wore the brown garb of the desert. The whole scene was a fearful exhibition of the blasting of the breath of the Almighty's displeasure!

In the centre of the plain stood a huge vulture, looking like the evil genius of the place, who suffered us to approach within pistol-shot, then sullenly rose with a loud scream of indignation at our invasion of his territories, and sailed slowly away over the lake to his eyry in the mountains of Moab. Enormous locusts, three and four inches in length, of a yellowish-green colour, were flying about; they were so large that, by the uncertain light of the early morning, I at first mistook them for birds; and a miserable hare, no larger than a rabbit, of a dusty gray colour, started from beneath a bush. These were the only wild creatures that we saw.

The shores at this northern extremity are remarkably flat, and strewed with vast quantities of drift-wood, white and bleached by the sun, which is brought down by "the swellings of Jordan." I did not perceive any bitumen lying about; but, as I was unable to dismount, I could not make a narrow inspection. There were a considerable number of shells resembling the cockle along the shore. It was a sore disappointment to me that I was compelled to relinquish my intention of bathing in these memorable waters; one of my companions, however, did so, and his experience corroborated the accounts of their extraordinary buoyancy, which enabled him to float with a facility which he had never experienced in the sea. The lake was so shallow that he was obliged to wade a long way before he could obtain sufficient depth for swimming; the bottom. when stirred, threw out quantities of fixed air bubbles, and the water, as it dried upon his skin, left a slight white incrustation, and was intolerably nauseous to the taste. My fellow-traveller related the result of his bath to one of [the Frenchmen in company, who never went within two hundred yards of the lake, though he was there for the purpose of writing a book. "Ah, bah! monsier," replied he, "it is all a fable." So much for accuracy of investigation!

Proceeding along the shore of the Dead Sea, we arrived at the mouth of the river, which was not more than fifty or sixty yards across, flowing between steep banks about fourteen feet in height, with sedges growing thickly at the bottom; higher up, the stream is overshadowed by willows and other shrubs. Riding along the bank for a couple of miles, and passing through a thicket of tamarisks and oleanders, at a bend of the river thickly shaded with willows, we found the spot which tradition marks as that where the Israelites marched over Jordan, and where our Saviour was baptised. It was here fordable, being not more than four feet deep; the current rapid. The pilgrims immediately stripped, and rushing down the steep bank, plunged into the sacred stream. Many had brought a white robe with them to wear at this ceremony, among whom was a Greek priest, who was busily engaged in dipping his compatriots "seven times in Jordan." The process of ablution lasted half an hour, which, if it did not, as they fondly imagined, wash their souls white, had that very desirable effect upon their bodies, which was in most instances highly needful. When they were re-clad, and had filled their bottles with the holy water, and out down branches of the willows to be carried off as mementoes of the place, we returned towards Rihhah by a more direct route.

At some distance from the present bank of the Jordan, is another line of bank. Whether this has been formed by inundations, or whether in ancient times the Jordan was a far more considerable stream than it is at present, is a question which I am unable to determine. The river was very low, although at this time of year (the middle of April) one might suppose that the melting of the snows of Lebanon would have increased the body of its waters, if it ever did so.

Three Weeks in Palestine and Lebanon.

THE OCEAN.

Who ever gazed upon the broad Sea without emotion?   Whether seen in stern majesty, hoary with the tempest, rolling its giant waves upon the rocks, and dashing with resistless fury some gallant bark on an iron-bound coast; or sleeping beneath the silver moon, its broad bosom broken but by a gentle ripple, just enough to reflect a long line of light, a path of gold upon a pavement of sapphire;—who has looked upon the Sea without feeling that it has power

"To stir the soul with thoughts profound."

Perhaps there is no earthly object, not even the cloud-cleaving mountains of an Alpine country, so sublime as the Sea in its severe and naked simplicity.   Standing on some promontory, whence the eye roams far out upon the unbounded Ocean, we may conceive a nobler idea of the majesty of that God, who holdeth "the waters in the hollow of his hand."   But it is only when on a long voyage, climbing day after day to the giddy elevation of the mast-head, one still discerns nothing in the wide circumference but the same boundless waste of waters, that the mind grasps anything approaching an adequate idea of the grandeur of the Ocean.   There is a certain indefiniteness and mystery connected with it in various aspects, that gives it a character widely different from that of the land.   At times, in peculiar states of the atmosphere, the the boundary of the horizon becomes undistinguishable, and the surface, perfectly calm, reflects the pure light of heaven in every part, and we seem alone in infinite space, with nothing around that appears tangible and real save the ship beneath our feet.   At other times, particularly in the clear waters of the tropical seas, we look downward unmeasured fathoms beneath the vessel's keel, but still find no boundary; the sight is lost in one uniform transparent blueness. Mailed and glittering creatures of strange forms suddenly appear, play a moment in our sight, and with the velocity of a thought have vanished in their boundless depths.   The very birds we see in the wild waste are mysterious: we wonder whence they come, whither they go, how they sleep, homeless and shelterless as they seem to be.   The breeze, so fickle in its visitings, rises and dies away; but "thou knowest not whence it cometh and whither it goeth;" the night-wind moaning by, soothes the watchful helmsman with gentle sounds, that remind him of the voices of beloved ones far away; or the tempest shrieking and groaning among the cordage turns him pale with the idea of agony and death. But God is there; lonely though the mariner feel, and isolated in his separation from home and friends, God is with him, often unrecognised and forgotten, but surrounding him with mercy, protecting him and guiding him, and willing to cheer him by the visitation of His grace, and the assurance of His love. "If I take the wings of the morning, and dwell in the uttermost parts of the sea; even there shall Thy hand lead me, and Thy right hand shall hold me."

POETRY.

[In Original Poetry, the name, (real or assumed) of the Author, is printed in Small Capitals, under the title; in Selections it is printed in Italics at the end.]

AN O'ER TRUE TALE.
Scott.

She drank of Pleasure's cup, that quickly turned
To bitterness and death, Now o'er her grave,
The night-wind sighs, but whispers not her name

In fashion's maze I found her,
  Light sparkled on her brow,
With beauty's smiles around her,
  Alas! how alter'd now.

The false one, he had seen her,
  To him, each art was known,
From virtue's path to wean her,
  And mark'd her for his own.

Of reason he bereav'd her,
  In passions melting tone;
He flatter'd, he deceived her,
  She lov'd that faithless one.

In triumph he departed,
  Abandon'd to her fate,
Deserted—broken hearted,
  Her soul was desolate.

The tempest howl'd—she heard not,
  The thunder-cloud had burst;
The lightning flash'd, she fear'd not,
  For fate had done its worst.

Again the false one sought her,
  But came too late to save,
And where her grief had brought her,
  He perish'd—on her grave.*

* The elegant and accomplished Captain S——, after a brief but libertine career, terminated his existence upon the grave of his victim.

Soham.

LINES
Written in pencil on the "Anglesey Column," near the Menai Bridge, North Wales, in 1826.

* Where Anglesey his laurels gained
  This column rose to tell,
Could "Cimric" gratitude, no more,
  And say where Picton fell?
For him no cenotaph is rais'd,
  No requiem o'er his grave,—
E'en envy wrote his epitaph,
  "He died, as die the brave." †

* Since the above was written a national Testimonial has been erected, to commemorate the military services of that gallant soldier; whose name will ever be enrolled in the imperishable records of the military historian.
† Vide the Waterloo Despatch.

THE SUMMER'S PAST.
JAMES HAZLEWOOD.

The summer's past, the flower's decay'd,
  Its richest foliage pale and sere;
Nature in russet robes array'd,
  Proclaims approach of winter near:
The perfumed bower, the sylvan shade,
  Of sweetest flowers, are all decay'd.

The summer's past, the vernal breeze,
  That gladden'd nature's wild domain,
And fann'd the form of pale disease,
  Must yield to winter's chilling reign.
The summer's past, and life's short bloom,
  Is hastening onward to the tomb.

The summer's past, and wintry rains
  May hush the music of the grove;
Yet spring will renovate the plains.
  The woods shall hear the voice of love:
So when death's dreary winter's o'er,
  Spring will the conqueror's spoil restore.

Liverpool.

TO MY FIRST GREY HAIRS.

Blossoms of death! why here so soon,
Startling and sad as snow in June?
My summers are but thirty-three,
Why come ye then so soon to me?

Blossoms of death! whence do ye grow?
Why do ye come, but never go?
Winter's white flowers give place in
    spring;
You to the last in your place cling!

Blossoms of death! then why so soon—
Why come to me before life's noon?
Few years—how few!—have passed me
    by!
Why come to one so young as I?

Blossoms of death! although to me
Solemn your early mission be,
I'll take it friendly, since your bloom
Bespeaks a life beyond the tomb!

All things have use: as snowdrops bring
Some tidings of a coming spring,
Blossoms of death! ye say—"Prepare
To leave this dull, cold scene of care!"

And as, when spring breaks on your gaze,
The snowdrop withers and decays,
Blossoms of death; so your decay
Shall come, but with a brighter day!

Thus whether, blossoms pale! with me
Your season short or long may be,
Still let me trust, as you grow rife,
The fruit will be immortal life!

    S. T. Hall, the "Sherwood Forester."

LINES TO A FRIEND.

J. GOODFELLOW.

'Tis Virtue that adorns the life,
Gives peace in trouble, joy in strife,
    And elevates the man:
The spirit pure; the mind serene,
Present a blissful pleasing scene,
    Which angels well may scan.

'Tis virtue spreads celestial light,
In this our world of sin and night,
    Dispensing moral gloom:
Yes, she will live when nature dies,
And flourish in her native skies,
    In all her lovely bloom.

The sun may loose his glorious light,
The moon no more illume the night,
    The stars may cease to shine:
But virtue lives, undimm'd with age,
Surviving nature's latest stage,
    Outlasting latest time.

May this thy richest portion be,
In time, and through eternity,
    The joys that ne'er decay;
And when thy earthly course is run,
To view the uncreated sun
    Through one eternal day.

    Guelph.

ODE TO FAITH.

HENRY PALMER
Remember me. Luke XXIII. v. 42.

Death to disarm, the wounded soul to heal;
    Of all its terrors to deprive the grave,
What charm more potent than the last appeal,
    That could on Calvary the Culprit save?

"Remember me" can give a second birth,
    Can cause all past offence to be forgiv'n;
Can burst the bonds that chain it to the earth,
    And raise the soul triumphantly to Heav'n.

Divine effulgence come, possess my soul;
    To thee, O saving Faith, I bend the knee;
Oh! guide me to the Cross, the Christian's goal,
    That my Redeemer may "Remember me."

Soham Cottage.

MISCELLANY AND EXTRACTS.

SERPENT CHARMER.—One of these jugglers, or charmers, was by far the most expert and daring fellow I had seen perform with snakes; and he completely astonished us by the manner in which he pulled about, and treated with the greatest indifference and coolness, a very fine Cobra de Capello, or Noya, as the Kandyans call it, about three feet and a half long, which he had brought with him. He handled it with great roughness. yet perfect confidence: he also struck and threatened it in so daring a way, that at last I suspected its poisonfangs had been broken or extracted; but this I found was not the case; for after he had taken much pains in order to irritate it, and soothe it when enraged, and had even put into his bosom, I told one of the servants to desire him to open its mouth,—not expecting that he would do so—and show me whether the poison fangs were extracted or not. He did so without the least hesitation, and there they certainly were, and in the most perfect state! Indeed I confess that in even going up to examine them, a strange sort of thrilling sensation ran through my whole frame, at the idea of being bitten by such a terrible yet beautiful creature. I then desired the servant to ask him if the snake would bite me if I touched it. He instantly replied, that it certainly would do so, and seemingly afraid lest I should venture too near it, he, in great haste, put it back into the bag in which he had brought it. —*From Col. Campbell's Excursions in Ceylon.* E.

THE Rev. Mr. Ferryman, a clergyman, who once resided at Qnorn, in Leicestershire, narrates two very singular anecdotes about the common English rat, which are worthy of being recorded as evidences of the great sagacity of that animal. Walking out in some meadows one evening, he observed a great number of rats in the act of migrating from one place to another, which it is known they are in the habit of doing occasionally. He stood perfectly still, and the whole assemblage passed close to him. His astonishment, however, was very great when he saw amongst the number an old blind rat, which held a piece of stick by one end in his mouth, whilst another rat had hold of the other end of it, and thus conducted its blind companion.

The other anecdote is the following :— Mr. Ferryman had an old friend of retired and studious habits, who, when sitting in his room one day saw an English rat come out of a hole at the bottom of the wainscot. He threw it a piece of bread, and in process of time he had so familiarized the animal that it became perfectly tame, ran about him, was his constant companion, and appeared much attached to him. He was in the habit of reading in bed at night, and was on one occasion awoke by feeling a sharp bite on the cheek. On looking round he discovered the curtain of his bed to be on fire. He made his escape, but the house was burnt down, and he saw no more of his rat. He was, however, convinced, and remained so for the rest of his life, that his old companion had saved him from being burnt to death by biting his cheek, and thus making him aware of his danger. The reader may put what faith he pleases in the tale. The gentleman himself was always indignant if any one doubted it, and certainly the marks of teeth were visible on his cheek.

That rats are endowed with an extraordinary degree of ingenuity and cunning, there are numerous well-attested facts to prove: the following is one of them. A ship on her voyage was not only much infested with rats, but proved so unfit for sea, that her stores were directed to be made over to another vessel. In doing this the greatest care was taken that the rats should not gain access to the other ship; and in order to prevent it, the two vessels were anchored at some distance from each other, and the stores were removed in boats. When the crew were about to quit the vessel, the whole body of rats were seen to make their way down its sides into the sea, and to swim to the ship into which the stores had been conveyed. They would have effected their object, had not the vigilance of the crew prevented them. The vessel got under weigh, and the rats were left to their fate. E.

CALLS OF AMERICAN BIRDS.—If superstition takes alarm at our familiar and simple species, what would be thought by the ignorant of a South American kind, large as the wood-owl, which, in the forests of Demerara, about midnight, breaks out, lamenting like one in deep distress, and in a tone more dismal even than the painful hexachord of the slothful *Aï*. The sounds, like the expiring sighs of some agonizing victim, begins with a high loud note, *ha! ha! ha! ha! ha! ha! ha!* each tone falling lower and lower, till the last syllable is scarcely heard, pausing a moment or two between the reiterated tale of seeming sadness. Four other species of the Goatsucker, according to Waterton, also inhabit this tropical wilderness, among which also is included the *Whip-poor-will*. Figure to yourselves the surprise and wonder of the stranger who takes up his solitary abode for the first night amidst those awful and interminable forests, when at twilight he begins to be assailed familiarly with a spectral equivocal bird, approaching within a few yards, and then accosting him with, *who-are-you, who-who-who-are-you?*—Another approaches and bids him, as if a slave under the lash, *work-away, work-work-work-away!*—A third mournfully cries, *willy-come-go! willy-willy-willy-come-go!*—And as you get among the high-lands, our old acquaintance vociferates, *whip-poor-will, whip-whip-whip-poor-will!* It is therefore not surprising that such unearthly sounds should be considered in the light of supernatural forebodings, issuing from spectres in the guise of birds.—*Nuttall's Ornithology.*

E.

CRAB-CATCHING ON THE SCOTTISH COAST.—We soon perceived two men in a small craft: their little boat hung motionless on the then waveless mirror of the bay, in about ten feet depth of water; and after for a minute or thereby holding their faces close upon the surface, they seemed suddenly to pull a long pole out of the water, with something adhering to its extremity. We soon found that they were taking advantage of the glassy stillness of the water, to overlook the early walks of the crabs. They no sooner saw these crusty crustaceans on the subaqueous sands, than they poked them behind with their long staves: the crabs turned round and seized upon the poles. These latter were slightly shaken by the fishermen, as if in pain or terror; the angry creatures clung all the closer, and were then rapidly hoisted into the boats.—*From Wilson's Voyage.*

E.

CANTERBURY CATHEDRAL was built by Sanfranc, with stone from the beautiful quarries near Caen, in Normandy. Sanfranc was an Italian, and Abbot of St. Stephen's, at Caen.

E.

MONTHLY NOTICES.

DECEMBER.

24th.—Savings' Bank Accounts made up about this time.

15th.—County Court, held at the Court House, Soham.

Printed by WILLIAM PLAYFORD, Soham, Cambridgeshire.

CPSIA information can be obtained at www.ICGtesting.com
Printed in the USA
BVOW04s0528120215

387449BV00017B/181/P